Road atlas of Britain

GW00373230

CONTENTS

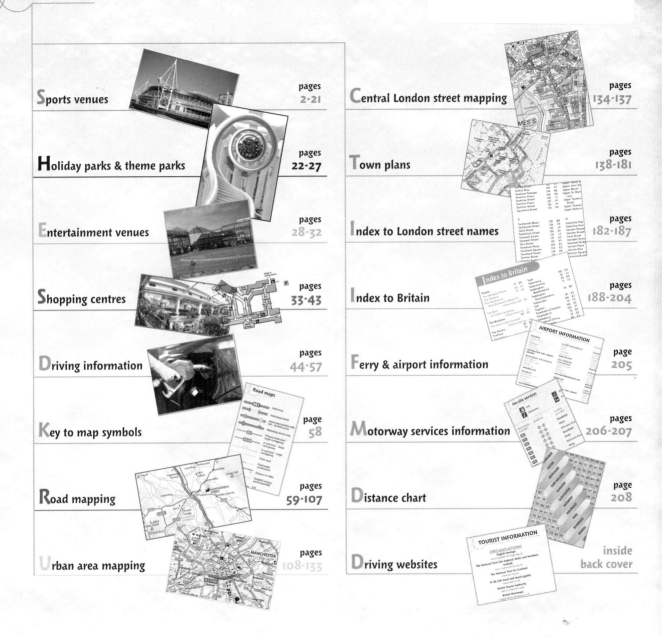

PHOTO CREDITS

Photographs were supplied by the following:
Aintree page 15; Alton Towers page 24; Amanda Berry pages 45, 52; Bicester Village page 37; Bluewater page 33; Butlins page 23;
Center Parcs page 22; Cheltenham Racecourse pages 15, 16; Chessington World of Adventures page 25; Darren Middleditch pages 5, 8;
Drayton Manor page 25; Durham County Cricket Club page 12; Empics Ltd pages 2, 3, 4, 5, 6, 7, 8, 9, 10, 11, 14, 16, 17, 18, 19, 20;
ExCeL page 29; Ford pages 44, 50, 54; Freeport pages 38, 39; Greater Glasgow & Clyde Valley Tourist Board page 31;
Lancashire County Cricket Club page 13; Loch Lomond Outlet Centre page 40; McArthur Glen pages 41, 42; MetroCentre page 35;
NEC Group pages 2, 30; Neil Forrest pages 43, 46, 47, 48, 49, 50, 51, 53, 55, 56; Norman Samuels pages 7, 28, 31;
Oakwood Park page 27; Sonia Kolaszynska page 47; Thorpe Park page 27; Trafford Centre page 36;
Warwickshire County Cricket Club pages 12, 14; Wembley page 32.

The town descriptions on pages 138-181 were researched and written by Karen Lloyd.

Whether you're a football fanatic or a racing guru, you'll find all the info you need on the biggest sporting venues around the country:

Cardiff Millennium Stadium

CARDIFF MILLENNIUM STADIUM

Cardiff Arms Park, Westgate Street, Cardiff, CF10 1NS
Tel: 029 2023 2661
Tickets: 0870 582 582

Map ref
112 B4

www.millenniumstadium.sportcentric.com

- On site of the old Cardiff Arms Park, home of Welsh rugby, in Cardiff city centre.
- International and national rugby and football including Six Nations Championship, Heineken Cup, F.A. Cup Final, League Cup Final.
- Boxing and speedway.
- Stadium has 72,000 seating capacity with a fully retractable roof.
- Concert and exhibition venue.
- Stadium tours.
- Adjoining retail and leisure plaza.

HAMPDEN PARK

Somerville Drive, Glasgow, G42 9BA
Tel: 0141 620 4000
www.hampdenpark.co.uk

Map ref
117 D4

- Scotland's national stadium.
- Home of Scottish national football and Queen's Park F.C..
- Hosted UEFA Champions League Final in 2002.
- Seating capacity 52,000.
- Scottish football museum and stadium tours.
- American football and concert venue.
- 4 miles south of Glasgow city centre.

MURRAYFIELD

Murrayfield, Edinburgh, EH12 5PJ
Tel: 0131 346 5000
www.sru.org.uk

Map ref
114 B2

- Home of Scottish Rugby Union.
- National and international matches including Six Nations Championship.
- 2 miles west of Edinburgh city centre.
- Stadium capacity of 67,500.
- Tours by request.
- Library with exhibitions open Mon - Fri 9am - 5pm
- Scotland achieved 'Grand Slam' here in 1925, 1984 and 1990.

National Indoor Arena - Birmingham

NATIONAL INDOOR ARENA

King Edward's Road, Birmingham, B1 2AA
Tel: 0121 780 3127
Box Office: 0870 909 4144
www.necgroup/nia/

Map ref
108 C3

- In Birmingham city centre, a short distance from New Street railway station
- Designed to accommodate more than 30 different sports.
- Has hosted 5 World and 3 European Championships.
- 6 lane 200 metre athletics track, dismantled for other events.
- Concerts, entertainment and exhibitions.
- T.V. Gladiators series filmed here and Eurovision Song Contest in 1998.
- Multi-storey pay and display car park.

NATIONAL WATER SPORTS CENTRE HOLME PIERREPONT

Map ref
77 E2

Adbolton Lane, Holme Pierrepont,
Nottingham,
NG12 2LU
0115 982 1212

www.nationalwatersports.co.uk

- Set in 270 acres of country parkland beside River Trent.
- 2000m regatta lake.
- 700m artificial white water canoe slalom course, also used for rafting.

- Slalom course floodlit evenings September to April.
- British Olympic Committee accredited centre for canoeing.
- Water ski lagoon with a cable tow.
- Fitness training centre.
- Residential complex and campsite.
- 3 miles west of Nottingham city centre, signposted from A52.

WIMBLEDON

Map ref
131 C6

All England Lawn Tennis and Croquet Club,
Church Road,
Wimbledon,
SW19 5AE
020 8944 1066
Tickets: 020 8971 2473
Museum: 020 8946 6131

www.wimbledon.org

- The Lawn Tennis Championships, the world's leading tennis tournament, first started here in 1877.
- Around 60 nations take part in the 2 week championship held over 2 weeks in June and July.
- 20 grass courts including Centre and Number 1 court.
- Tickets allocated by ballot.
- Club grounds cover 42 acres and include a further 30 courts.
- Located in south west London with shuttle buses running between the ground and Southfields London underground and Wimbledon main line stations during the championships.
- Wimbledon Lawn Tennis Museum open daily 10.30am - 5.00pm.

TWICKENHAM

Rugby Road, Twickenham,
Middlesex
TW1 1DZ
020 8892 2000
Tickets: 020 8831 6666

Map ref
66 A1

www.rfu.com

- Home of England Rugby Union.
- International and national cup and league matches.
- 10 miles from central London.
- Shuttle Bus runs between Richmond London Underground station and ground on match days.
- Museum of rugby with interactive exhibits and the Calcutta Cup on display.
- Stadium tours.
- Restaurants, bars, rugby merchandise shop.

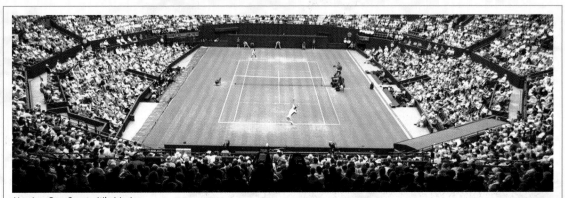

Number One Court - Wimbledon

Anfield (Liverpool F.C.)

ANFIELD, LIVERPOOL

Anfield Road,
Liverpool
L4 0TH
Tel: 0151 263 2361
Box office phone number:
0151 260 8680

Map ref
120 B1

www.liverpoolfc.tv

○ 4 miles from the end of the M62.

○ 45,362 seated capacity.

○ Originally home to Everton FC, Anfield has been home to Liverpool FC for over 100 years.

○ Stadium tours available and the museum is full of Anfield memorabilia.

○ Plans for new stadium to be built 300 yards down the road at Stanley Park, possibly in time for start of 2005/06 season.

○ Club nickname: The Reds.

CRAVEN COTTAGE, FULHAM

Map ref
131 B5

Stevenage Road
London
SW6 6HH
Tel: 020 7893 8383
Box office phone number:
020 7834 4710

www.fulhamfc.com

○ Stadium is undergoing redevelopment and is due to be completed for the start of the 2004/05 season.

○ Fulham's home games to be played at Loftus Road (home of QPR) until then.

○ Club nickname: The Cottagers.

EWOOD PARK, BLACKBURN ROVERS

Map ref
81 D3

Blackburn,
Lancashire, BB2 4JF
Tel: 01254 698888
Box office phone number:
01254 671666

www.rovers.co.uk

○ A mile from junction 4 of the M65.

○ 10-15 minute walk from Mill Hill railway station.

○ 31,367 seated capacity.

○ Ewood park ground tours are available on weekdays.

ELLAND ROAD, LEEDS UNITED

Leeds
LS11 0ES
Tel: 0113 226 6000
Box office phone number:
0113 226 1000

Map ref
119 E3

www.leedsunited.com

○ Just off junction 2 of the M621.

○ 20 minute walk from Leeds railway station, shuttle buses available.

○ 40,204 seated capacity.

○ The East Stand is the biggest cantilever stand in the world.

○ Was one of the 8 grounds to host Euro '96 games.

○ Stadium tours are available, booking is essential on 0113 226 6223.

○ Club nickname: The Whites.

GOODISON PARK, EVERTON

Map ref
120 B1

Goodison Road,
Liverpool, L4 4EL
Tel: 0151 330 2200
Box office phone number:
0151 330 2300

www.evertonfc.com

- 4-5 miles from junction 4 of the M57.
- 15-20 minutes walk from Kirkdale rail station.
- 40,260 seated capacity.
- Goodison Park was first opened in 1892 and was the first purpose built football stadium.
- Club nickname: The Toffeemen.

HIGHBURY (ARSENAL STADIUM), ARSENAL

Arsenal Stadium,
Avenell Road,
London
N5 1BU
Tel: 020 7704 4000
Box office phone number:
020 7413 3366

www.arsenal.com

Map ref
132 A2

- Next to Arsenal Underground Station.
- 38,500 seated capacity.
- Club Nickname: The Gunners.
- Arsenal FC began life when a group of workers at the Woolwich Arsenal Armament Factory formed a team in 1886.
- Museum located in the North Bank stand has extensive archive of Arsenal memorabilia.

Highbury (Arsenal F.C.)

MAINE ROAD, MANCHESTER CITY

Map ref
122 C3

Manchester
M14 7WN
Tel: 0161 232 3000
Box office phone number:
0161 226 2224

www.mcfc.co.uk

- 2-3 miles from junction 5 of the M60 and junction 3 of the M56.
- 34,996 seated capacity.
- Club nickname: The Blues/Citizens.
- Manchester City are due to move to the new City of Manchester stadium in time for the 2003/04 season.

OLD TRAFFORD, MANCHESTER UNITED

Sir Matt Busby Way,
Manchester M16 0RA
Tel: 0161 868 8000
Box office phone number: 0161 868 8010

www.manutd.com

Map ref
122 C3

- 2 miles from junction 7 and 9 of the M60.
- Station adjacent to Old Trafford Stadium (trains on match days only) and close to Old Trafford Metrolink station.
- 67,603 seated capacity.
- Pre-bookable stadium tours available and can also visit the museum charting the club's history from 1878.
- Club nickname: The Red Devils.

Old Trafford (Manchester United F.C.)

REEBOK STADIUM, BOLTON WANDERERS

Burnden Way,
Bolton,
Lancashire,
BL6 6JW
Tel: 01204 673750
Box office phone number:
01204 673601

**Map ref
81 D3**

www.bwfc.co.uk

- Just off junction 6 of the M61.
- A few minutes walk from Horwich Parkway railway station.
- 28,000 seated capacity.
- Reebok Stadium opened in 1997.
- Club nickname: The Trotters.

RIVERSIDE STADIUM, MIDDLESBROUGH

**Map ref
85 E3**

Middlesbrough,
TS3 6RS
Tel: 01642 877700
Box office phone number:
01642 877809

www.mfc.co.uk

- A mile east of Middlesbrough town centre off the A66.
- 15 – 20 minutes walk from Middlesbrough railway station.
- 35,100 seated capacity.
- Stadium built in 1995 and was the first constructed to comply with the Taylor report.
- Club nickname: Boro.

Stadium of Light (Sunderland A.F.C.)

ST. ANDREWS STADIUM, BIRMINGHAM CITY

**Map ref
109 D3**

St. Andrews Stadium,
Birmingham
B9 4NH
Tel: 0121 772 0101
Box office phone number:
09068 332988

www.bcfc.com

- About 2 miles from junction 6 of the M6.
- 10 minutes walk from Bordesley railway station.
- 30,200 seated capacity.
- Club Nickname: The Blues.
- Club was formed in 1875 by a group of cricketers from a local church.

ST. JAMES' PARK, NEWCASTLE UNITED

Newcastle-upon-Tyne,
NE1 4ST
Tel: 0191 201 8400
Box office phone number:
0191 261 1571

**Map ref
124 B2**

www.nufc.co.uk

- Half a mile north east of Newcastle city centre.
- Adjacent to St. James' Park Metro station.
- Over the road from the Newcastle Brewery famous for its Newcastle Brown Ale.
- 52,173 seated capacity.
- Club nickname: The Magpies.

St. Mary's Stadium - Southampton F.C.

ST. MARY'S STADIUM, SOUTHAMPTON

Britannia Road,
Southampton SO14 5FP
Tel: 0870 2200 000
Box office phone number:
0870 2200 150

Map ref
129 B2

www.saintsfc.co.uk

- 2-3 miles from junction 14 of the M3 and junction 5 of the M27.
- 30 minutes walk from Southampton railway station, or take the shuttle bus.
- 32,251 seated capacity.
- Club nickname: The Saints.

STADIUM OF LIGHT, SUNDERLAND

Map ref
125 F4

Sunderland,
SR5 1BT
Tel: 0191 551 5000
Box office phone number:
0191 551 5151

www.safc.com

- Half a mile north of Sunderland City centre across the River Wear.
- The Stadium of Light has its own Metro station with trains from both Sunderland and Tyneside.
- 48,300 seated capacity.
- First game in the Stadium of Light was played in 1997.
- Stadium tours available, ring 0191 551 5055 for details.
- Club nickname: The Black Cats.

STAMFORD BRIDGE, CHELSEA

Fulham Road,
London SW6 1HS
Tel: 020 7385 5545
Box office phone number:
020 7386 7799

Map ref
131 C5

www.chelseafc.co.uk

- Close to Fulham Broadway Underground Station.
- 43,000 seated capacity.
- Club nickname: The Blues.
- Stadium tours available.
- Stamford Bridge is part of the Chelsea Village complex which also includes the World of Sport visitor attraction.

THE HAWTHORNS, WEST BROMWICH ALBION

Map ref
108 B2

Halfords Lane,
West Bromwich,
B71 4LF
Tel: 0121 525 8888
Box office phone number:
0121 525 8888

www.wba.co.uk

- Half a mile from junction 1 of the M5.
- Five minutes walk from The Hawthorns Metro station.
- 27,200 seated capacity.
- Club nickname: The Baggies.

Stamford Bridge - Chelsea F.C.

THE VALLEY, CHARLTON ATHLETIC

Floyd Road,
Charlton,
SE7 8BL
Tel: 020 8333 4000
Box office phone number: 020 8333 4010

www.cafc.co.uk

Map ref
133 D5

- Off the A102 at junction of A206.
- Close to Charlton railway station or a short bus ride from North Greenwich Underground station.
- 26,500 seated capacity.
- Club nickname: The Addicks.

UPTON PARK (BOLEYN GROUND), WEST HAM UNITED

Map ref
132 D3

Green Street, Upton Park,
London E13 9AZ
Tel: 020 8548 2748
Box office phone number:
020 8548 2700

www.whufc.co.uk

- A mile west of the North Circular Road at the A124 junction.
- Five minutes walk from Upton Park Underground station.
- 35,647 seated capacity.
- Club nickname: The Hammers/Irons.

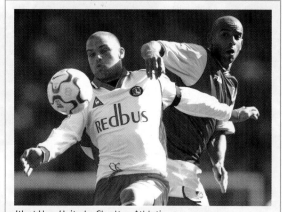
West Ham United v Charlton Athletic

- A mile from junction 6 of the M6.
- A few minutes walk from Witton railway station.
- 43,000 seated capacity.
- Club Nickname: The Villans.
- Ground was used during Euro '96.
- Tours of the ground are available.

VILLA PARK, ASTON VILLA

Villa Park, Trinity Road,
Birmingham B6 6HE
Tel: 0121 327 2299
Box office phone number:
0121 327 5353

Map ref
108 C2

www.astonvilla-fc.co.uk

WHITE HART LANE,
TOTTENHAM HOTSPUR

Map ref
132 B2

748 High Road, Tottenham,
London N17 0AP
Tel: 020 8365 5000
Box office phone number:
08700 112222

www.spurs.co.uk

- Half a mile south of the North Circular on the A1010.
- Five minutes walk from White Hart Lane railway station or half an hour from Seven Sisters Underground station.
- Stadium tours are available on weekdays.
- 36,214 seated capacity.
- Club nickname: Spurs.

Villa Park (Aston Villa F.C.)

ALMONDVALE STADIUM, LIVINGSTON

Map ref
90 B2

Almondvale Stadium Road,
Livingston,
West Lothian
EH54 7DN
Tel: 01506 417000
Box office phone number:
01506 417000

www.livingstonfc.co.uk

- 2 – 3 miles from junction 3 of the M8.
- 15 minutes walk from both Livingston North and Livingston South railway stations.
- 10,000 seated capacity.
- Club Nickname: Livi Lions.
- Livingston F.C., formerly Meadowbank Thistle, played their first game in this new stadium in November 1995 after the team relocated from Edinburgh.

Celtic Park (Celtic F.C.)

CELTIC PARK, CELTIC

Glasgow, G40 3RE
Tel: 0141 556 2611
Box office phone number:
0141 551 8653

Map ref
117 E3

www.celticfc.co.uk

- 1 – 2 miles from junction 1 of the M74 and from Glasgow City centre on the A74.
- 30 minutes walk from Glasgow City centre railway stations.
- 60,832 seated capacity.
- Club Nickname: The Bhoys.

DENS PARK, DUNDEE

Sandeman Street,
Dundee
DD3 7JY
Tel: 01382 889966
Box office phone number:
01382 889966

Map ref
95 D3

www.dundeefc.co.uk

- A mile north of Dundee City centre off the B960 Dens Road.
- 12,085 seated capacity.
- Club Nickname: Dark Blues.
- Main stand is an unusual oval shape so those seated on the touchline are furthest from the pitch.
- Practically next door to Tannadice Park, home to rivals Dundee United.

EAST END PARK, DUNFERMLINE ATHLETIC

Map ref
90 B1

Halbeath Road,
Dunfermline,
Fife,
KY12 7RB
Tel: 01383 724295
Box office phone number:
01383 724295

www.dunfermline-athletic.com

- 2 miles from junction 3 of the M90 on the A907.
- 15 minutes walk from Dunfermline railway station.
- 12,558 seated capacity.
- Club Nickname: The Pars.

— Dundee United v Rangers —

EASTER ROAD, HIBERNIAN

12 Albion Place,
Edinburgh EH7 5QG
Tel: 0131 661 2159
Box office phone number:
0131 661 1875

Map ref
115 D1

www.hibs.co.uk

- 1-2 miles north east of Edinburgh city centre.
- 15 minutes walk from Edinburgh Waverley railway station.
- 17,500 seated capacity.
- Club was formed by a group of Irish Immigrants, hence the name Hibernian, the Roman name for Ireland.
- Club Nickname: The Hibees.

FIRHILL STADIUM, PARTICK THISTLE

Map ref
117 D2

Glasgow,
G20 7AL
Tel: 0141 579 1971
Box office phone number: 0141 579 1971

www.ptfc.co.uk

- A mile from junction 16 and 17 of the M8.
- 10-15 minutes walk from St. George's Cross underground station.
- 14,538 seated capacity.
- Club Nickname: The Jags.

FIR PARK, MOTHERWELL

Firpark Street,
Motherwell
ML1 2QN
Tel: 01698 333333
Box office phone number:
01698 333033

Map ref
89 G2

www.motherwellfc.co.uk

- A mile from junction 6 of the M74.
- 15 minutes walk from Motherwell railway station or 5 – 10 minutes from Airbles station.
- 13,742 seated capacity.
- Club Nickname: The Well.

IBROX STADIUM, RANGERS

Map ref
116 C3

Glasgow,
G51 2XD
Tel: 0141 580 8500
Box office phone number:
0870 600 1972

www.rangers.co.uk

- Just off the M8 at junction 23 (westbound traffic only) or 24.
- A few minutes walk from Ibrox underground station.
- 50,411 seated capacity.
- Club Nickname: The Gers/Teddy Bears.

— Ibrox (Rangers F.C.) —

PITTODRIE STADIUM, ABERDEEN

Map ref
99 F4

Pittodrie Street,
Aberdeen
AB24 5QH
Tel: 01224 650400
Box office phone number:
01224 631903

www.afc.co.uk

- Half a mile north of Aberdeen City centre off the A956.
- 30 minutes walk from Aberdeen railway station.
- 22,199 seated capacity.
- Club Nickname: The Dons.

Pittodrie (Aberdeen F.C.)

RUGBY PARK, KILMARNOCK

Map ref
89 E3

Rugby Road,
Kilmarnock KA1 2DP
Tel: 01563 545300
Box office phone number:
09001 633249

www.kilmarnockfc.co.uk

- Just to the south west of Kilmarnock town centre.
- 15 – 20 minutes walk from Kilmarnock railway station.
- 18,128 seated capacity.
- Club Nickname: Killie.

Livingston v Heart of Midlothian

TANNADICE PARK, DUNDEE UNITED

Tannadice Street,
Dundee DD3 7JW
Tel: 01382 833166
Box office phone number:
01382 833166

Map ref
95 D3

www.dundeeunitedfc.co.uk

- A mile north of Dundee City centre off the B960 Dens Road.
- 14,209 seated capacity.
- Club Nickname: The Terrors.
- Practically next door to Dens Park, home to rivals Dundee.

TYNECASTLE STADIUM, HEART OF MIDLOTHIAN

Map ref
114 C2

Gorgie Road,
Edinburgh EH11 2NL
Tel: 0131 200 7200
Box office phone number:
0131 200 7209

www.heartsfc.co.uk

- 1-2 miles west of Edinburgh city centre on A71.
- 15 minutes walk from Edinburgh Haymarket railway station.
- 18,008 seated capacity.
- The club was formed in 1874 and was named after the Royal Mile dance hall frequented by the founders.
- Club Nickname: The Jam Tarts.

Riverside, County Ground (Durham C.C.C.)

COUNTY GROUND BRISTOL

Gloucestershire County Cricket Club,
Nevil Road, Bristol, BS7 9EJ
Tel: 0117 910 8000
Tickets: 0117 910 8010

Map ref
110 C3

www.glosccc.co.uk

- Headquarters ground of Gloucestershire County Cricket Club.
- 2 miles north of Bristol City Centre, close to Junction 2 of M32.
- 8,000 capacity ground.
- Second largest playing area in England.
- England v Australia match played in 2001 attracted record 15,000 spectators.

COUNTY GROUND DURHAM

Map ref
85 D2

Durham County Cricket Club,
County Ground, Riverside,
Chester-le-Street,
County Durham,
DH3 3QR
Tel: 0191 387 1717

www.durham-ccc.org.uk

- Riverside became Durham's permanent home in 1995.
- Hosts international, county championships and league matches.
- Floodlit games.
- Bistro and bar.
- Accessible from junction 63 of A1(M).

EDGBASTON

The County Ground,
Edgbaston Road, Birmingham,
West Midlands, B5 7QU
Tel: 0121 446 4422

Map ref
108 C3

www.warwickccc.org.uk

- County ground for Warwickshire County Cricket Club since 1886.
- Test match venue since 1902 when Australia were bowled out for 36.
- 17,500 capacity.
- End names: Pavilion End, City End.
- 2 miles south of Birmingham city centre.
- Good car parking facilities.
- £2.5m Edgbaston Cricket Centre opened in 2000 with main arena, restaurants, bars, showroom, shop, viewing gallery and balcony.
- Museum open on match days.
- Brian Lara scored a world record 501 not out, here in 1994.

Edgbaston (Warwickshire C.C.C.)

HEADINGLEY

Map ref
119 E1

Headingley Cricket Ground,
St. Michael's Lane, Leeds,
West Yorkshire, LS6 3BR
Tel: 0113 278 7394

www.yorkshireccc.org.uk

- Home of Yorkshire County Cricket Club.
- Established 1888 with test cricket since 1899.
- End names: Football Stand End, Kirkstall Lane End.
- Yorkshire batsman Geoff Boycott made his hundredth hundred here against Australia in 1977.
- Capacity of 14,000.

- Adjacent to Headingley Stadium rugby ground, home to the Leeds Rhinos (Rugby League) and the Leeds Tykes (Rugby Union).
- 2 miles north west of Leeds city centre.

Lord's Cricket Ground,
St. John's Wood,
London NW8 8QN
Tel: 020 7286 8011
Tickets: 020 7432 1066

www.middlesexccc.com

LORD'S

Map ref
130 C3

- World renowned cricket ground.
- Owned and run by Marylebone Cricket Club (MCC).
- Home to Middlesex County Cricket Club since 1877.
- Hosts Test matches, one-day internationals, domestic one-day finals, most of Middlesex's home games and village and club cricket finals.
- End names: Pavilion End, Nursery End.

- Museum with the Ashes on display.
- Brian Johnston Memorial Theatre shows historical cricket footage.
- Ground tours.
- MCC Indoor School.
- Lord's Tavern pub beside Grace Gate on St. John's Wood Road.
- No car parks. Nearest London underground station is St. John's Wood.

Old Trafford (Lancashire C.C.C.)

OLD TRAFFORD

Map ref
122 C3

Old Trafford Cricket Ground,
Talbot Road,
Manchester,
M16 0PX
Tel: 0161 282 4000
Tickets: 0161 282 4040

www.lccc.co.uk

- Home of Lancashire County Cricket Club.
- Tests played here since 1884.
- Capacity 19,000.
- End names: Stretford End, Warwick Road End.
- Museum open on International and 1st Xl match days.
- Indoor cricket centre.
- Located to the west of Manchester city centre, five miles from junction 9 of M60.
- Linked to north, central and south Manchester by tram service, MetroLink.

Edgbaston (Warwickshire C.C.C.)

SOPHIA GARDENS, CARDIFF

Cathedral Road,
Cardiff,
CF1 9XR
Tel: 029 2040 9380

Map ref
112 B4

www.glamorgancricket.com

- Home of Glamorgan County Cricket Club since 1967.
- In parkland on west bank of the River Taff 1 mile north west of Cardiff city centre.
- International and county championship and league matches.
- Capacity for 5,500 spectators.
- Glamorgan National Cricket Centre in Sophia Gardens has extensive indoor facilities.

THE OVAL

Map ref
131 D5

The Oval Cricket Ground,
Kennington,
London, SE11 5SS
Tel: 020 7582 6660
Tickets: 020 7582 7764

www.surreycricket.com

- Home of Surrey County Cricket Club, founded 1845.
- Test series in England usually end here.
- End names: Pavilion End, Vauxhall End.
- Current capacity 18,500 – undergoing redevelopment.
- Vauxhall nearest mainline station, Oval nearest tube.
- First Test in England played here in 1880 with an England win over Australia by 5 wickets.
- Ken Barrington Cricket Centre with multi-purpose sports hall.
- Health & Fitness club.

The Oval (Surrey C.C.C.)

TRENT BRIDGE

Trent Bridge,
Nottingham,
NG2 6AG
Tel: 0115 982 3000
Tickets: 0870 168 8888

Map ref
126 C3

www.trentbridge.co.uk

- Home ground of Nottinghamshire County Cricket Club since 1841.
- Test and county cricket venue.
- 15,300 capacity.
- End names: Radcliffe Road End, Pavilion End.
- New Fox Road and Radcliffe Road stands.

- Trent Bridge Cricket Centre with indoor cricket halls, leisure, conference and accommodation facilities.
- Located just to south of Nottingham city centre across River Trent.
- Can be approached from M1 and A1 without travelling through city centre.

Sporting venues - RACECOURSES

AINTREE

Map ref
80 C4

Aintree Racecourse,
Ormskirk Road, Aintree,
Liverpool L9 5AS
Tel: 0151 5232600

www.aintree.co.uk

- World renowned Grand National takes place at 3 day National meeting in April.
- Four and a half mile course with 30 fences including Becher's Brook and The Chair.
- The Grand National is the richest National Hunt race in Europe and attracts worldwide T.V. audiences of 600 million.
- Red Rum, the only horse to have won the National 3 times, is buried near the winning post.
- 3 further race meetings held each year.
- Visitor centre 'The Grand National Experience' open May-October.
- Aintree railway station opposite the racecourse entrance. Located on the A59, one mile from M57/M58 junction, linking to the M62 and M6.

Grand National - Aintree

ASCOT

Ascot Racecourse,
Ascot,
Berkshire, **Map ref
66 A1**
SL5 7JN
Tel: 01344 622211
Tickets: 01344 876876

www.ascot.co.uk

- 25 days of racing.
- Flat racing May-October, National Hunt November-April.
- Prestigious Royal Ascot 4 day meeting in mid June is highlight of flat racing and social calendar.
- King George VI and Queen Elizabeth Diamond Stakes in July.
- Queen Elizabeth II stakes in September.
- On A329 to west of Ascot close to M3 junction 3 and M4 junction 6.
- First race meeting at Ascot held 1711.

Aintree Racecourse

AYR

Map ref
89 E4

Ayr Racecourse
2 Whitletts Road,
Ayr, KA8 0JE
Tel: 01292 264179

www.ayr-racecourse.co.uk

- Scotland's premier racecourse with flat and jump racing over 12 months.
- The Scottish Grand National held in April.
- Red Rum is the only horse to have won both the Scottish Grand National and the Grand National at Aintree within the same year (1974).
- Ayr Gold Cup, 6 furlong sprint, run in September during Western Meeting.
- Close to Ayr town centre, 1 mile from A77.
- Children's play areas.
- Free parking.

Cheltenham Racecourse

Cheltenham Racecourse

CHELTENHAM

The Steeplechase Company,
Prestbury Park, Cheltenham,
Gloucestershire, GL50 4SH
Tel: 01242 513014
Booking Office: 01242 226226
www.cheltenham.co.uk

Map ref
70 B2

- World's leading National Hunt course.
- Cheltenham Festival in March attracts 150,000 spectators over 3 days, and is a favourite with the Irish.
- Cheltenham Gold Cup and Champion Hurdle the most prestigious races of the Festival.
- 2 undulating courses with uphill finish.
- Located at foot of Cotswold Hills, 1 mile north of Cheltenham town centre on A435.
- Free parking, except for Cheltenham Festival.
- Return bus link from Cheltenham Spa railway station from 2 hours before racing.
- Hall of Fame illustrates story of steeplechasing. Open Mon-Fri 9.30am-4.30pm, Sat-Sun 10.00am-2.00pm.

DONCASTER

Map ref
82 C4

Doncaster Racecourse,
Grand Stand, Leger Way,
Doncaster, DN2 6BB
Tel: 01302 320066
www.britishracing.com

- St. Leger Stakes, the oldest English Classic, run in September at 4 day Festival meeting.
- Lincoln Handicap Stakes opens summer flat racing season.
- November Handicap closes season.
- Best known for flat racing but National Hunt meetings during winter.
- Town Moor course a mile south of Doncaster town centre at junction of A18 and A638. Signposted from junctions 3 and 4 of M18.

GOODWOOD

Goodwood Racecourse,
Goodwood, Chichester,
W. Sussex, PO18 OPS
Tel: 01243 755022 /
0800 018 8191
www.gloriousgoodwood.co.uk

Map ref
65 F3

- 20 days of top class flat racing a year.
- 'Glorious Goodwood' festival in July and August includes the 1 mile Sussex Stakes, 2 mile Goodwood Cup, and 6 furlong Richmond Stakes.
- Excellent bar, restaurant and entertainment facilities.
- Frankie Dettori had his first winner here in 1987 at the age of 16.
- Situated on the Sussex Downs 5 miles north of Chichester with free parking.

EPSOM DOWNS

Map ref
66 B2

The Grandstand,
Epsom Downs,
Surrey, KT18 5LQ
Tel: 01372 726311
Tickets: 01372 470047

www.epsomderby.co.uk

- The Epsom Derby, the blue riband event of the flat racing world, is a mile and a half race for three year olds. First staged 1790.
- The Queen and Royal Party traditionally drive down the course at 1pm on Derby Day.
- The Oaks and Coronation Cup also run at 2 day June Derby meeting.
- Entertainment including funfair and bands add to festive atmosphere.
- Epsom Downs undulating course notorious for uphill climb from start and steep descent into Tattenham corner.
- On B290 2 miles from Epsom town centre, reached from junction 8 or 9 of M25.

Derby Day - Epsom

Sporting venues - RACECOURSES

KEMPTON PARK

Map ref 66 A1

Kempton Park Racecourse,
Sunbury-on-Thames,
Middlesex,
TW16 5AQ
Tel: 01932 782292
Tickets: 01372 470047

www.kempton.co.uk

- Well known for National Hunt racing but has more flat racing days.
- Highlight is the 2 day Christmas Meeting with the King George VI Chase run on Boxing Day.
- Statue of Desert Orchid, 4 times winner of the King George, beside the paddock.
- 15 miles from central London and close to junction 1 of M3. Approached by A308 or A316.

NEWBURY

Newbury Racecourse,
Newbury,
Berkshire, RG14 7NZ
Tel: 01635 528354

Map ref 65 E1

www.newbury-racecourse.co.uk

- 28 race days, National Hunt and flat.
- Prestigious Hennessy Gold Cup run over jumps in November.
- Greenham Stakes in April, one of the flat racing highlights.
- Nursery available to racegoers with children.
- 18 hole golf course.
- Approached from the A34 one mile south east of Newbury. Newbury railway station is adjacent to the course.

Watching the Pertemps 1000 Guineas Stakes - Newmarket

NEWMARKET

Map ref 72 C1

Newmarket Racecourse,
Westfield House, The Links,
Newmarket,
Suffolk,
CB8 0TG
Tel: 01638 663482
Tickets: 01638 675500

www.newmarketracecourses.co.uk

- Two adjacent courses with a total of 36 race days.
- Racing on the Rowley Mile course in spring and autumn, summer racing on the July Course.
- The 1,000 and 2,000 Guineas run in May are the first classics of the racing calendar.
- 3 day July meeting features the valuable July Cup.
- Autumn Cambridgeshire meeting.
- Champions Day with Cesarawitch and Champion Stakes in October.
- King Charles II inaugurated horseracing in England at Newmarket in 1664.
- Located off the A11, 2 miles south west of Newmarket.

SANDOWN PARK

Map ref 66 A2

Sandown Park Racecourse,
Esher, Surrey, KT10 9AJ
Tel: 01372 470427
Tickets: 01372 470047

www.sandown.co.uk

- Flat and jump racing in parkland setting.
- Mixed card at Whitbread Gold Cup meeting in April.
- Eclipse Stakes in July.
- 7,600 capacity stand.
- Children's play area.
- 15 miles from central London on north side of Esher. Nearest motorway access, M25 junction 10.
- First racecourse to have live televised racing (1947).

Babraham Handicap Stakes - Newmarket

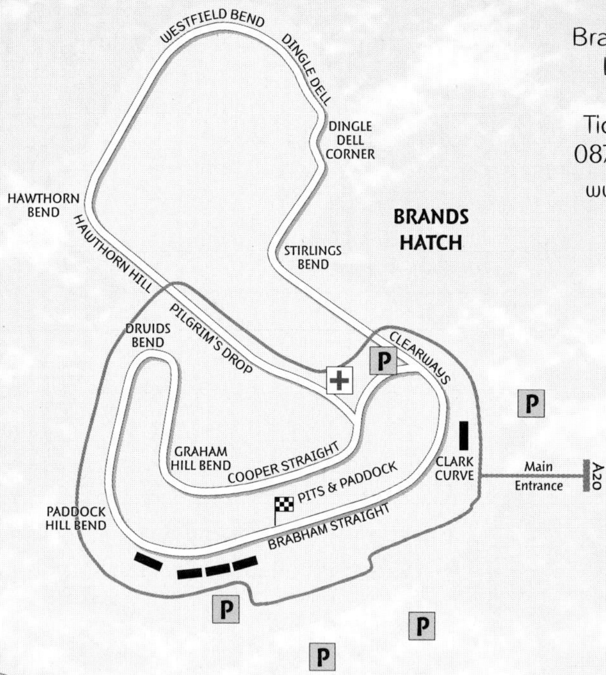

BRANDS HATCH

Brands Hatch Road, Fawkham,
Longfield, Kent, DA3 8NG
Tel: 01474 872331
Tickets & Booking enquiries:
0870 6060 611 or 01327 857273
www.octagonmotorsports.com

Map ref
66 C2

BRANDS HATCH

(circuit map with labels: Westfield Bend, Dingle Dell, Dingle Dell Corner, Hawthorn Bend, Hawthorn Hill, Stirlings Bend, Druids Bend, Pilgrim's Drop, Clearways, Graham Hill Bend, Cooper Straight, Clark Curve, Paddock Hill Bend, Pits & Paddock, Brabham Straight, Main Entrance, A20)

- Grand Prix circuit 2.6 miles, Indy circuit 1.2 miles, Rallycross circuit 0.9 miles.
- Venue for European round of FIM World Superbike Championship and British Touring Car Championship.
- Started in 1926 as bicycle racing grass track.
- First British Grand Prix held at Brands Hatch 1964.
- Nigel Mansell won his first World Championship race here in 1985.
- Yamaha Track and Race School, racing and off road rally schools, 4x4 course.
- Located on A20, 3 miles from M25 junction 3.

CADWELL PARK

Map ref
78 A1

Cadwell, Louth,
Lincolnshire, LN11 9SE
Tel: 01507 343248
Tickets & Booking enquiries:
0870 6060 611 or 01327 857273

www.octagonmotorsports.com

- Principally a motorcycle circuit, 'Bikers Paradise'.
- Hilly, twisting, narrow track with woodland section.
- Full circuit 2.2 miles, Club circuit 1.5 miles, Woodlands circuit 0.8 miles.
- British Superbike Championship event is the highlight of the racing calendar.
- Vintage and classic car racing.
- Yamaha Track and Race School.
- 7 miles south of Louth on A153.

CASTLE COMBE

Castle Combe,
Chippenham,
Wiltshire,
SN14 7EY
Tel: 01249 782417/782929

Map ref
70 B4

www.castlecombecircuit.co.uk

- 1.9 mile circuit, first opened 1950.
- British Formula 3 Championship and British GT Championship venue.
- Formula Ford, saloon car, mini, historic sports car and motorcycle racing.
- Outdoor karting track, skid pan, 4x4 challenge course, racing school on site.
- Circuit driving shows with track passes, club and trade stands, auto jumble.
- 5 miles north west of Chippenham on B4039, signposted from M4 junctions 17 and 18.

CROFT

Croft on Tees,
North Yorkshire, DL2 2PN
Tel: 01325 721819
Tickets: 01325 721815

Map ref
85 D4

www.croftcircuit.co.uk

- International 2.1 mile circuit.
- Formula 3 and British GT Championship events.
- Club car, club motorcycle, British touring car, classic motorcycle and rallycross meetings.
- Car and motorcycle track days giving public access to circuit.
- Free parking.
- Located 6 miles south of Darlington.
- Signposted from A1 (M) junctions 57 and 58.

RAC British Touring Car Championships - Brands Hatch

DONINGTON PARK

Map ref
77 D3

Castle Donington,
Derby, DE74 2RP
Tel: 01332 810048

www.donington-park.co.uk

- International Grand Prix class circuit with car and motorcycle meetings held most Sundays mid-March to November.
- Grand Prix circuit 2.5 miles long, National circuit 2 miles.
- Home of British Motorcycle Grand Prix.
- Hosted European Grand Prix in 1993, won by Ayrton Senna.
- 'Donington Grand Prix Collection' with over 150 cars from 1930s to present.
- Collection museum open daily from 10am-5pm (except Christmas period).
- Motorcycle racing school, club motorcycle riding, car track days.
- Park's natural amphitheatre used as venue for large concerts and music festivals.
- Extensive car parking - normally free except at music events.
- 3 miles from M1 (junctions 23a and 24) and M42/A42 (junction 14).

GOODWOOD

Map ref
65 F3

Goodwood House,
Chichester,
West Sussex, PO18 0PH
Tel: 01243 755000
Tickets: 01243 755055

www.goodwood.co.uk

- 2 major events each year in parkland surrounding Goodwood House, 3 miles north of Chichester.
- Festival of Speed Meeting in July is world's biggest and most diverse classic motor sports event.
- Main attraction of Festival is 1.2 mile hill climb.
- Classes for earliest racing cars through to modern day F1 with famous riders from past and present.
- Over 200 cars take part from all disciplines of motorsport, also motorcycle and downhill soapbox races.
- Motor Circuit Revival Meeting in September is series of races for historic cars on restored 1948 Goodwood circuit with race officials and competitors in 1948-1966 period clothing.

World Superbike Championships

ISLE OF MAN TOURIST TROPHY CIRCUIT

Isle of Man Department of Tourism & Leisure,
Grandstand, Douglas, Isle of Man, IM2 4TB
Tel: 01624 644644

www.iomtt.com

Map ref
80 B3

- Isle of Man Tourist Trophy Races held annually in the last week of May, first week of June.
- 37.8 mile road race circuit for motorcycles on public roads closed for the event.
- Starts and finishes in Douglas.
- Lap record of 17 minutes 47 seconds (127.29mph average speed) set by David Jefferies in 2002.
- Oldest road racing event in the world - first started 1907.
- Attracts 40,000 visitors to the island.

KNOCKHILL

by Dunfermline,
Fife, KT12 9TF
Tel: 01383 723337

www.knockhill.co.uk

Map ref
94 C4

- Scotland's national motorsport centre.
- 1.3 mile long circuit.
- Motorcycle and car racing all season including stock cars and rallycross.
- Highlight events: F3/GT PowerTour, British Superbikes, British Touring Cars.
- Driving and riding courses and track days.
- Located on A823, 5 miles north of Dunfermline.

— Start of the British Grand Prix 2001 - Silverstone —

LYDDEN

Wootton,
Canterbury,
Kent,
CT4 6RX
Tel: 01304 830557/830174
www.lyddenracecircuit.co.uk

Map ref
67 F2

- Rallycross, sports car and motorcycle racing.
- Rallycross at Easter and August Bank Holiday.
- Lord of Lydden and Sidecar Burn-up events at October meeting.
- Short 1 mile circuit.
- Set within natural amphitheatre giving spectators a good view of most of the course.
- Free parking. Dogs allowed on a lead.
- Located off A2, 7 miles south east of Canterbury.

MALLORY PARK

Kirkby Mallory,
Leicester, LE9 7QE
Tel: 01455 842931/2/3
www.mallorypark.co.uk

Map ref
77 D4

- Motorsport every weekend during racing season - over 40 meetings.
- Major events are for motorcycles: Race of the Year, Post TT, British Superbikes, Sidecar Festival.
- Plum Pudding meeting on Boxing Day for cars and motorcycles.
- Full circuit 1.4 miles, oval circuit 1 mile.
- Set in natural amphitheatre with excellent spectator viewing from grassy banks.
- Driving activity days for every kind of motorsport.
- 8 miles west of Leicester off A47 Leicester to Hinkley Road.
- Signposted from M1 junction 21.

PEMBREY

Burry Port, Llanelli,
Carmarthenshire, SA16 OHZ
Tel: 01554 891042
www.barc.net

Map ref
62 B1

OULTON PARK

Map ref
75 F2

Little Budworth, Tarporley,
Cheshire, CW6 9BW
Tel: 01829 760301
Tickets & Booking enquiries:
0870 6060 611 or 01327 857273
www.octagonmotorsports.com

- Undulating track set in wooded Cheshire countryside.
- Full circuit 2.8 miles, Island circuit 2.4 miles, Fosters circuit 1.7 miles.
- Spectators can view from within the perimeter of the circuit.
- British Touring Car and British Superbike Championships events.
- Rally and racing school and 'new driver' courses.
- Signposted from A54/A49 interchange, 13 miles west of M6 junction 18.

- Home of Welsh motorsport and British Automobile Racing Club Wales.
- Club car, motorcycle, kart and truck racing all season.
- British Kart Grand Prix, British Truck Racing Championships, European Motorcycle Sidecar Championships.
- Hosts rallies and sprints.
- 1.5 mile circuit, 0.9 mile rallycross circuit.
- Performance driving school.
- 10 miles from M4 junction 48. Follow brown chequered flags.

ROCKINGHAM

Map ref
77 F4

Mitchell Road,
Corby,
Northamptonshire,
NN17 5AF
Tel: 08700 134044
www.rockingham.co.uk

- £55 million all-seater motorsport venue opened 2000.
- Spectator capacity 130,000.
- One of the largest outdoor stadiums in Europe.
- 1.5 mile banked oval track with 10 versions of infield and combined road racing courses.
- Formula 3, British GT, British Superbikes race meetings, Ascar Championships.
- Indoor and outdoor karting tracks.
- Track driving and passenger events.
- Johnny Herbert Rockingham Experience racing school.
- 2 miles north of Corby off A6116.

Sporting venues - MOTOR RACING CIRCUITS

SANTA POD

Airfield Road,
Podington, Wellingborough,
Northants, NN29 7XA
Tel: 08700 782828

www.santapod.com

Map ref
71 F1

- Home of European Drag Racing.
- Record of 4.89 seconds by Top Fuel dragster set June 2002.
- Most famous raceway outside the United States.
- Opened in 1966 on former US airbase.
- Major events: FIA European Drag Racing Championships, MSA Top Alcohol Championship, British Pro Modified Championship, ACU Drag Bike Championship, Santa Pod Racers Club Sportsman Drag Racing Championships.
- Located between villages of Hinwick and Podington.
- 14 miles north from M1 junction 14, 2 miles east of A509.

SILVERSTONE

Map ref
71 E2   Silverstone,
Northamptonshire,
NN12 8TN
Tel: 01327 857271
Tickets & Booking enquiries:
0870 6060 611 or 01327 857273

www.octagonmotorsports.com

- Home of British Formula 1 Grand Prix which attracts crowds of over 250,000.
- F1 started in 1950 and first race was at Silverstone.
- One of the fastest racing circuits in Europe, Grand Prix circuit 3.2 miles.
- Michael Schumacher holds current Grand Prix lap record of 1 minute 24 seconds, average speed 136mph.
- F1 testing takes place all season, open to spectators.
- Other major annual events: International GT Spectacular, World Superbikes, Best of British Motorsport, Silverstone Classic Festival.
- 7 circuits in total at Silverstone.
- Driving school and track days.
- 30,000 car parking spaces.
- Located on A43 between Towcester and Brackley, 7 miles from junction 15a of M1.

SNETTERTON

Norwich,
Norfolk, NR16 2JU
Tel: 01953 887303
Tickets & Booking enquiries:
0870 6060 611 or 01327 857273

www.octagonmotorsports.com

Map ref
79 D4

- Circuit 2 miles.
- 2 of the longest straights in the UK and one of the fastest circuits.
- Racing for cars, bikes, karts and rally cars.
- Major British Championships visit here: British Superbikes, British Formula 3, British GTs.
- Hosts British Touring Car night race.
- Used for long distance record attempts, speed trials, 24-hour events.
- Located off A11, 10 miles north east of Thetford.

THRUXTON

Map ref
65 D1   Andover,
Hampshire,
SP11 8PN
Tel: 01264 882222

www.barc.net

- 2.4 mile circuit is UK's fastest.
- Car, classic car, motorcycle and truck racing.
- British Superbikes, F3/GT Championships, MRO Championships events.
- British Automobile Racing Club HQ here.
- Thruxton Motor Sports Centre has racing school, 4x4 facility, outdoor karting centre.
- 5 miles west of Andover adjacent to A303.

If you're looking for white-knuckle days out or weekends away with your mates then this is the section for you. Info on the major theme and holiday parks:
Holiday parks pages 22-23

Theme parks pages 24-27

— Center Parcs - rapids —

CENTER PARCS LONGLEAT FOREST

Center Parcs Longleat Forest,
Warminster,
Wiltshire,
BA12 7PU
Tel: 08705 200 300

Map ref
64 B2

www.centerparcs.com

- Holiday villas in woodland landscape which has notable giant redwood trees.
- 'Sub tropical swimming paradise' at the Plaza.
- Indoor sports and leisure activities.
- Outdoor activities, including abseiling, mountain bike trekking, the 3G swing and seasonal watersports.
- Multi-sensory Roman-themed Spa – the Aqua Sana.
- Restaurants, bars, shops.

OASIS WHINFELL FOREST

Oasis Whinfell Forest,
Temple Sowerby, Penrith,
Cumbria, CA10 2DW
Tel: 08705 200 300

Map ref
86 A3

www.centreparcs.com

- Set in 400 acres of pine forest on the edge of the Lake District National Park.
- Lakeside apartments and forest lodges.
- Over 100 indoor and outdoor activities.
- Spa.
- On A66 5 miles east of Penrith (M6 junction 40).

CENTER PARCS SHERWOOD FOREST

Center Parcs Sherwood Forest,
Rufford, Newark,
Nottinghamshire,
NG22 9DN
Tel: 08705 200 300

Map ref
77 E1

www.centerparcs.com

- Holiday villas in heath and woodland landscape.
- Domed 'sub tropical swimming paradise'.
- Indoor sports and leisure activities.
- Outdoor activities and seasonal watersports.
- Fantasy 'Greenwood' theme for tenpin bowling and adventure golf.
- Health and beauty facilities and treatments.
- Restaurants, bars, shops.
- 25 minutes drive from A1 or MI junction 31.

CENTER PARCS ELVEDON FOREST

Center Parcs Elvedon Forest
Tel: 08705 200 300

www.centerparcs.com

- This holiday village is currently being refurbished, see the website or phone the booking line for information about when it will re-open.

— Center Parcs - biking —

Holiday parks

BUTLINS, BOGNOR REGIS

Map ref
66 A4

Butlins, Bognor Regis,
West Sussex
PO21 1JJ
Tel: 01243 820202

www.butlins.co.uk

- Situated on Sussex coast, 1 mile east of Bognor Regis on A259.
- Skyline Pavilion with bars, restaurants, shops.
- Splash Waterworld and numerous sports facilities.
- Go Karts, Funfair, Megazone laser arena, cinema, tenpin bowling, live entertainment, dance floors.
- Facilities for numerous sports.
- Day visitor passes.

— Butlins - Minehead —

BUTLINS, MINEHEAD

Butlins, Minehead,
Somerset TA24 5SH
Tel: 01643 703331
www.butlins.co.uk

Map ref
63 D3

- Located on seafront at Minehead. Nearest M5 junctions - 24 & 25.
- Large sandy beach, lake with boating and angling.
- Indian restaurant on site.
- Skyline Pavilion with bars, restaurants, shops.
- Splash Waterworld and numerous sports facilities.

- Go Karts, Funfair, Megazone laser arena, cinema, tenpin bowling, live entertainment, dance floors.
- Facilities for numerous sports.
- Day visitor passes.

BUTLINS, SKEGNESS

Map ref
78 B1

Butlins,
Skegness,
Lincolnshire,
PE25 1NJ
Tel: 01754 762311

www.butlins.co.uk

- 3 miles north of Skegness on A52.
- Close to sandy beach, Beach Club swimming pool, indoor sports facilities.
- Original 1950s holiday chalet, now Grade 2 listed building.
- Skyline Pavilion with bars, restaurants, shops.
- Splash Waterworld and numerous sports facilities.
- Go Karts, Funfair, Megazone laser arena, cinema, tenpin bowling, live entertainment, dance floors.
- Day visitor passes.

— Butlins - Waterslide —

- Open daily from 9.30am March-November.
- Britain's premier theme park with over 30 state-of-the-art rides.
- Air-flying coaster new in 2002.
- Nemesis - first suspended 'legs free' coaster.
- Oblivion - first 'face first' vertical drop coaster.

Alton, Stoke-on-Trent, Staffordshire, ST10 4DB
Tel: 01538 702200
Tel: 08705 20 40 60
www.altontowers.com

ALTON TOWERS

Map ref
76 C2

- Ticket prices: 12 years and over from £18.50. Advance booking discounts for peak times.
- £2.00 car parking charge
- Submission - double inverter.
- Illusion Ice Show in Big Top.
- 500 acre grounds include gardens and remains of Alton Towers mansion.
- Signposted from M1 junctions 23a & 28, from M6 junctions 15 & 16.
- Alton Towers Hotel adjacent.

Nemesis - Alton Towers

AMERICAN ADVENTURE

Map ref
77 D2

Pit Lane, Ilkeston,
Derbyshire, DE7 5SX
Tel: 0845 330 2929
www.adventureworld.co.uk

- Open daily from 10am March-November.
- Ticket price: 13 years and over £13.99
- Surrounds 32 acre lake with woodland setting.
- Nightmare Niagara - world's tallest triple drop log flume.
- Missile rollercoaster, sky coaster and twin looper.
- Runaway Train, Rocky Mountain Rapids, Santa Fe Railway, Buffalo Stampede.
- Shows in 'Western Saloon Bar'.
- 2 miles north of Ilkeston, signposted from M1 junction 26.
- Free car parking.

BLACKPOOL PLEASURE BEACH

Ocean Boulevard, Blackpool,
Lancashire, FY4 1EZ
Tel: 01253 341033
Opening times: 0870 444 5566

Map ref
80 C3

www.bpbltd.com

- Open March-November, opening times vary.
- Ticket prices: Unlimited ride wristband £25, admission to park is free. Individual ride tickets £1 (number required per ride varies).
- Wristband discounts on Fridays and for advance purchase.
- 45 acres of amusements, rides and shows located on Blackpool's sea front.
- 10 rollercoasters including classic wooden Big Dipper built 1923, high speed turbulent 71m high hypercoaster Pepsi Max Big One, 360 degree loop coaster Revolution and Grand National twin track coaster.
- Children's 'Beaver Creek' theme park.
- Exit M6 junction 32 onto M55. Follow signs for Blackpool South Shore and then Blackpool Pleasure Beach.
- 1,000 spaces in 5 car parks - charges apply.

CAMELOT

Map ref
81 D3

Park Hall Road, Charnock Richard,
Chorley, Lancashire, PR7 5LP
Tel: 01257 452100
www.camelotthemepark.co.uk

- Open daily from 10am June-August, open weekends only March-May and September-October. Additional weekday opening Easter week and Autumn half term. Open May Bank Holiday.
- Ticket price: £13.50
- Family entertainment park based on Arthurian legend.

- White-knuckle rides: The Gauntlet looping rollercoaster; New Century Excalibur 2 gyro inverter; The Rack - Europe's only split rollercoaster.
- Merlin's playground for young children, log flume, dodgems, jousting arena.
- Situated close to M6 (junctions 27 and 28) and M61 (junction 8).
- Free car parking.
- Park Hall Hotel adjacent.

Theme parks

CHESSINGTON WORLD OF ADVENTURES

Map ref 66 A2

Leatherhead Road, Chessington,
Surrey KT9 2NE
Tel: 0870 444 7777
www.chessington.com

- Open March-November (excluding some off-peak days).
- Opening times vary from 10am-5/6pm. Open till 7pm in August.
- Ticket prices: 12 years and over, from £17.00.
- Discounts for advance booking.
- New action rides in 2002: New Vampire swinging rollercoaster, interactive Tomb Blaster, Dennis's Madhouse in Beanoland.
- Animal enclosure, sea lion and penguin shows.
- 12 miles south west of London on A243, 2 miles from the A3 and M25 (junction 9 or 10).

Vampire Ride - Chessington

FLAMINGO LAND

Map ref 82 C1

Kirby Misperton, Malton,
North Yorkshire, YO17 6PZ
Tel: 01653 668287
Tel: 0870 752 8000
www.flamingoland.co.uk

- Open daily from 10am March-November. Closes 5pm weekdays and 6pm at weekends, Bank Holidays and throughout July and August.
- Ticket prices: £13.50
- 100 rides, shows and attractions.
- 5 rollercoasters including Magnum Force, Europe's only triple looping rollercoaster, The Bullet and Wild Mouse.
- The Terroriser thrill ride.
- Zoo with large flock of pink flamingos and over 1,000 animals including tigers, camels and monkeys.
- Adjoining holiday village and leisure complex.
- Signposted off A169 Malton to Pickering Road.

LIGHTWATER VALLEY

Map ref 82 A1

North Stainley, Ripon,
North Yorkshire, HG4 3HT
Tel: 01756 635368
www.lightwatervalley.co.uk

- Opens 10am, rides 10.30am, closes from 4.30pm.
- Open daily June-August, Easter week, Autumn half term. Open weekends only April and September. Open May Bank Holiday.
- Ticket prices: over 1.1m tall £13.50
- Rides classified as Jaw Droppers, Whipper Snappers or Nippers.
- The Ultimate, 1.48 mile long wooden roller coaster, claimed to be the world's longest.
- Batflyer suspended hang glider, Falls of Terror water ride, The Rat subterranean rollercoaster, The Twister, Black Widow's Web.
- Set in rural parkland 3 miles north of Ripon.
- 15 minute drive from A1 following A61 to Ripon and then A6108.
- Location of Lightwater Valley Shopping Village.

DRAYTON MANOR THEME PARK

Map ref 76 C4

Nr. Tamworth,
Staffordshire, B78 3TW
Tel: 01827 252400/287979
Bookings: 0870 010 8446
www.draytommanor.co.uk

- Open daily March-November.
- Gates open 9am, rides from 10.30am.
- Closes 5pm-7pm.
- Ticket prices: over 14 years £15.00 - £17.50. Admission only passes available.
- Discounts for advance booking.
- Family run with over 100 rides, amusements and live entertainment.
- Set in wooded parkland around a lake.
- Major rides: Apocalypse, the world's first stand-up tower drop; Stormforce 10; the gyro swing Maelstrom; Shockwave, Europe's only stand-up rollercoaster.
- Robinsons Land for children's rides.
- Get around by cable car or miniature train.
- Drayton Zoo with over 1000 animals, reptiles and exotic birds.
- Near Tamworth on A4091, close to junctions 9 & 10 of M42.

Apocalypse - Drayton Manor

LOUDON CASTLE

Galston,
Ayrshire, KA4 8PE
Tel: 01563 822296

www.loudoncastle.co.uk

Map ref 89 F3

- Open daily 10am-5pm April-September.
- Ticket prices: Over 1.25m tall £12.00
- Set in 500 acres of parkland with ruined 19c Loudon Castle a feature.
- The Drop Zone, 45m vertical plunge through trees.
- Traditional Galloping Carousel, possibly Britain's biggest.
- Splash Mountain log flume.
- Rory's Animal Kingdom zoo.
- 5 miles east of Kilmarnock off A71.

M&D'S

Map ref 89 G2

Hamilton Road,
Motherwell,
ML1 3RT
Tel: 01698 333777

www.scotlandsthemepark.co.uk

- Theme park and indoor family entertainment centre at Motherwell.
- Ticket prices: Free admission, rides from £2.00 with pay as you go tokens. Unlimited ride wristband £12.50
- Over 40 major rides and attractions.
- Jammin - world's first spinning coaster, Tornado double looping coaster, Freefall drop ride, Moby's Revenge water ride.
- Scotland's largest indoor soft play area, bingo, games arcade.
- Cosmic Bowl: 16 lane glow-in-the dark tenpin bowling.
- Located in Strathclyde Country Park close to M74 junction 5.
- Free parking.

MAGICAL WORLD OF FANTASY ISLAND

Sea Lane, Ingoldmells,
Nr. Skegness,
Lincolnshire, PE12 1RH
Tel: 01754 872030

www.fantasyisland.co.uk

Map ref 78 B1

- Open daily May-November from 10am.
- Closes 5.30pm / 6pm early and late season; closes 10pm Sunday-Thursday and 11pm Fri & Sat main season.
- Ticket prices: Free admission, rides from 50p with pay as you go tokens.
- Britain's first indoor theme park largely housed within 30m high glass and metallic pyramid structure.
- Jubilee Odyssey - Europe's longest suspended rollercoaster with 6 inversions and reaching speeds up to 160 km/h.
- More thrills on G Force, Volcanic Eruption, Millennium Coaster and Simex Movie Ride with motion simulation.
- Entertainment programme including evening cabaret in main season.
- 7 day a week indoor and outdoor market adjacent.
- 4 miles north of Skegness on sea front at Ingoldmells.

NEW PLEASUREWOOD HILLS

Map ref 79 F4

Leisure Way,
Corton, Lowestoft,
Suffolk, NR32 5DZ
Tel: 01502 508200

www.pleasurewoodhills.co.uk

- Open daily from 10am June-August, Easter week, Autumn half term. Open weekends only April, May, September.
- Ticket prices: Over 1.3m tall £12.99. Discounts for advance purchase

- Over 50 rides and attractions in 50 acre leisure park.
- Thrill rides: Drop Zone, Cannonball rollercoaster, Magic Mouse thrillcoaster, Mega Dance.
- Formula K raceway (extra charge).
- Sea lion and parrot shows, circus reviews.
- Halloween and Christmas events.
- Just off A12 between Lowestoft and Great Yarmouth.

OAKWOOD PARK

Map ref 68 B2

Canaston Bridge, Narberth,
Perthshire, SA67 8DE
24 hour Information Line:
08712 206 233
Bookings: 08712 206 211
www.oakwood-leisure.com

- Ticket prices: 10 years and over £12.25
- Prices include all rides excluding Vertigo, supplementary charge varies according to number of flyers.
- Open daily from 10.00am March-September.
- Wales's premier theme park.
- Modern wooden rollercoaster Megafobia, built 1996.
- 50m high sky coaster Vertigo.
- The Bounce, UK's only shot 'n drop tower coaster reaching 70km/h in 2 seconds.
- Europe's tallest, steepest, wettest water ride Hydro.
- Mardi Gras festival in June, After Dark summer season with live entertainment, fireworks and light shows, children's event at Christmas.
- 20 miles west of Carmarthen.

Hydro - Oakwood Park

PLEASURE ISLAND

Kings Road, Cleethorpes,
South Humberside,
DN35 0PL
Tel: 01472 211511
www.pleasure-island.co.uk

Map ref 88 E3

- White Knuckle Valley with Hyper Blaster, Terror Rack, Boomerang, Crazy Loop and Alkazam.
- Spanish, Moroccan and African themed areas.
- Music and animal shows and entertainment.
- Located in east coast resort of Cleethorpes.
- Free car parking.

- Open daily from 10am March-September and during Autumn half term. Open weekends only September and October. Closes 5pm / 6pm depending on time of year.
- Ticket price: £10.50

THORPE PARK

Map ref 66 A1

Staines Road,
Chertsey,
Surrey, KT16 8PN
Tel: 0870 444 4466
www.thorpepark.com

- Open daily March-September (excluding some off-peak days).
- Opening times vary from 9.30/10am-5/6pm. Open till 7.30pm in August.
- Ticket prices: 12 years and over from £17.00 - £23.00. Discounts for advance booking.
- New in 2002 Colossus - world's first 10 inversion rollercoaster.
- Other major rides: Detonator mega drop, Vortex, Zodiac, Tidal Wave - plunge 26m into wall of water.
- Located in 500 acre park on A320 between Staines and Chertsey.
- Signposted from M25, junctions 11 &13.
- Free car parking.

Colossus - Thorpe Park

Heading to a model train exhibition or a Cliff Richard concert ? - you can tell, there's nothing to be embarrassed about. This is the who, what, when, where, why section for all the big exhibition and concert venues.

ABERDEEN ECC

Bridge of Don,
Aberdeen, AB23 8B4
Tel: 01224 824824

Map ref
99 F4

www.aecc.co.uk

○ Exhibition and conference centre opened 1985.
○ Major rock and pop music venue.
○ Permanent home of biennial 'Offshore Europe' exhibition which attracted 24,000 visitors from 77 countries in 2001.
○ Redevelopment will increase conference delegate capacity to 2,000 by 2003.
○ 2 miles north of Aberdeen at Bridge of Don, just off A90.
○ Free parking.

ALEXANDRA PALACE

Map ref
130 D1

Alexandra Palace Way,
Wood Green,
London N22 7AY
Tel: 020 8365 2121

www.alexanderpalace.com

○ Versatile venue hosting awards ceremonies, banquets, concerts, conferences, exhibitions.
○ Historic building set in 198 acres of parkland and gardens with boating lake and panoramic views over London.
○ First public television broadcast made from here by B.B.C. in 1936.
○ Victorian Palm Court conservatory entrance foyer.
○ Great Hall with Henry Willis organ and rose window has capacity of more than 7,000 people.
○ Indoor ice rink.
○ Annual events: Road Racing & Superbike Show, London Garden Show, New London Classic Motor Show, RYA Sailboat and Windsurf Show, Knitting & Stitching Show.
○ 5 miles north of central London and 5 miles west of M1 junction 2.
○ Free parking for 2,000 cars.
○ Wood Green (Piccadilly line) nearest London Underground station.

Alexandra Palace

BOURNEMOUTH INTERNATIONAL CENTRE

Exeter Road, Bournemouth, BH2 5BH
Tel: 01202 456400

Map ref
64 C4

www.bic.co.uk

○ Conference, exhibition, entertainment and leisure centre on Bournemouth's seafront.
○ Used in conjunction with refurbished 1930s Pavilion Theatre and Ballroom.
○ 3 large halls including Windsor Hall with retractable tiered seating.
○ Annual wedding, ideal home, antiques, craft, and holiday exhibitions.
○ Fitness Zone and leisure pool with giant slide and wave machine.
○ Pay and display multi-storey car park.

BRIGHTON CENTRE

Map ref
66 B4

Kings Road,
Brighton,
East Sussex,
BN1 2GR
Tel: 01273 290131
Box office: 0870 900 9100

www.brightoncentre.co.uk

○ Purpose-built international conference, entertainment and exhibition centre.
○ Largest in south of England.
○ Superstar rock and pop concerts, world sporting events and major political conferences held here.
○ Main Hall can be transformed into ice rink, tennis court, theatre or disco.
○ Located on the seafront at Brighton close to the city centre.
○ 2 NCP car parks close by.

CARDIFF INTERNATIONAL ARENA

Map ref 112 B4

Mary Ann Street, Cardiff, CF10 2EQ
Tel: 029 2023 4500
Box office: 029 2022 4488
www.uk.cc.com/cia

- Cardiff's premier conference, exhibition and live entertainment centre.
- Opened 1993.
- Concerts, sporting events, ice shows, dance and comedy events.
- Capacity of main arena is 6,700 standing, 5,000 all seated.
- Major annual events include Regal Welsh Snooker Tournament, Welsh Caravan Show, Holiday on Ice, World Pool Championships, Creative Stitches and Crafts Alive Exhibition.
- Home to Cardiff World Trade Centre.
- In Cardiff city centre close to Cardiff central station.
- Use city centre car parks.

EARLS COURT

Warwick Road, London, SW5 9TA
Tel: 020 7385 1200
www.eco.co.uk

Map ref 66 B1

- Trade and consumer exhibitions, conventions, pop concerts, sporting events.
- Comprises Earls Court 1 and 2 exhibition halls and Conference Centre.
- Earls Court 1 opened 1937; Earls Court 2 opened 1999 with Europe's biggest unsupported roof span.
- London Boat Show, Tomorrow's World Roadshow, Daily Mail Ideal Home Exhibition, Stuff LIVE and Caravan & Outdoor Leisure Show among regular events.
- Car parking can be pre-booked.
- Close to Earls Court (Piccadilly & District Lines) and West Brompton (District Line) London Underground stations.

EXCEL

London, E16 1XL
Tel: 020 7476 0101
www.excel-london.co.uk

Map ref 133 C4

- New international exhibition, conference and event centre.
- Largest venue on a single site in London.
- Largest column-free halls in Europe.
- Major events include World Travel Market, International Food & Drink, British Power Boat Grand Prix, The Toy Fair, International Wine & Spirits Fair.
- The London Boat Show will become an annual event from January 2004.
- Venue for Pop Idol TV series and music video shoots by Westlife and Jamiroquai.
- Located on 100-acre site on north side of Royal Victoria Dock close to London City Airport.
- Served by Docklands Light Railway; Royal Victoria, Custom House and Prince Regent stations.
- Sunborn Yacht, custom built luxury hotel, berthed alongside ExCel's eastern entrance.
- 3 car parks with 5,700 spaces which can be pre-booked.

ExCel

G-MEX

Windmill Street, Manchester, M2 3GX
Tel: 0161 834 2700
www.gmex.co.uk

Map ref 122 C2

- In Central Manchester on the site of Central station which closed in 1969.
- G-Mex opened 1986 with exhibition halls, meeting rooms and auditorium.
- Victorian facade of the station retained.
- Adjacent Manchester International Convention Centre opened 2001.
- Hosts leisure activities, business meetings, sporting events, academic gatherings.
- Banquets can seat up to 3,500.
- 2002 Commonwealth Games venue for gymnastics, judo and wrestling.
- NCP car park directly below G-Mex/MICC has 2,136 spaces which can be pre-booked.
- Linked to Manchester Piccadilly station by Metrolink tram system.

- Major venue for conferences, trade fairs, exhibitions and entertainment.
- 2,000 seat auditorium and 8 interlinked halls including Edwardian Royal Hall.
- Major regular events include Home & Gift, Royal College of Nursing and Chartered Institute of Personnel & Development conferences and exhibitions.
- More than 300,000 attend events annually at HIC.

HARROGATE INTERNATIONAL CENTRE

Kings Road, Harrogate, HG1 5LA
Tel: 01423 500500
Box office: 01423 537230

Map ref
82 A2

www.harrogateinternationalcentre.co.uk

- Located centrally in Harrogate.
- 450 car parking spaces at HIC underground car park. Charges apply.
- Harrogate Moat House Hotel adjacent.

LONDON ARENA

Map ref
133 C4

36 Limeharbour,
London, E14 9TH
Tel: 020 7538 8880
Box office: 020 7538 1212

www.londonarena.co.uk

- Holds major public and trade events in heart of London Docklands.
- Comprises main arena with 9,000 square metres of pillar free floor space, conference rooms and numerous V.I.P. suites.
- Banqueting capacity of 5,000.
- Annual events include The London Marathon Expo and MOBO awards.
- Brit Awards held here 1998 and 1999.
- Home of London Knights Ice Hockey team.
- Docklands Light Railway connections from Canary Wharf or Heron Quays stations.
- Nearest London Underground at Canary Wharf (Jubilee Line).
- 1,000 car parking spaces in local NCP car parks.

MEN ARENA

21 Hunts Bank,
Manchester, M3 1AR
Tel: 0161 950 5000
Box office: 0161 930 8000

Map ref
122 C2

www.men-arena.com

- Europe's largest indoor concert venue with 19,500 seats.
- Attracts world class performers and 1.2 million visitors annually.
- Sporting events include boxing, basketball and ice hockey.
- Host to netball and boxing in Commonwealth Games 2002.
- Home to Manchester Storm Ice Hockey club.
- Located in Manchester City Centre adjacent to Victoria Station.
- Metrolink tram services to Manchester Piccadilly intercity station.
- On A56 3 miles from M62 junction 17.
- Multi-storey car park on site with 1,500 spaces; a further 7,000 spaces within 500m.

NEC AND NEC ARENA

Map ref
109 F4

Birmingham, B40 1NT
Tel: 0121 780 4141
Box office: 0870 909 4133

www.necgroup.co.uk

- One of Europe's busiest exhibition and events centres.
- UK's largest exhibition venue.
- 600-acre site with 20 interconnected halls, arena and outdoor exhibition area.
- Around 260 events held each year, the majority trade fairs.
- Regular events include Spring Fair Birmingham, BBC Gardeners' World, British International Motor Show, The Clothes Show and Crufts.
- Over 3 million exhibition visitors annually ranks the NEC second only to Paris Expo in Europe.
- NEC Arena is one of the UK's top venues for rock and pop concerts, seating 12,000.
- World Figure Skating Championships held in NEC Arena in 1995.
- Car parking on site with 24,000 parking spaces. Charges apply. Shuttle bus to main entrances.
- Easy access from M42 junction 6.
- Close to Birmingham International Station and Birmingham International Airport.

NEC

Entertainment venues

NOTTINGHAM ARENA

Map ref 126 C2

The National Ice Centre,
Lower Parliament Street,
Nottingham, NG1 1LA
Tel: 0115 853 3000

www.nottingham-arena.com

- Major music and indoor sports venue opened 2000.
- Seating capacity up to 10,000.
- Housed within National Ice Centre open 364 days a year.
- 2 Olympic sized ice pads, one of which transforms into the Arena.
- Ice galas and children's shows also staged.
- Home of Nottingham Panthers ice hockey team.
- Health and Fitness club.
- Located in Nottingham City Centre at edge of the Lace Market.

77 Hammersmith Road,
London W14 8UX
Box office: 020 7385 1200
www.eco.co.uk

OLYMPIA

Map ref 131 C4

- Trade and consumer exhibitions, conventions, pop concerts, sporting events.
- Together with Earls Court, London's leading major events venue.
- Comprises Olympia 1 and 2 exhibition halls and Conference Centre.
- Olympia 1 opened as the Grand Hall in 1886 with a performance by the Paris Hippodrome Circus.
- Venue for Olympia International Show Jumping Championships in December.
- Also Daily Mail House & Garden Fair, Ski & Snowboard Show, National Cat Club Show and Fine Art & Antiques fairs.
- Car parking can be pre-booked.
- Served by Kensington Olympia mainline station and London Underground Kensington Olympia (District Line) station.

Olympia

SECC

Map ref 116 C3

Glasgow, G3 8YW
Tel: 0141 248 3000
Box office: 0870 040 4000
www.secc.co.uk

- Concert, exhibition, conference and special events centre with more than 200 annual events.
- Hosts concerts with major rock stars, opera, ballet, sporting events, circus and carnivals, animal shows, ice shows, and flower shows.
- Major public events include Christmas and New Year Carnival, FoodFest and Scottish Wedding Show.
- 5 halls and 2 purpose built auditoriums.
- Main hall has concert arena capacity of 10,000.
- SECC opened in 1985 and 3,000 seat Clyde auditorium in 1997.
- Clyde auditorium known locally as the Armadillo because of its distinctive shape.
- 1 mile west of Glasgow city centre, just off junction 19 of M8.
- Own bus terminus and railway station linking to Glasgow Central Station.
- Parking for 3,000 vehicles off Finnieston Street.
- 2 hotels, casino and business centre on site.

SECC

Broughton Lane,
Sheffield, S9 2DF
Tel: 0114 256 5656
www.sheffield-arena.co.uk

SHEFFIELD ARENA

Map ref 128 C2

- One of the largest indoor entertainment centres in the UK.
- Opened 1991 to host World Student Games.
- 12,000 capacity concert arena with permanent ice floor.
- Hosts concerts, theatrical productions, ice hockey, ice shows, basketball, exhibitions and conferences.

- Home to Steelers ice-hockey team.
- International Supercross track created by dumping soil on ice floor.
- 3 miles north west of Sheffield city centre, close to junctions 33 & 34 of M1.
- On site parking for 1,200 cars; overspill car park with 800 spaces.
- Linked to Sheffield railway station by Supertram.

Wembley Arena

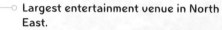

TELEWEST ARENA, NEWCASTLE

Arena Way,
Newcastle-upon-Tyne,
NE4 7NA
Tel: 0191 260 5000
Box office: 0870 707 8000
www.telewestarena.co.uk

Map ref
124 B3

- Largest entertainment venue in North East.
- Hosts music and sports events, exhibitions and conferences.
- Concert arena seats more than 11,000.
- Opened November 1995 with basketball, first concert in December 1995 featured David Bowie.
- Regular premier league basketball, ice hockey with Newcastle Vipers home team.
- Rock@Arena club in foyer.
- Close to the city centre on north bank of River Tyne.
- From A1 follow A184 to city centre, then A189 across Redheugh Bridge.
- 600 space car park on site.

WEMBLEY ARENA

Map ref
130 A3

Empire Way,
Wembley,
Middlesex,
HA9 0DW
Tel: 0870 739 0739

www.wembley.co.uk

- One of the most well known indoor music arenas in the UK.
- Capacity of 11,000.
- Also hosts sporting and other special events.
- Can accommodate basketball courts, ice rinks and playing fields.
- Just off A404 North Circular Road (B4557 Great Central Way).
- Nearest London Underground is Wembley Park (Metropolitan and Jubilee lines).
- Also served by Wembley Central (Bakerloo Line) and Wembley Stadium railway station (connects to London Marylebone).
- 6,000 on site parking spaces for Wembley complex.

WEMBLEY EXHIBITION CENTRE

Stadium Way,
Wembley,
Middlesex,
HA9 0DW
Tel: 0870 730 0739

Map ref
130 A3

www.wembley.co.uk

- Conference centre and 3 interlinked exhibition halls.
- Exhibitions include Rock n' Pop Fair, Wembley Antiques and Collector's Fair, UK Wedding Show.
- Grand Hall auditorium used for concerts and sporting events as well as conferences.
- Located just off A404 North Circular Road (B4557 Great Central Way).
- Nearest London Underground is Wembley Park (Metropolitan and Jubilee lines).
- Also served by Wembley Central (Bakerloo Line) and Wembley Stadium railway station (connects to London Marylebone).
- 6,000 on site parking spaces for Wembley complex.

Wembley Exhibition Centre

Calling all shopaholics! The major out-of-town shopping centres and, for those looking for a bargain, all the outlet villages are listed here with the details that will make your shopping experience a dream, until you get the credit card bill anyway!

Out-of-town shopping centres pages 33-36   Outlet villages pages 37-43

BLUEWATER

Greenhithe, Kent, DA9 9ST
Tel: 0845 6021021

www.bluewater.co.uk

Map ref
66 C1

- Over 330 shops and restaurants
- Three leisure villages
- 13 screen Showcase cinema.
- Boating lake, climbing wall, cycle and tandem hire, golf pro tour putting and Land Rover Adventure Zone.
- A mile from junction 2 of the M25.
- 13000 free parking spaces.

Open:
Mon–Fri   10am–9pm
Sat   9am–8pm
Sun   11am–5pm
(Many of the restaurants remain open until 11pm)

First Floor

Ground Floor

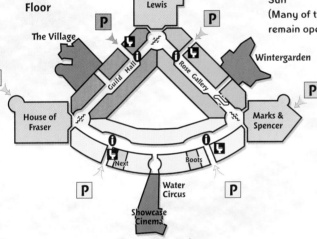

— Bluewater —

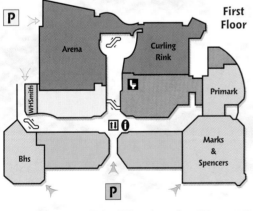

First Floor

- Located off the M8 at junction 25a (westbound traffic only) and 26.
- Over 100 shops and restaurants.
- An ice-skating and 8-sheet curling rink.
- A 4000 seat international arena.
- A Maritime Heritage Centre and riverside broadwalk.
- 6500 free parking spaces.

BRAEHEAD SHOPPING CENTRE

Kings Inch Road,
Glasgow G51 4BN

www.braehead.co.uk

Map ref
116 B2

Open:
Mon–Fri   10am–9pm
Sat   9am–6.30pm
Sun   11am–6pm
Bank Hol   10am–6pm

Ground Floor

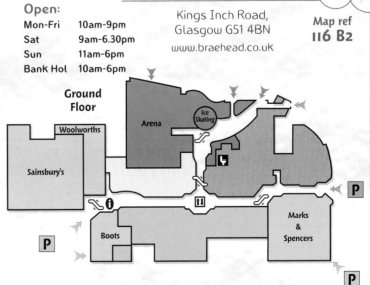

See page 34 for key to symbols on plans

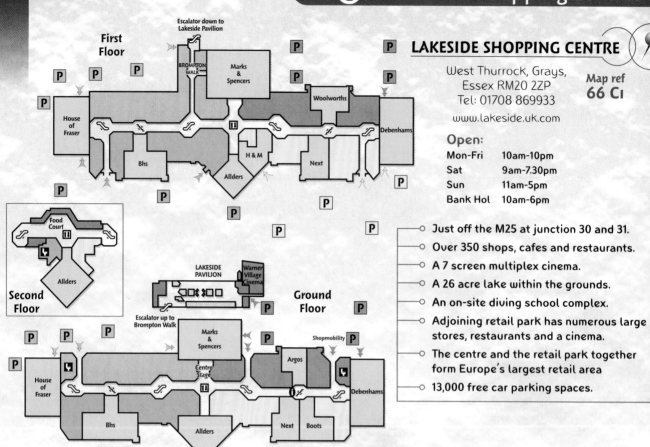

First Floor

Escalator down to Lakeside Pavilion

BROMPTON WALK

House of Fraser

Bhs

H & M

Marks & Spencers

Allders

Next

Woolworths

Debenhams

LAKESIDE SHOPPING CENTRE

West Thurrock, Grays,
Essex RM20 2ZP
Tel: 01708 869933
www.lakeside.uk.com

Map ref
66 C1

Open:
Mon-Fri   10am-10pm
Sat   9am-7.30pm
Sun   11am-5pm
Bank Hol   10am-6pm

Second Floor

Food Court

Allders

LAKESIDE PAVILION

Warner Village Cinema

Ground Floor

Escalator up to Brompton Walk

House of Fraser

Bhs

Marks & Spencers

Centre Stage

Allders

Argos

Next

Boots

Debenhams

Shopmobility

- Just off the M25 at junction 30 and 31.
- Over 350 shops, cafes and restaurants.
- A 7 screen multiplex cinema.
- A 26 acre lake within the grounds.
- An on-site diving school complex.
- Adjoining retail park has numerous large stores, restaurants and a cinema.
- The centre and the retail park together form Europe's largest retail area
- 13,000 free car parking spaces.

MEADOWHALL

Sheffield, S9 1EP
Tel: 0114 256 8800
www.meadowhall.co.uk

Map ref
128 C1

Open:
Mon-Fri   10am-9pm
Sat   9am-7pm
Sun   11am-5pm
Bank Hol   10am-6pm
Many of the leisure facilities open earlier and close later than the shops

- Just off the M1 at junction 34.
- Has its own tram and railway station.
- Over 200 shops and restaurants.
- An 11 screen cinema.
- Over 30 speciality stores in 'The Lanes'.
- Over 12,000 free parking spaces.

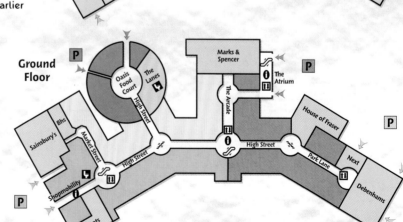

First Floor

Wonderpark/Le Grand Casino

Warner Village Cinema

Oasis Food Court

Marks & Spencer

The Atrium

The Arcade

High Street

House of Fraser

Park Lane

Next

Debenhams

W H Smith

Allders

Boots

Ground Floor

Oasis Food Court

The Lanes

Marks & Spencer

The Atrium

The Arcade

High Street

House of Fraser

Park Lane

Next

Debenhams

Bhs

Sainsbury's

Market Street

High Street

Shopmobility

Boots

 Stairs   Escalator   Lift   Toilet   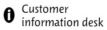 Customer information desk   Car park   Entrance

MERRY HILL CENTRE

Brierley Hill,
West Midlands, DY5 1QX
Tel: 01384 481141

Map ref
76 B4

www.merryhill.co.uk

Open:

Mon-Wed	10am-8pm	Sat	9am-7pm
Thurs-Fri	10am-9pm	Sun	11am-5pm

Opening hours for some stores extend beyond theses times.

- Approached from A4036, signposted from junctions 2 & 3 of M5.
- Over 250 stores.
- 7,000 free car parking spaces.
- Amphitheatre for entertainment and activities.
- Crèche.

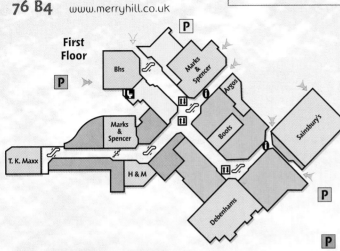

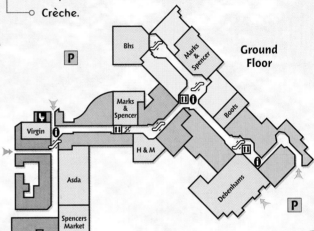

METROCENTRE

Gateshead, Tyne and Wear, NE11 9YG
Tel: 0191 493 0219
Tel: 0191 460 5299

Map ref
84 C1

www.metrocentre-gateshead.co.uk

- Themed areas with small unique shops together with major high street names.
- 50 eating places and several pubs.
- 11 screen UCI cinema, Megabowl entertainment centre, Metroland indoor theme park.
- 10,000 free parking spaces.

- On A1 west of Gateshead, 3 miles south west of Newcastle upon Tyne.
- One of the largest indoor shopping centres in the U.K. with 360 stores.

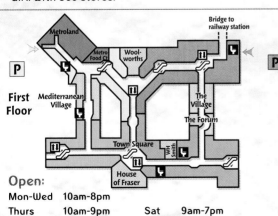

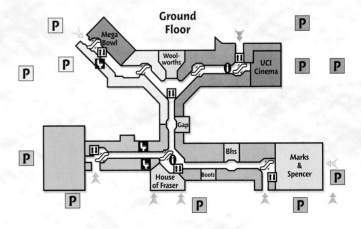

Open:

Mon-Wed	10am-8pm		
Thurs	10am-9pm	Sat	9am-7pm
Fri	10am-8pm	Sun	11am-5pm

Leisure facilities and some restaurants remain open later.

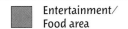 Entertainment/ Food area   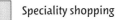 Speciality shopping   Major store    Other shopping

Out-of-town shopping centres

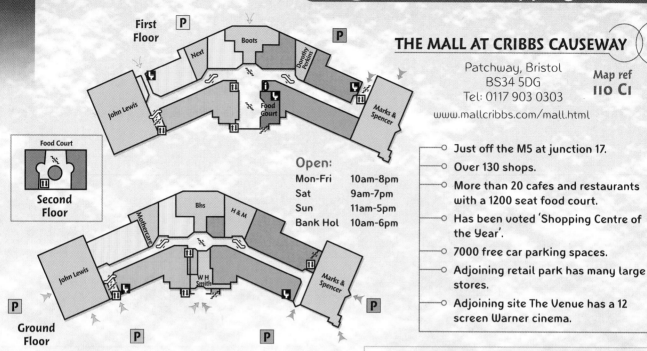

First Floor

Next • Boots • Dorothy Perkins

John Lewis • Food Court • Marks & Spencer

Food Court

Second Floor

Ground Floor

Mothercare • Bhs • H & M

John Lewis • W H Smith • Marks & Spencer

THE MALL AT CRIBBS CAUSEWAY

Patchway, Bristol
BS34 5DG
Tel: 0117 903 0303

Map ref **110 C1**

www.mallcribbs.com/mall.html

Open:

Mon-Fri	10am-8pm
Sat	9am-7pm
Sun	11am-5pm
Bank Hol	10am-6pm

- Just off the M5 at junction 17.
- Over 130 shops.
- More than 20 cafes and restaurants with a 1200 seat food court.
- Has been voted 'Shopping Centre of the Year'.
- 7000 free car parking spaces.
- Adjoining retail park has many large stores.
- Adjoining site The Venue has a 12 screen Warner cinema.

THE TRAFFORD CENTRE

Map ref **122 A3**

Manchester, M17 8AA
Tel: 0161 749 1717/1718
www.traffordcentre.co.uk

Open:

Mon-Fri	10am-9pm
Sat	9am-7pm
Sun	12pm-6pm
Bank Hol	10am-7pm

Many restaurants in The Orient open until midnight.
UCI cinema open until midnight, 3am Friday and Saturday.

First Floor

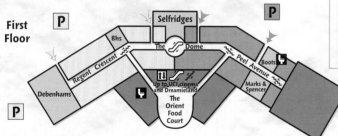

Selfridges • Bhs • The Dome • Peel Avenue • Boots

Regent Crescent • Up to UCI cinema and Dreamieland • Marks & Spencer

Debenhams • The Orient Food Court

Ground Floor

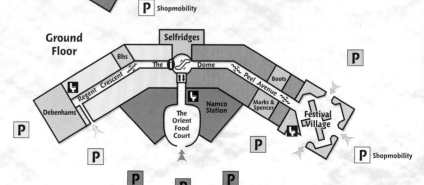

Selfridges • Bhs • The • Dome • Peel Avenue • Boots

Regent Crescent • Namco Station • Marks & Spencer • Festival Village

Debenhams • The Orient Food Court

Shopmobility

Shopmobility

- At junctions 9 & 10 of M60.
- 280 stores.
- Largest multiplex in the U.K. with 20 screen UCI cinema.
- Namco Station has tenpin bowling and bumper cars.
- Dreamieland - Europe's first shopping-centre based ride.
- Crèche and children's soft play area.
- Shopmobility and access services.
- 10,000 free car parking spaces.

— Trafford Centre

See page 34 for key to symbols on plans

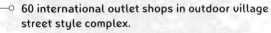

BICESTER VILLAGE

Map ref
71 E3

50 Pingle Drive,
Bicester,
Oxon,
OX6 7WD
Tel: 01869 323200

www.bicestervillage.com

Open:

Mon-Sun   10am-6pm

- 60 international outlet shops in outdoor village street style complex.
- Many famous brand names from Knightsbridge and Bond Street.
- Savings of at least 25% on normal retail prices.
- 2 miles from M40 junction 9.
- Free parking in 5 large car parks.
- Limousine service offered from UK airports, London and regional addresses.

— Bicester Village —

CLACTON FACTORY SHOPPING VILLAGE

Stephenson Road West,
Clacton-on-Sea,
Essex,
CO15 4TL
Tel: 01255 479595

Map ref
73 E3

www.clactonvillage.co.uk

Open:

Mon-Sat   10am-6pm
Sun   11am-5pm

- 48 outlet shops in outdoor village street style complex.
- Traditional French Carousel for children.
- Savings of up to 50% all year round.
- Located next to A133 Clacton by-pass which provides a link to the A120 and M11 (junction 8), A12 and M25 (junction 28).
- 1,000 free car parking spaces.

CLARKS VILLAGE OUTLET CENTRE

Map ref
63 F3

Farm Road,
Street,
Somerset,
BA16 0BB
Tel: 01458 840064

www.clarksvillage.co.uk

Open:

Mon-Sat   9am-6pm
Sun   10am-5pm
(Nov-March closes 5.30pm
Mon-Sat)

- 57 outlet shops.
- Up to 50% off all year round.

- Food court, tourist information, indoor and outdoor children's play areas.
- Wildlife events presented by Secret World Wildlife Rescue.
- Next to Clarks shoe factory at Street, 12 miles from junction 23 of M5.
- Pay and display car parking with 1400 spaces.
- Next to outdoor swimming pool.

DE BRADELEI MILL SHOP

Chapel Street,
Belper,
Derbyshire,
DE56 1AR
Tel: 01773 829830

Map ref
77 D2

Open:

Mon-Fri   9.30am-5.30pm
Sat   9.30am-6pm
Sun   10.30am-4.30pm

- Designer and brand name discount outlet.
- Up to 70% discount on top fashion and designer labels.
- Located in historic old mill where Queen Victoria's coronation stockings were made.
- Shops and coffee shop set around mill courtyard.
- Small free car park.

DE BRADELEI WHARF

Cambridge Road,
Dover,
Kent,
CT17 9BJ
Tel: 01304 226616

Map ref 67 F3

Open:
Mon-Fri	9.30am-5.30pm
Sat	9.30am-6pm
Sun	11am-5pm

- Over 20 factory outlet fashion and furnishings units and coffee shop.
- Located in former dockside building in historic Wellington Dock behind Dover's Marine Parade.
- Car parking available.

FESTIVAL PARK FACTORY SHOPPING VILLAGE

Map ref 63 E1

Ebbw Vale,
Gwent,
NP23 8FP
Tel: 01495 350350

Open:
Mon-Sat	9.30am-5.30pm
	(Open until 7pm on Thurs)
Sun	11am-5pm

- Over 40 factory outlet shops.
- Many shops sell stock at half the recommended retail price.
- Next to Festival Park, landscaped gardens created for 1992 Garden Festival Wales.
- Located on A4046 Ebbw Vale to Newport Road.
- Signposted from M4 junction 28 and from A465 Abergavenny to Swansea road.
- Free parking.

FREEPORT BRAINTREE

Charter Way,
Chapel Hill,
Braintree,
Essex CM77 8YH
Tel: 01376 348867

Map ref 72 C3

www.freeportplc.com

Open:
Mon-Sat	10am-6pm
	(Open until 8pm on Thurs)
Sun	11am-5pm

- Over 80 designer outlet shops.
- Internet café, health & beauty salon, indoor golf simulator, mini-cinema.
- Adventure playground and indoor play area.
- Located off A120, signposted from Braintree. Use M11 junction 8.
- 1,200 free car parking spaces.

Freeport - Braintree

- Over 85 designer outlet shops.
- Internet café, health & beauty salon, indoor golf simulator, mini-cinema.
- Indoor and outdoor play areas.
- Close to M62 junction 32.
- 3,500 free car parking spaces.

FREEPORT CASTLEFORD

Castleford,
West Yorkshire,
WF10 4FR
Tel: 01977 520153

Map ref 82 A3

www.freeportplc.com

Open:
Mon-Fri	10am-8pm
Sat	10am-6pm
Sun	11am-5pm

FREEPORT FLEETWOOD

Map ref
80 C2

Anchorage Road, Fleetwood,
Lancashire, FY7 6AE
Tel: 01253 877377

www.freeportplc.com

Open:
Mon-Wed   10am-6pm
Thurs-Fri   10am-8pm
Sat-Sun   10am-6pm

- Outlet village with over 40 shops.
- Children's Go Karts and adventure play area.
- Follow A585 to Fleetwood from M55 junction 3.
- 1,000 free car parking spaces.

FREEPORT HORNSEA

Rolston Road,
Hornsea,
North Humberside
HU18 1UT
Tel: 01964 534211

Map ref
83 D2

www.freeportplc.com

Open:
Mon-Sun   9.30am-6pm

- Outlet village with over 45 shops.
- Butterfly World with free-flying butterflies.
- Adventure playground, model village, crazy golf, electronic games for children.
- From M62 junction 38 follow B1230 to Beverley, then A1035 to Hornsea.
- 1,600 free car parking spaces.

FREEPORT SCOTLAND

Map ref
90 A2

Five Sisters,
Westwood,
West Calder,
West Lothian,
EH55 8QB
Tel: 01501 763488

Open:
Mon-Sun   10am-6pm.

www.freeportplc.com

- Over 40 designer outlet shops.
- Amazonia comprising indoor tropical house with free-flying butterflies, small mammals, reptiles and insects.
- Indoor and outdoor play areas, Go Karts, fairground rides.
- Between Edinburgh and Glasgow, signposted from M8 junction 4.
- 1,500 free car parking spaces.

FREEPORT TALKE

Pit Lane,
Talke Pits,
Stoke-on-Trent,
ST7 1XD
Tel: 01782 774113

Map ref
76 B1

www.freeportplc.com

Open:
Mon-Fri   9.30am-8pm
Sat   9.30am-6pm
Sun   11am-7pm

- Outlet mall with over 40 shops.
- Children's soft play area.
- 4 miles east of M6 junction 1. Follow A500, then A34 to Talke.
- 1,000 free car parking spaces.

— Freeport - Braintree —

GRETNA GATEWAY

Glasgow Road,
Gretna,
Dumfries-shire,
DG16 5GG
Tel: 01461 339100

www.gretnagateway.com

Map ref
85 F1

Open:
Mon - Sun   10am-6pm

- 27 factory outlet shops with more planned.
- Several brand names have their only outlet shops in Scotland here.
- Up to 50% off retail prices.
- 8 miles north of Carlisle at Gretna, close to A(74M) junction 22.
- Around 1,000 free car parking spaces.

K VILLAGE

Map ref
86 A4

Kendal,
Cumbria,
LA9 7DA
Tel: 01539 732363

www.kvillage.co.uk

Open:
Mon-Fri   9.30am-6pm
Sat   9am-6pm
(Closes 5.30pm in winter)
Sun   11am-5pm

- Discount outlet centre with 13 shops including fashion and houshold goods.
- Up to 50% off recommended retail prices.
- Heritage centre illustrating history of K shoemaking in Kendal and reconstructed K Shoe Shop.
- Restaurant, picnic and outdoor play areas.
- Located just to the south of Kendal, approached from M1 junction 36.

LIGHTWATER VILLAGE

North Stainley,
Ripon,
North Yorkshire,
HG4 3HT
Tel: 01765 635321

Map ref
82 A1

Open:
Mon-Sun   10am-5pm

- Retail and factory outlet complex with 13 shops.
- Fashions and homeware at almost half the retail price.
- Located at Lightwater Valley Theme Park, 3 miles north of Ripon.
- Free parking.

LOCH LOMOND OUTLET CENTRE

Map ref
89 E1

Main Street,
Alexandria,
Dunbartonshire,
G83 0UG
Tel: 01389 710077

www.lochlomondoutletcentre.co.uk

Open:
Mon-Sun   9.30-5.30

- 20 outlet units in Grade A listed building.
- Discounts of up to 50% off original prices.
- Argyll Motor Company factory opened here in 1905, turned over to torpedo production in World War II.
- Motoring heritage museum.
- Café.
- Free parking.

Loch Lomond Outlet Centre

McARTHUR GLEN DESIGNER OUTLET
- ASHFORD

Map ref
67 E3

Kimberley Way,
Ashford,
Kent, TN24 0SD
Tel: 01233 895900

www.mcarthurglen.com

Open:

Mon-Wed	10am-6pm
Thurs	10am-8pm
Fri	10am-6pm
Sat	9am-6pm
Sun	11am-5pm

- Over 70 designer outlet stores.
- Tented structure designed by Millennium Dome architect Richard Rogers.
- Food court and cafés.
- Children's play area, tourist and visitor information with tickets to local attractions.
- Exit M20 at junction 10, following signs for International Station and Designer Outlet.
- Free parking.

McArthur Glen Designer Outlet - Ashford

McARTHUR GLEN DESIGNER OUTLET
- CHESHIRE OAKS

Map ref
75 E1

Open:

Mon-Fri	10am-8pm
Sat	10am-6pm
Sun	11am-5pm

Kinsey Road,
Ellesmere Port,
The Wirral,
Cheshire, CH65 9JJ
Tel: 0151 348 5600

www.mcarthurglen.com

- Europe's largest designer outlet with over 140 stores.
- Restaurants and food court.
- Children's play areas, tourist information centre.
- Follow signs from junction 10 of M53.
- 3,000 free car parking spaces.
- 30 million visitors since opening in 1995.
- Bowling alley, multi-screen cinema and nightclub in adjacent Coliseum entertainment complex.

McArthur Glen Designer Outlet - Great Western

McARTHUR GLEN DESIGNER OUTLET
- BRIDGEND

Open:

Mon-Fri	10am-8pm
Sat	10am-6pm
Sun	11am-5pm

The Derwen,
Bridgend,
South Wales,
CF32 9SU
Tel: 01656 665700

Map ref
63 D2

www.mcarthurglen.com

- Wales's largest designer outlet with 90 shops.
- Village street style with 800 seat food court.
- 9 screen Odeon cinema.
- Entertainment programme, children's play areas, tourist information centre.
- Close to junction 36 of M4.
- 2,000 free car parking spaces.

McARTHUR GLEN DESIGNER OUTLET
- GREAT WESTERN

Open:

Mon-Wed	10am-6pm
Thurs	10am-8pm
Fri	10am-6pm
Sat	9am-6pm
Sun	11am-5pm

Kemble Drive,
Swindon,
Wiltshire,
SN2 2DY
Tel: 01793 507600

Map ref
70 C4

www.mcarthurglen.com

- Over 110 designer outlet stores in former Great Western Railway works.
- Largest covered designer outlet in Europe.
- Food court and cafés.
- Crèche and children's play area.
- Follow signs for Outlet Centre from junction 16 of M4.
- Car parking charges - over 3,000 spaces.
- Adjacent to STEAM, museum of the Great Western Railway.

McArthur Glen Designer Outlet - Livingston

McARTHUR GLEN DESIGNER OUTLET
- LIVINGSTON

Almondvale Avenue,
Livingston,
West Lothian,
EH54 6QX
Tel: 01506 423600

Map ref
90 A2

www.mcarthurglen.com

Open:
Mon-Wed 10am-6pm
Thurs 10am-8pm
Fri-Sun 10am-6pm
Cathedral Mall open until 8pm Wed-Fri;
Food court open Mon-Fri 9am-8pm &
Sat-Sun 9am-6pm.

- Scotland's largest designer outlet with over 80 stores.
- Restaurants, pub, cinema and fitness centre.
- 13 miles west of Edinburgh, signposted from M8 junction 3.
- 2,000 free parking spaces.
- Water sculpture by celebrated Japanese artist Susumu Shingu a feature.

McARTHUR GLEN DESIGNER OUTLET
- MANSFIELD

Map ref
77 D1

Mansfield Road,
South Normanton,
Derbyshire,
DE55 2ER
Tel: 01773 545000

www.mcarthurglen.com

Open:
Mon-Wed 10am-6pm
Thurs 10am-8pm
Fri 10am-6pm
Sat 9am-6pm
Sun 11am-5pm

- 65 shops and food court.
- Sherwood Forest themed children's play area.
- Annual brass band festival in August.
- Located on A38, close to M1 junction 28.
- Free parking with over 1,000 spaces.

McARTHUR GLEN DESIGNER OUTLET
- YORK

Open:
Mon-Wed 10am-6pm
Thurs 10am-8pm
Fri-Sat 10am-6pm
Sun 11am-5pm

St. Nicholas Avenue,
Fulford,
York,
YO19 4TA
Tel: 01904 682720

Map ref
82 B2

www.mcarthurglen.com

- More than 110 designer outlet stores in former hospital building.
- Grounds planted with over 400 trees.
- Viking-themed food court.
- 4 miles south of York close to A64/A19 interchange.
- Free parking with 2,700 spaces.
- Park and Ride to York city centre.

McArthur Glen Designer Outlet - York

Outlet villages

ROYAL QUAYS OUTLET CENTRE

Map ref
125 E2

Coble Dene Road,
North Shields,
Tyne and Wear,
NE29 6DW
Tel: 0191 296 3743

www.royalquaysoutletcentre.co.uk

Open:

Mon-Wed	10am-6pm	Fri-Sat	10am-6pm
Thurs	10am-8pm	Sun	11am-5pm

- Over 50 stores, food court, outdoor children's play area.
- Home to the 'Lightning Clock' moving sculpture which strikes on the hour.
- Just off the A19 next to the International Ferry Terminal at North Shields, 1 mile from the Tyne Tunnel.
- Free parking.

STERLING MILLS DESIGNER OUTLET VILLAGE

Map ref
94 D4

Devon Vale,
Tillicoultry,
Clackmannanshire,
FK13 6HQ
Tel: 01259 752100

www.sterlingmills.com

Open:

Mon-Sun   10am-6pm

- Outlet for internationally renowned designer brand names.
- Between 30% and 70% off High Street prices.
- 39 shops and restaurant.
- Nike's only Scottish outlet store.
- Just off A91, 8 miles west of Stirling.
- Free parking with over 500 spaces.

THE DESIGNER ROOM

Jacksons Landing,
The Highlight,
Hartlepool,
Cleveland,
TS24 0XN
Tel: 01429 275308

Map ref
85 E3

www.jacksonslanding.co.uk

Open:

Mon-Sat	10.0am-6pm
Sun	11am-5pm

- Designer discount department store.
- Up to 70% off most purchases.
- Located on Hartlepool Marina next to historic 18th century quay and Hartlepool Museum.
- First floor café has panoramic views over harbour.
- 1 million visitors annually.
- 2,500 free parking spaces.

THE GALLERIA

Map ref
72 A3

Comet Way, Hatfield,
Hertfordshire,
AL10 0XR
Tel: 01707 278301

www.factory-outlets.co.uk

Open:

Mon-Fri	10am-8pm
Sat	10am-6pm
Sun	11am-5pm

- 60 designer and brand outlet stores on 2 levels.
- 20% to 60% off normal prices.
- Well known for menswear.
- A mall dedicated to furniture and furnishings.
- 6 restaurants and cafés.
- 9 screen UCI cinema.
- Situated over the A1(M) at Hatfield between junctions 3 & 4, 6 miles north of M25 junction 23.
- 1,800 free car parking spaces with easy access for visitors with children and the disabled.
- 5 million shoppers annually.

Everything you'll ever need to know about cars and driving. From the techie stuff (lots of three letter abbreviations) to what to do if you have an accident (apart from panic!):

ANTI-LOCK BRAKING SYSTEMS (ABS)

Have you ever pressed hard on the brake pedal to reduce speed and felt a grating, vibrating sensation through your right foot. There is no fault with the brakes! **Chances are you've activated the ABS**, which you've seen on car ads and on the car dashboard when starting up and wondered what it was all about.

ABS detects when any one or more wheels (i.e. tyres) is about to skid under braking and is activated to put the brakes on and off

ABS

up to **20 times a second** (hence the grating feeling). Speed is reduced but ABS allows the wheel/s to continue to rotate. So what does that enable the driver to do?

Imagine braking hard and skidding. Without ABS, the wheels would 'lock up' and the car 'plough on' in a straight line! Turning the steering wheel will make no difference to your direction whatsoever. With ABS, the wheels are allowed to rotate under braking, enabling you to emergency brake and steer. An easy way to remember the main benefit: **ABS, A**llows **B**raking and **S**teering.

So do ABS brakes shorten stopping distances? **NO!** They don't. Think about how they work again. ABS puts the brakes on and off up to 20 times a second. So the brakes are **on 50%** of the time and **off 50%**. If you release a little brake pedal pressure to just de-activate ABS, creating 100% braking effect but less hard, you will brake in a shorter distance.

If you are braking under ABS in an emergency, look for the 'escape' space to steer towards. Don't look at whatever caused the problem as you will always end up steering towards what you are looking at!

ACTION FOLLOWING AN ACCIDENT

If you are involved in a crash, hopefully, whatever 'Passive' safety systems (e.g. Seat Belts, Air Bags, Impact Protection Systems, etc) there may be in your car have done their job and you and any passengers are uninjured.

Use your hazard warning lights to warn other traffic and ask other drivers to switch off their engines and stop smoking. Move uninjured people away from the vehicles to safety and do not move injured people from their vehicles unless they are in immediate danger from fire or explosion. Be prepared to give first aid.

Two emergency items you may well wish to carry in your car and which are readily available from motorist shops are:

1) A **Fire Extinguisher** - check it is easily accessible and servicable.

2) A **Life Hammer** - a small, red plastic hammer, housing both a tungsten steel tip to break into toughened glass (side windows and rear screen usually) and a safety blade to cut through seat belt webbing to release occupants who may be trapped.

If any party is injured the Police and Emergency Services must be contacted, however, onlookers may well have already done this, especially if the accident is causing traffic congestion, but don't assume that this is the case. If it is a low speed 'shunt' accident with no serious damage or injuries, rather than having an argument in the middle of the road as to whose fault it was, causing congestion and high risk to yourselves and other road users, just drive your vehicles to a safe area and exchange details there.

If you are involved in an accident which causes damage or injury to any other person, vehicle, animal or property, **you must and are legally required to STOP!**

Exchange names, addresses, registration numbers and insurance companies with the other drivers. If you do not do this, the accident must be reported to the police, as soon as possible and within 24 hours

Take a look at the Highway Code (very readable little book these days!) Rules 255 to 261, for an excellent and comprehensive guide to actions.

ACTION FOLLOWING A BREAKDOWN

Why is it that some drivers, when they're breaking down, brake sharply and stop right in the middle of the road or lane creating congestion and mayhem for the rest of us motorists? In many cases, the momentum of the vehicle and/or the downhill slope of the road could have easily been used for the driver to pull up somewhere safe off the carriageway.

The Highway Code gives sound advice. If your vehicle breaks down, get it off the road if possible and put your hazard warning lights on to warn of any obstruction. If it's dark put your sidelights on and don't stand between your vehicle and oncoming traffic.

If you are breaking down on the motorway, try to get your vehicle to 'limp' to the next exit or service area. Why? **Because the hard shoulder is the most dangerous place to be on the motorway**. Even though motorways are the safest roads in the UK, there are more fatalities on the hard shoulder than any of the other three lanes!

If you have broken down on the hard shoulder, ensure you park with the cars wheels pointing to the left. Walk to the nearest emergency phone, following the arrows on the white posts with blue tops, or get out of the car on the passenger side and use your mobile phone. The emergency phones are free, go straight through to police emergency control and, as you call, your exact location will be known. Give as many details as you can (let them know if you are a lone woman) then return to your car and await the breakdown service. **Don't get in your car unless you feel unsafe**, in which case sit on the passenger side of the car with the seatbelt on and lock all the doors.

On any other road, try to get the car out of the way of other traffic, switch on your hazard lights and raise the bonnet. Call your motoring organisation giving as many details as possible (let them know if you feel at risk) and get back into the car, unless there is danger of a collision.

Take a look at the Highway Code (a very readable little book!) Rules 248 to 254, for an excellent and comprehensive guide to actions.

Action following a breakdown

AIR CONDITIONING

It's one of those rare, hot sultry August days. You're in the rush hour queue, with all the windows open, choking on car fumes. In spite of having the fan on full, on 'cold', you're still sweating buckets! The chap in the car next to you looks as cool as a cucumber and has all the windows closed. This is when you wish you had air conditioning!

Air conditioning makes driving more comfortable, and you can have a system fitted if your car doesn't have one as standard. They now come with **automatic temperature control**, and **computers** that can provide different temperatures for the driver and passenger! From a safety viewpoint, above 38.5 degrees C, you don't function too well!

A quick trip round the technology

Coolant is pumped to a chamber where it cools hot air from the car interior by evaporation (remember your fizzics?) The cool air is blown back into the car. The evaporated coolant is then compressed, forcing it back into being a liquid again, which is pumped to the chamber.... **This is a closed system, so it shouldn't leak.**

What you should know...basic care

If you have air conditioning, it needs to be **switched on** for five minutes **every week** or the seals dry out and leak coolant – keep an eye on the level. **Have it serviced** every 30,000 miles, or every two years.

Environmental considerations

Your fuel consumption will be higher and there are other environmental considerations as well. Older cars used R12, the infamous **CFC** (chlorofluorocarbon, trade name Freon) as a coolant, which basically wrecks the ozone layer. Today, R134a is used, an HFC (hydroflurocarbon) which doesn't contain the ozone damaging chlorine bit but which **does** contribute to global warming – you can't win!

More air conditioning = Warmer atmosphere = More air conditioning!

But there are still those hot August days!!

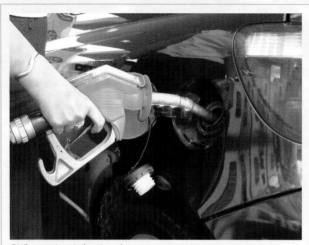
BHP, petrol and diesel engines

BHP, PETROL & DIESEL ENGINES

For those of us who are into **TLA's** (Three Letter Abbreviations), **BHP** means Brake Horse Power. Simply put, this is the maximum power delivered by an engine at a particular engine speed, denoted in **RPM** (Revolutions Per Minute). Also, if you ever see that the max. power output is, say, 150PS, and you did GCSE German, PS means Pferde Starke, Horse Power auf Deutsch, sorry, in German. So it's the same thing!

Due to rapid developments in engine design technology, the choice between buying a petrol or diesel powered car is becoming more difficult. Modern diesel powered cars are clean and can deliver amazing performance. Not only that, but you can get 65 - 70 miles per gallon.

Diesel powered cars can cost more to buy and may require more frequent engine oil and filter changes than petrol cars. However, from a taxation viewpoint, modern diesel engine emissions are low, providing significant benefits to the personal allowances of company car drivers. Diesel engines are not only very reliable (no spark plugs or electrical ignition timing involved) but they also last a long time - see how old some of your local diesel powered buses are !

DEFENSIVE DRIVING (STAYING ALIVE, STAYING ALIVE, AH, AH, AH, HONEY!)

You've passed your driving test and everyone knowingly says; "Now you've got to learn to drive!" Patronising or what - especially as they probably mean 'go faster and shout a lot!'

However, there are things that you can learn the hard way, like being hit by a car that was signalling and didn't turn. Or perhaps you could have observed that in spite of the 'blinking' light, the car couldn't make that turn at that speed without rolling it over.

Defensive driving is about assuming everyone else using the road is an idiot – and not being one yourself! Never assume anything is going to do what it indicates. Expect the unexpected, assess the situation and be ready to take 'evasive action'. Above all, **put safety first – You are in charge of a potentially lethal weapon.**

        Observe

        Anticipate

        Stay in Control (of the vehicle and yourself!)

        Tolerate

        Be Responsible

        Be Courteous

Re-read the Highway Code (drive at a safe speed for the conditions). Use your common sense (little old ladies take longer to cross the road and might be deaf – you'll be old one day, hopefully!).

Being able to assess a situation, make a decision and act safely and quickly comes with practice and experience. The most difficult skill to master is being tolerant and staying in control of your emotions when another driver does something **really stupid**. This can lead to **ROAD RAGE**, which makes good television viewing, but which causes serious accidents - and you feel a **real idiot** when you've calmed down!

Stay in control, pull yourself back from your immediate feelings (does it really matter compared to the number of people starving in the world/being killed and maimed by senseless wars/dying from terrible illnesses?) – of course not, let it go, stay calm – **and stay alive!**

Driving information

DRINKING/DRUGS AND DRIVING

As members of the modern human race, **we love to socialise.** We love to go out and meet up with friends in pubs and clubs and have a great night out. We want to relax, lose those inhibitions and get away from all those constraints, disciplines, rules and regulations imposed upon us during the weekday work/home routine. Perfectly understandable.

As qualified drivers we all passed a basic test. This test did **NOT** cover driving at night, driving with your mates talking away (loudly, because they've all had a drink!), driving under some influence of alcohol, not necessarily excessive, and driving at speed round your favourite bend in the wet.

Alcohol affects your driving judgement and abilities, creates a false sense of confidence, reduces co-ordination, decreases your reaction time, affects judgement of speed, distance, risk and reduces your driving skill, even if you are below the legal limit. **So, it doesn't affect much then!**

Drinking, drugs and driving

Imagine you are a rear passenger in the car above, with the driver approaching his favourite bend. Oh, by the way, that afternoon he had been playing Monaco Grand Prix on his Playstation at home and he's told you he now knows all about how to take a bend properly! What odds will you give yourself for survival now?

Don't get in the car with a driver, even if it's a good friend, if you suspect they are under the influence of alcohol and/or drugs. Why should you place your life in their unskilled hands?

We are all individuals with varying physiological make-ups! The influence of different levels and types of alcohol and drugs, even prescribed ones, or indeed a mix of both, is really an unknown. If there is any chance that your driving ability is impaired then PLEASE, DON'T DRIVE! Just arrange for a taxi or use another means of transport.

OK, now the serious stuff. **What does the law say?** It says 'You **MUST NOT** drive under the influence of drugs or medicine' and 'You **MUST NOT** drive with a breath alcohol level higher than 35 microgrammes per 100 ml or a blood alcohol level of more than 80 mg per 100 ml'.

There are more drink/drive fatalities in Summer than Winter, even including Christmas. Why? Warm weather creates thirst and when combined with extended daylight hours tempts drivers out onto the roads.

When you're driving, look out for the driving behaviour of other motorists which suggests they may well be under the influence of drink or drugs. Position to keep well away from their potential crash!

If You Drink, Please Don't Drive!

DRIVING WITH CHILDREN - SAFETY

Apart from 'don't!' if you have to transport children, little cherubs under the age of fourteen have to be physically restrained – whether they like it or not! The driver carries the **legal** responsibility for making sure children are appropriately secured - and stay that way!

How do you choose a child car seat? For babies and small children, it depends on the **weight** and not the **age** of the child – another reason for a strop "Sarah doesn't have to sit in a baby seat and she's younger than me - waaaaaaaah!" Anyway, the DTLR recommend which to use for what, (see their website www.dtlr.gov.uk). Only buy a second-hand child seat if you know its full history and it has the fitting instructions.

Where do you put it? The best place is in the middle of the rear seat if possible (to minimise injury from side impact). Don't put a rear facing child car seat (or any other, unless it's okay with the car manufacturer) in a front passenger seat, which is fitted with an airbag. When the child is in the seat, you should only be able to get two fingers between the collarbones and harness straps - without being bitten!

Driving with children

For all children, the **legal** requirements are listed in the latest 'Highway Code' – **make sure you know them.**

Keeping kids happy, comfortable and amused is not covered here, but unless they are, you will constantly be distracted from driving safely. Remember that in a hot car, a young child's body temperature will increase three to five times **faster** than an adult, good reason to scream! As for amusing them on long journeys, besides games and food, you may even have to throw street cred to the wind and sing along with "Old MacDonald"!

ERGONOMICS – ARE YOU SITTING COMFORTABLY?

Can you reach the steering wheel and foot pedals easily, or do you have to lean forward or sit with your knees under your chin? (They are not supposed to be higher than the pelvis!). Do you have to slump in your seat because the roof is too low? Is your head on the headrest? (If not, a rear end collision could result in serious whiplash injury). Can you reach all the controls without having to take your eyes off the road? You can end up with all sorts of back problems if you drive a lot; so take note aspiring sales reps!

Get comfy before you start!

If your seat adjusts, move it so you don't need to stretch for instruments or pedals. Try cushions or purpose made foam wedges. Adjust the headrest if possible, if not, get an add-on headrest support. If the steering wheel is thin, you can get repetitive strain injury; get a padded cover for it (good one for the Christmas list!). Adjust the seat belt so it's safe and comfortable (e.g. not twisted).

To avoid a pain in the bum, put your wallet in the glove box, just don't forget you've left it there! Drinking water keeps muscles more relaxed – but take a sports bottle, it's easier to use, and only drink whilst stationary. Don't wear tight clothes and wear 'comfy' shoes (keep a trendier pair in the back for when you get out!). Take breaks on long journeys; don't just sleep, get out and stretch a bit.

...And if you notice you can't see out of the rear view mirror while you're driving, don't alter it, **SIT UP**, you've probably slumped!

Don't twiddle while you drive!

If all your knobs are the same size, make sure you know which does what before you start. Anyway, it's embarrassing to squirt the windscreen when you meant to indicate left!

EXHAUST EMISSIONS / CATALYTIC CONVERTERS

In the 'Old Days' (1950's) places like London often suffered from, given particular circumstances, a choking atmosphere called SMOG (SMoke and fOG). This was witnessed in other European cities and across the Atlantic, a 'heat haze' of sunshine refracting through a deep layer of car exhaust fumes often blanketed American cities. Laws to regulate emissions were brought in and began a technological revolution in engine efficiency leading to a reduction in emissions of harmful exhaust gases.

Here comes the science . . .

The main emissions of a petrol car engine are:-

1) Nitrogen gas - air is 78% Nitrogen so most passes straight through the engine.

2) Carbon Dioxide - a product of combustion.

3) Water vapour - another product of combustion.

Exhaust emissions and catalytic converters

These emissions are mostly harmless, although Carbon Dioxide is believed to contribute to global warming. Because the car engine combustion process is never perfect, some smaller amounts of more harmful emissions are also produced.

So what is a Catalytic Converter? This is a device that uses a catalyst to convert three harmful compounds in car exhaust into harmless compounds.

Harmful compounds are:-

4) Carbon Monoxide - a poisonous gas that is colourless and odourless

5) Hydrocarbons - produced mostly from unburnt fuel that evaporates

6) Oxides of Nitrogen (NOx) - contribute to smog and acid rain.

In a Catalytic Converter, the catalyst (in the form of Platinum and Palladium) is coated onto a ceramic honeycomb or ceramic beads that are housed in a muffler-like package linked into the exhaust system.

The catalyst helps to convert the Carbon Monoxide into Carbon Dioxide. It converts the Hydrocarbons into Carbon Dioxide and water. It also converts the Nitrogen Oxides back into Nitrogen and Oxygen.

So, we end up with very much cleaner exhaust emissions and air in our towns and cities we can actually breathe!

Exhaust emission levels now form the basis of company car 'Benefit In Kind' taxation and is now based on car and model exhaust emission levels and not annual mileage.

Even though globally, emissions from cars form a very small percentage of the total greenhouse gas emissions, car manufacturers believe that they have gone a long way to producing a product which more than meets their obligations under the Kyoto agreement.

Globally, as more old 'dirty' emission cars and vehicles are scrapped and replaced by new 'clean' ones, this situation can only get better!

Gear changing

GEAR CHANGING

Nothing to do with wearing a new outfit or exchanging illegal substances!!

Have you ever seen TV film reports on driving through towns and, when interviewed, the driver of a prestige, performance car says to the reporter, "This car won't do 30mph!!".

The car's top speed is probably 4 or 5 times that so it's not the driver complaining that the car is too slow. The problem is that he or she is trying to drive at 30mph in 4th, 5th or 6th gear and the speed is difficult to control. Selecting no higher than 3rd gear would give a lot more urban speed control, give more 'flexibility' with improved engine braking when decelerating and eliminate excessive braking and gear changing when negotiating hazards in towns.

"But my driving instructor told me to get into 'top' gear as soon as possible and my dad says 'top' saves fuel!". Firstly, when you learnt to drive in a small low-powered car with a 4-speed gearbox, 4th gear may well have been a much lower gear ratio than 3rd in most medium powered, 5 speed production cars.

Secondly, selecting a lower gear in 30mph limits does **not** use more fuel. Fuel consumption is not governed by the speed of the engine but by the position of the accelerator pedal. Pressing the accelerator down in too high a gear squirts excessive fuel into the engine which is then wasted. If you are fortunate enough to drive a vehicle with an instantaneous fuel consumption read-out, try it and watch the mpg drop dramatically.

Smooth gear changing up or down can be measured by what is termed the 'passenger test'. **Does your passenger 'bob' noticeably forwards and backwards every time you change gear?** When you accelerate, due to weight shift, the front of the car goes up and the back goes down. On changing gear, power to the wheels is momentarily removed then replaced and the car 'rocks' on its suspension. Try settling, balancing or 'plateauing' the power just prior to changing into each higher gear and you'll find that your passenger acts less like a 'nodding donkey' and may well praise you for a 'chauffeur-like drive!'.

So, use gears intelligently to improve driving and manage speed more effectively. Try this:-

No higher than 2nd gear in 20 mph limits

No higher than 3rd gear in 30 mph limits

No higher than 4th gear in 40 mph limits

and you may well keep a few penalty points off your driving licence!

IN-CAR ENTERTAINMENT – ICE!

Beware; this area is full of jargon. If you're buying, read lots of In-Car Entertainment mags and take a techno-head (and lots of money) with you!

Technology is moving so fast that state of the art today is state of the ark tomorrow!

However, to get you started, the main source of ICE is the 'Head Unit'; this just means the main radio/cassette etc. player in the middle of the front panel, which also controls all the other add-ons. Most head units have a removable faceplate for security.

If you really like your toys, it's now possible to play **audio** or **visual** material, from almost **any** recording media, via a whole range of clever output devices. You can have anything from an MP3 player, to in-car Dolby Digital surround sound **cinema!** You could even have a 'thin' screen mounted in the boot lid for those pre-match picnics! The boot will also need to house several amplifiers if you want lots of goodies, so not much room left for the smoked salmon and champagne!

In-car entertainment

To keep your back-seat passengers entertained; you could have screens mounted in the back of headrests or in roof-mounted pods (with headphones). They can watch films, TV or play games.

By the way...

If you do the installation **yourself** and there is an **electrical fire** as a result, your insurance company may not pay up!

Also, amplifiers are heavy, make sure they are fixed down and don't hit you in the back of the head in a crash! They also get warm, so don't enclose them.

Finally, all this stuff can be very distracting and the law in this country currently states that **you can have a video/TV screen anywhere in the car so long as the driver is unable to watch it.**

Go on.........!

LONE FEMALE DRIVER

Don't let all the hype about attacks on lone women scare you into never getting into your car without a male – inflatable or otherwise! Just be aware...

Have you got enough fuel/oil/water etc. for the journey? Does everything essential work? (Can you change a wheel? – Dad's are good at this!). Let someone know your plans. Do you know the route? Have you got a good (Collins) road atlas?

Breakdown. DON'T PANIC! Your car breakdown membership is up to date – isn't it? You have your fully charged mobile phone with you (and some change and a phone card). Ask for the name of the breakdown man, tell them you're a lone female, put on your hazard warning lights, lock yourself in the car and sit in the passenger seat – you're waiting for 'your man' to return aren't you! When rescue arrives, open the window a tiny bit and ask for his name and ID. On a motorway, use the phones provided, and don't wait in the car – there is a high risk of being driven into!! Make sure you can get back in quickly though.

Mobile phones

When parking:

Never leave anything 'girlie' in view (dead giveaway – here's a woman!)

Reverse into the space, ensuring a quick getaway.

Have your keys in your hand when returning (preferably with company).

Look in the back before you get in.

When driving:

Being followed? Drive to a police station or somewhere busy.

Lock doors/close windows in slow moving/stationary traffic.

Hide your bag.

In a queue, leave enough space to pull out.

Never stop if flagged down (unless it's by bona fide police!).

Never give lifts to strangers.

Consider a personal deterrent (e.g. screech alarm) and don't be afraid to **MAKE A NOISE!** if threatened.

MOBILE PHONES

Think of all the people, family and friends you know and you can probably count on less than one hand those who do not use a mobile phone. It's the biggest communication revolution in the last 10 years. We want to be accessible to others and that includes the time when we are driving our cars, however this can compromise safety.

Active mobile phone conversation when driving is like **counting to 100 out loud and writing the alphabet at the same time.** You'll do neither particularly well! Concentration is split between the two activities so not only is driving skill reduced but you often don't have a good conversation with a changing signal strength ("hang on, you're breaking up!!", type comments) or frustratingly, complete signal loss.

Is it illegal to drive when using a mobile phone? Even though there is no specific law, you will be prosecuted for **'Driving Without Due Care and Attention'** or **'Careless Driving'** if found 'juggling' with a phone and driving one-handed. A crash may well result in more serious charges. So what can you do?

Give yourself a break and use the mobile phone when stopped in a safe place, a lay-by or parking area. You may think it looks cool to be on the phone when driving, until you're mentally distracted and run into something solid! But you may say "That happens to other drivers, it won't happen to me!" Well you may be lucky, but **you'll be 10 times more likely to crash when 'phone-driving'!**

Finally, take seriously the signs at petrol stations warning about not using your mobile phone. A ringing mobile phone can cause petrol vapours to ignite resulting in serious injury to you, damage to your car and it doesn't do your phone much good either!

MOT TESTS

MOT tests

The words that bring terror to every car owner, "the car's due for its MOT"! Well, there's no avoiding it, just like the dentist, it has to be done!

By law, every car over three years old (from its first registration date) must have a valid vehicle test certificate, known as 'the MOT', there is a hefty fine for not having one.

Introduced by the old Ministry of Transport (Mr. Cholmondley-Warner!) this annual test makes sure that the car is safe to use on the roads and is environmentally sound on the day of the test. An authorised testing station must carry out the test – look for the blue triangle on the garage wall. As with all things compulsory, there is a fee!

There are some exemptions and exceptions, contact the Vehicle Inspectorate if you're unsure (their website is www.via.gov.uk/mot). You can drive the car to a testing station for its MOT, or for repairs following an MOT failure (or tow it to a scrap yard!) without a certificate, but you **must** have made a prior appointment.

Not only is it against the law not to have an MOT, you also have to produce it, along with your insurance certificate, to obtain your tax disc. Driving without an MOT can also make your insurance invalid if you have an accident.

Unlike insurance and road tax, you don't get a reminder through the post, so **write the date in blood in your diary!** - you can have the car tested up to one month before the expiry date. The police won't wear the excuse "sorry officer, I forgot", the reply is "You're nicked"!

If you buy a car, remember, the MOT certificate is no indication that the car is in a roadworthy condition, so be warned!

MOTORWAY SERVICES

Motorway services

It's one o'clock in the morning, you've been driving for a couple of hours and you could just do with a coffee. The sign on the motorway says 'Services 1 mile'. What can you expect to find there?

Well, all motorway service areas must provide fuel, free toilets, and free short term parking (usually up to two hours), 24 hours a day, 365 days a year, for all users – including those with disabilities. However, prices and standards of service are set by the individual operators – the big three being Moto, Welcome Break and Roadchef.

Besides the above, you can eat at a variety of outlets, play on games machines, get some cash from a hole-in-the-wall, feed and change the baby (well the nappy anyway!). You can shop for snacks, magazines, and bits 'n bobs, even stop overnight in a motel, **and** if you're 'upwardly mobile', you can take advantage of the 'Workspace' in some service stations, where you can fax, photocopy, use your laptop and even hold a conference (for a small fee)!

Remember, it's illegal to stop anywhere else on the motorway unless it's an emergency.

Tiredness. Sleep driving, due to sleep deprivation, is the cause of more car crashes than drink or drug driving. Opening the window and playing loud music (no matter how much your Mother wouldn't like it!) just **does not wake you up, so stop at motorway services if you're feeling tired:**

> Plan to stop for at least 15 minutes every two hours.
>
> Have a coffee or two and a nap of about 15 minutes (the caffeine doesn't start to work for at least 20 minutes).
>
> Swap drivers if possible.
>
> Your most vulnerable time is between 2am and 6am, try to avoid this.
>
> And get a good night's sleep before you even start.
>
> So, 'enjoy', as they say!

THE POINTS SYSTEM

You really don't want to be part of this system; it's very bad news. Points don't mean prizes; they mean possible disqualification from driving.

If you are convicted of a motoring offence, besides any fines or sentences, the courts will also issue 'penalty points' or a period of disqualification, depending on the seriousness of the offence. The DVLA adds these to your records and your licence ('endorsing' it with the penalty points). What's more, if you incur 12 or more points within three years, you will be automatically disqualified – like public transport do you?

If the offence was to do with drinking/drugs and driving, (there are several categories), the endorsements may remain on your licence for 11 years from the date of conviction. Other offences will mean the points remain for four years from the date of the offence or conviction.

To add insult to injury, when the endorsement period has expired, if you want to remove the points from your licence, you must fill in another driving licence application form and send it off with other bits and pieces **and a fee!**

There is a similar process if you were disqualified, only this time you will be sent the forms. If it was to do with drink/drugs, then the DVLA may want to make all sorts of medical enquiries first, which will take more time. You can grovel and apply to have a disqualification removed under certain circumstances, but it's at the discretion of the court that disqualified you in the first place.

New drivers. Now, if you are still in the **two year probationary period after passing your first driving test** and you commit an offence which leads to you having **six** or more penalty points (including any incurred before passing), you will have your **full entitlement to drive all categories revoked.** You then have to take another driving test, but the penalty points stay on your licence – and there is **no right of appeal!**

BE GOOD!

REGULAR CHECKS

Cars do breakdown occasionally and it's inconvenient and usually pretty expensive to put right. But there are some things that can be done to ensure your car doesn't fail because of something stupid.

Tyres – know the correct tyre pressures for your car, or at least have them written down somewhere, and check the pressure of your tyres at least once a fortnight. Make sure you know where your car's basic toolkit is, even if you don't intend actually changing a wheel yourself!, and if you've got locking wheel nuts make sure you've got the key!

Engine oil – check the dipstick at least every fortnight. Running out of oil is very bad news for your car's engine and for your wallet! If you're constantly having to top up, it's an indication that you could have engine problems.

Coolant – check the level regularly and use anti-freeze all year round as it 'does exactly what it says on the tin' and stops the cooling system corroding.

Regular checks - checking your oil

Windscreen – make sure your wipers are clearing the window properly and replace them if they become worn. Check you've got enough screenwash as it's better at cleaning the dirt than water alone and finally inspect the screen for chips and try and get them repaired before they cause the whole window to crack!

Lights – check all your lights regularly, driving on a motorway at two in the morning is not the time to find out your headlights aren't working!

Bodywork – if you don't want your car to turn into a rust bucket on wheels make sure you repair any damage to the bodywork as soon as possible.

Petrol – it's obvious, of course it is, who'd be that stupid?, but before setting off on a journey make sure you've got enough petrol. It's time-consuming and, quite frankly, embarrassing to run out miles from the nearest garage.

SEATBELTS

Newton said that if thou hits yon tree in thy car and thou hast disregarded thy seatbelt, thy body will fly forth until it meets with a solid object. Don't try to disprove him; he was a clever chap!

You've heard this before – but...

A 10 stone person, crashing at 30mph (48 km/hr), not wearing a seatbelt, hits the steering wheel at an average of 45 times their weight. Things like your liver, brain, heart etc. will tear and move – Yuk! Your passengers could also go through the windscreen and get run over by a passing lorry...Enough?

The Law

In the UK, **you must wear a seatbelt, if one is available,** unless you're exempt. If your passengers are under 14, you are responsible for making sure they are appropriately 'restrained'. See the latest 'Highway Code' for laws relating to children.

How seatbelts work

1) Retractor mechanism. One end of the seatbelt webbing is attached to a spool inside this mechanism. A spring enables the spool to take up any slack. Pull the seatbelt and it untwists the spring, let it go, the webbing is tightened.

2) Locking mechanism. Located in the retractor and activated by the car's or the belt's movement, this 'pawl and ratchet' arrangement stops the spool rotating in a crash and the webbing unwinding.

Newer seatbelts might have:

3) Pretensioner. This actually pulls on the belt in a crash, rather than just stopping it extending further.

4) Load limiter. All designs release a little more webbing if a very high force is applied to the belt. This minimises injuries caused by the seatbelt itself.

Wearing them

Keep the seat upright and don't let a three point (ordinary) belt cross your neck or arms. Position a lapbelt across the pelvis. Adjust it correctly, make sure it's not twisted and inspect it for damage occasionally. Make sure you hear that **Klunk Klick!**

Finally... Put animals in safe cages. You can get seatbelts for dogs – daft? Ask a paramedic trying to get into a car containing a panic stricken unrestrained large dog!

Speeding

SPEEDING

At the risk of being controversial, perhaps we should approach this topic with the following statement: **SPEED KILLS** – but does it? Speed alone is not the problem!!

We go on holiday and fly at over 550mph! Japan has 200 mph trains! Michael Schumacher drives at 180 mph on race circuits! BUT, he obeys the 120kph (72mph) speed limit in the pit lane during the Formula One Grand Prix race to avoid a 10 second Stop/Go penalty. So why has this speed limit been introduced? In a word – SAFETY.

Imagine this. You're driving past your local Junior school, it's 3.30pm on a Wednesday afternoon in term time, the end of lessons bell has gone off and all the children are running out onto the pavement for the school bus and parent's cars. It's a 30mph limit.

Is it safe to drive towards this situation at 30mph? NO!! Maybe 12mph or less is the only safe speed for the 200 metres and 45 seconds or so, it will take to handle this situation safely.

Imagine this. Same stretch of road as above but now it's 2.15am in the early hours of a Thursday morning with no pedestrians, no 'clubbers', no traffic and no hazards. We may think that 45 or 50mph is now a 'safe' speed. Problem is there's a speed camera on this stretch and it's set at 35mph and you will end up with another kind of STOP/GO penalty - STOP at the local Magistrates Court and GO and get fined with 3 points on your driving licence!

What's the point being made here? It's not speed that's the problem! It's drivers using speed in the wrong place and at the wrong time - that's the problem!! Whatever the speed limit, as drivers, we must always drive to the hazard level. What does that mean? Have a look at Rule 105 in the Highway Code: **'Always drive at a speed that will allow you to stop well within the distance you can see to be clear.'**

Why do drivers slow down when they see a Police vehicle? Not always because they are speeding. Often they don't know what the speed limit is for that stretch of road because they didn't look for the speed limit change sign (situated on both sides of the road).

SUPPLEMENTARY RESTRAINT SYSTEMS

You have these if the steering wheel, seat, facia or door trim is marked 'SRS' or 'airbag'. This means your car is fitted with explosives!

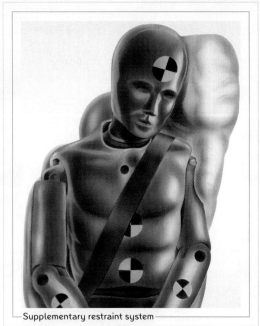
Supplementary restraint system

If you hit something, gas rushes into the airbag, inflating it in less than one second. It then instantly starts to deflate to cushion your inevitable journey towards the steering wheel - don't worry if you see 'smoke', this is part of the process in some cars!

NO, this does not mean you don't have to wear a seat belt, you'll still be in trouble with the people in blue if you don't belt up!

If the driver needs to sit closer than ten inches (25 cm) from the steering wheel, the airbag will hit them before it has fully inflated, with enough force to cause **serious injury or death**. Measure from the centre of the breastbone to the cover of the airbag, if you are in this danger zone, try moving the seat back or reclining it slightly. If these don't work, contact the manufacturer for advice.

Although the airbag may save your life, it can cause minor injuries such as abrasions and burns (the gas is hot), so don't try seeing if you can set it off for fun! The whole airbag module has to be replaced too, which costs an arm and a leg!

Finally, never put your feet on the dashboard or dangle your fluffy dice near the airbag! If you have seat airbags, make sure any covers have appropriate holes in them. Don't lean against the door if you have side airbags and **never ever** fit a rear facing child restraint in a passenger seat protected by an airbag.

TELEMATICS

You need to 'Open Your Mind' with this topic because it's very much the **'Tomorrow's World' of Motoring**. Let's start with what this modern word means. Telematics means telecommunications and computing. So what does that mean in relation to cars of the future?

Imagine voice activated and voice response systems in your car. "Not that far away from what I've seen in cars with Mobile Phones" you say! Now move on to the next stage. Imagine satellite positioning systems combined with Internet Access, entertainment and convenience services, such as **fully automatic electronic billing when filling up at a petrol station** or **immediate connection to an insurance company** in the event of an accident, or **emergency services if the airbag has been activated**!

Imagine asking, on the move, for your nearest, favourite style restaurant, receiving the menu in advance and ordering, or what about asking for your nearest cinema and 'what's on', booking tickets, then verbally receiving turn-by-turn directions to your choice of destination. How about hearing, then selecting and downloading to your 'ICE' your favourite music, on the move.

Imagine businesses receiving information from your vehicle and offering services based on that information. For example, an insurance or finance company could change a car insurance policy or repayments figures based on the mileage information it receives from your car. You may get a call from your garage who have been notified, by your car telematics, that you've got a slow puncture in your front nearside tyre!

As with most things, there are two schools of thought with Telematics. One says it's brilliant and I can't wait to be able to play with all these **'Boy's Toys'**. The other believes that it is becoming an imposition of personal and civil liberties. Some believe that, with careful selection of applications, Telematics is to the benefit of drivers, as long as accessing information on the move does not adversely affect concentration levels and safety.

Historically, a car has been seen as a transportation tool. In the future, Telematics will probably transform it into something more essential for day-to-day living.

TRAFFICMASTER

Did you drive along the same familiar route to work this morning, guessing how far the usual queue had moved back in your direction? Did your heart sink when the back of the queue was at junction 10 instead of 9?

A familiar tale to motoring millions, a kind of automotive roulette in which you bet upon where the back of the queue is today, place your chips on red or black and spin the wheel of fortune, for good or bad!

But what about all those great traffic reports we get on the radio? All very good but they are often telling you about the traffic jam you are currently stuck in! So what are your options? Use public transport, find another job or find an alternative route or 'rat run' when your normal route is congested. So how do you know when this is?

Trafficmaster plc, based in Milton Keynes, have been providing in-car traffic data for over 4 years. They are the people responsible for all those 'stalks' drivers see off motorway bridges and on A roads, dark blue poles which many people still think are speed cameras. In fact they're **Trafficmaster passive flow meters**. They work by reading number plates of cars as they pass then, when you pass a second unit the system produces an average speed based on a sample of vehicles. When compared to the standard journey time (at legal speeds) the system gives an accurate measure of delays caused by traffic congestion.

The Trafficmaster Freeway system gives this information to the driver by what some people consider to be a 'Doctor Who, Dalek sound-alike' female voice, **"M6, traffic flowing freely"** and the YQ unit based system uses an LCD display to show current average traffic speeds on all major roads and motorways.

If you want to know what the roads are like before you set off try Trafficmaster Online (www.trafficmaster-online.com). This well designed web-site with partial free membership allows the basic features to be used for gratis. Within the site, Traffic View produces a map of England, Scotland and Wales onto which the major highways are overlaid to provide an environment which you can zoom into to locate your particular area. This basically is an internet version of the YQ unit.

The additional services (where you do need to pay) include Journey Forecast and Journey Guard.

Trafficmaster is not perfect but it can be a very helpful tool with Britain's increasing road congestion. Also, the system can only monitor those roads where the flow meters have been installed, but this is increasing all the time.

So, take a closer look at Trafficmaster - especially now you know those dark blue posts aren't yet another type of speed camera!

VEHICLE SECURITY (THATCHAM, LOCKING, TRACKING)

Think of the oldest, ugliest, least cool, dirtiest and slowest car that you would rather run a mile away from rather than be seen driving and you've got one of the strongest anti-theft devices.

Fortunately, or unfortunately, most modern cars are desirable, especially performance based models. Significant improvements have been made by manufacturers to make new cars even more secure with built in immobilisers, sophisticated alarm systems, removable sound system facings, electronic signal ignition keys and keyless 'go' systems. As a result, there are more cars **stolen with keys** now than stolen without!

This introduces a new dimension into personal security. As a result we drivers need to be more vigilant and aware of our location, surroundings and any suspicious looking characters nearby. If you stop for fuel, ensure you take your car keys out of the ignition and keep them with you.

Vehicle security

If you are a woman and feel uneasy about anyone nearby where you have just stopped or parked, stay in the car with the doors locked. Consider a mobile phone call to the Police or drive off to somewhere public and safe. This may sound a bit OTT but is it really worth the risk not to?

How many times have we seen the posters **'Do Not Leave Valuables In Your Car'** and do we always follow the advice? Indeed, anything on show through the window glass will attract the 'would-be' car thief so remove it to somewhere out of sight. Remember, most car insurance policies do not cover vehicle contents.

How much care do we really take about choosing a fairly safe and secure parking space? How many householders with garages regularly leave the car overnight on the drive leaving the garage empty? One current sinister development is that of car thieves, in the early hours when everyone's asleep, using a stick through the house letter box to 'hook' car keys off the hall table!

The Thatcham Motor Insurance Repair Research Centre evaluates the effectiveness of car security products against the British Insurance Industry's criteria for Vehicle Security. Tracker is a device which allows the police to track a stolen vehicle via an electronic signal emitted from a sensor concealed in the car. Up to a 10% discount off your car insurance premium is available if your vehicle is fitted with a Thatcham One security device or a Tracker system.

Back to basics then. When you leave your vehicle you should:

Remove the ignition key and engage the steering lock

Consider fitting a high visibility external steering lock

Lock the car, even if you only leave it a few minutes

Close the windows completely

NEVER leave children or pets in an unventilated car

Finally, read your car insurance policy. When you come to claim after theft, you may get an unpleasant shock if the circumstances just happen to be listed in the EXCLUSIONS!

WHEELS & TYRES

Big and important topic, this one! Look at the palm of your hand. Not that big is it? But that's the size of the 'contact patch' between each properly inflated tyre and the road. Unless you're on a motorbike, or driving a three wheeler, you have got four of these helping you brake and corner.

When manufacturers develop cars, a lot of research and testing time goes into correct types and sizes of wheels and tyres to give optimum performance, at correct tyre pressures, under braking, cornering and accelerating. But you've just looked in the local motor discount shop and seen a superb looking set of wide alloy wheels that will impress your mates and help you look cool. Take great care! Unless wheels and tyres are approved for your car, you may end up with less grip than you started with!

Wheels and tyres

It's time for a quick Q&A test on tyres. Here goes:-

Q1) What is the legal minimum tyre tread depth in the UK?

A1) 1.6mm, across the central 3/4 of the tread, all the way round.

Q2) Who is legally responsible for tyres, driver or owner?

A2) Always the driver, with possible incrimination of the owner.

Q3) What is the maximum fine per illegal tyre, in points and money?

A3) 3 penalty points and up to £2,500 per illegal tyre!

Q4) How often should we check tyre condition and pressures?

A4) Weekly as a minimum, but check before driving after someone else has - they may have 'kerbed' the front, nearside tyre and damaged it!

Q5) Why is it that screw or nail punctures happen more often in rear tyres?

A5) The front tyre runs over the screw or nail, flicks it upright and the rear tyre runs onto it!

In the wet, incorrect tyre pressures and shallow tread depth reduce tyre performance dramatically. Please check your tyres frequently.

YEOMAN NAVIGATION

The joy and freedom for a driver having the use of a car just cannot be beaten! Going anywhere, whenever you like, with whoever you choose, just knocks the spots off public transport. That is, until you get stuck in a traffic jam or end up getting lost, trying to choose whether to turn left or right at this junction, to get to your destination.

Some people have a brilliant sense of direction, it's nothing to do with being male or female either, just as poor and skilled drivers cross both sexes. What some of us need is a little help. Yeoman Navigation could just be the friend we need.

Used hands free or with a passenger making the call, this mobile phone based, pay-for-use navigation service is **brilliant for drivers born without a biological compass!**

Phone Yeoman on 09050 50 50 50 and try the system. A REAL person will ask where you are travelling from and to. The voice system then gives an overview of the route, distance, estimated journey time and any current delays. It takes less than a minute to set-up a journey, then hang up when you've heard what you need.

Yeoman keep your information (automatically from your mobile phone number) so you can call back at any time for the latest traffic or turn-by-turn directions. It doesn't take long - most people spend under 3 minutes a journey - and only one minute for just traffic reports. Free text messages warn of any new delays on your route. Simply call back in for a new ETA or faster route.

So how much is it? Calls cost 1p a second but only while you're connected, so most journeys cost less than the price of a sandwich.

So DON'T GET LOST. Ring 09050 50 50 50 AND GET THERE.

Visit www.yeomannavigation.com for more details.

CREDIT LINE

The information in this driving section was researched and written by Karen Lloyd (Air conditioning; Defensive driving; Driving with children; Ergonomics; In-car entertainment; Lone female driver; Motorway services, The points system; Seatbelts and Supplementary restraint systems) and Alan White of DriverSkill (ABS; BHP, Petrol and diesel engines; Drinking, drugs and driving; Exhaust emissions and catalytic converters; Gear changing; Mobile phones; Speeding; Telematics; Trafficmaster; Vehicle security; Wheels and tyres and Yeoman Navigation).

DriverSkill is one of the UK's leading advanced and performance driving consultancy and training companies. Founded in 1989, DriverSkill is dedicated to enhancing the driving experience on road, race circuit or proving ground, through improved skill levels and increased awareness with maximum safety.

Only a select few are able to train to the highest of standards required by DriverSkill. Clients who have benefited from this expert training include Toyota, Porsche Cars GB, Lexus, Rolls Royce and Mercedes.

DriverSkill is run by Alan White and was formed to improve customers' driving skills. For the past 6 years Alan has been a full time advanced and high performance driving consultant. His skills and expertise continue to be called upon from a wide range of manufacturers and organisations.

Alan is the holder of a RoSPA Diploma, IAM, HPC, MSA National Car Race and ARDS Licences and is also a Fellow of the Institute of Sales and Marketing. He is dedicated to developing the skill levels of all drivers for maximum enjoyment and safety.

To find out more, visit the website at www.driverskill.co.uk
Driving Skills for Life

Road maps

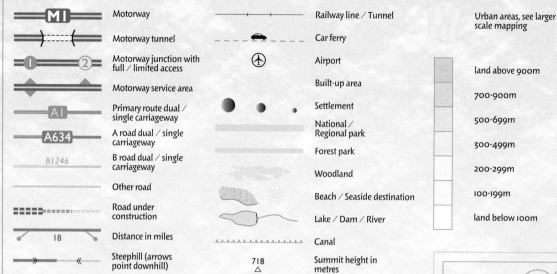

M1	Motorway
	Motorway tunnel
1 / 2	Motorway junction with full / limited access
	Motorway service area
A1	Primary route dual / single carriageway
A634	A road dual / single carriageway
B1246	B road dual / single carriageway
	Other road
	Road under construction
18	Distance in miles
	Steephill (arrows point downhill)
	Toll

	Railway line / Tunnel
	Car ferry
	Airport
	Built-up area
	Settlement
	National / Regional park
	Forest park
	Woodland
	Beach / Seaside destination
	Lake / Dam / River
	Canal
718	Summit height in metres
☆	Place of interest

Urban areas, see larger scale mapping

- land above 900m
- 700-900m
- 500-699m
- 300-499m
- 200-299m
- 100-199m
- land below 100m

Urban area maps

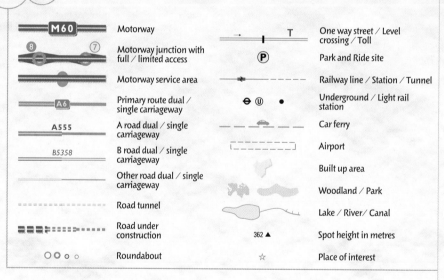

M60	Motorway
8 / 7	Motorway junction with full / limited access
	Motorway service area
A6	Primary route dual / single carriageway
A555	A road dual / single carriageway
B5358	B road dual / single carriageway
	Other road dual / single carriageway
	Road tunnel
	Road under construction
	Roundabout

T	One way street / Level crossing / Toll
P	Park and Ride site
	Railway line / Station / Tunnel
	Underground / Light rail station
	Car ferry
	Airport
	Built up area
	Woodland / Park
	Lake / River / Canal
362 ▲	Spot height in metres
☆	Place of interest

Featured place of interest

OLD TRAFFORD — Sports stadium / venue

ALTON TOWERS — Holiday park / Theme park

EXCEL — Entertainment venue

BLUEWATER — Out of town shopping centre / Outlet shopping village

City and town centre plans

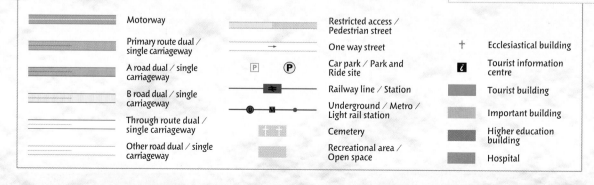

	Motorway
	Primary route dual / single carriageway
	A road dual / single carriageway
	B road dual / single carriageway
	Through route dual / single carriageway
	Other road dual / single carriageway

	Restricted access / Pedestrian street
	One way street
P	Car park / Park and Ride site
	Railway line / Station
M	Underground / Metro / Light rail station
	Cemetery
	Recreational area / Open space

†	Ecclesiastical building
i	Tourist information centre
	Tourist building
	Important building
	Higher education building
	Hospital

10 miles

20 km

1:440,000 7 miles to 1 inch / 4.4 km to 1 cm

D **E** **F**

I

Bo

TINTAGEL CASTLE ☆

Tintagel

Delabole

St Tea

St Endellion

A39

11

Port Isaac Bay

Pentire Point

Trevose Head

Padstow

St Merryn 7

Wadebridge

A389 A389

B33/4

B3266

B3276

A39 12 7

Trenance

A39

odmin

2

St Columb Major

Lanivet

13

B3274

Newquay A3059

SEA-LIFE CENTRE ☆ 8

A392 A30

Roche

Luxulya

St Enoder

St Dennis

EDEN PROJECT ☆

A3075

Perranporth

Goonhavern

13

St Stephen

A3058

A391

60

16

St Austell

St Agnes

CALLESTOCK CIDER FARM ☆

13 11

10

A390

A39 B3275

Probus 13 Grampound

LOST GARDENS OF HELIGAN ☆

St Aus Bay

Portreath

TEHIDY C. PARK

B3277

5

A30 A390

Truro

Tregony

Mevagissey

8

St Day

TRURO CATHEDRAL

Fal

B3287

Gwithian

CORNISH GOLDSMITHS ☆

Redruth

A39

A3078

St Ives

B3301

Camborne

8

3

St Ives Bay

13

11

A393

Dodman Poin

Zennor

A3074

Hayle

B3311

B3302

10

Leedstown

10

Penryn

St Just in Roseland

Pendeen

B3306

Ludgvan

A30

B3280

Wendron

3

St Mawes

Cape Cornwall

Madron

Marazion

A394

Breage

A394

Falmouth

St Just

A3071

Penzance

Newlyn

Constantine

Falmouth Bay

Longships

A30

ST. MICHAEL'S MOUNT

13

Helston

Sennen 9

St Buryan

B3315

Mount's Bay

Porthleven

St Keverne

Land's End

LAND'S END C. PARK

FLAMBARDS VILLAGE THEME PARK ☆

A3083

B3293

Mullion 11

Coverack

Black Head

4

Lizard Point Lizard

D **E** **F**

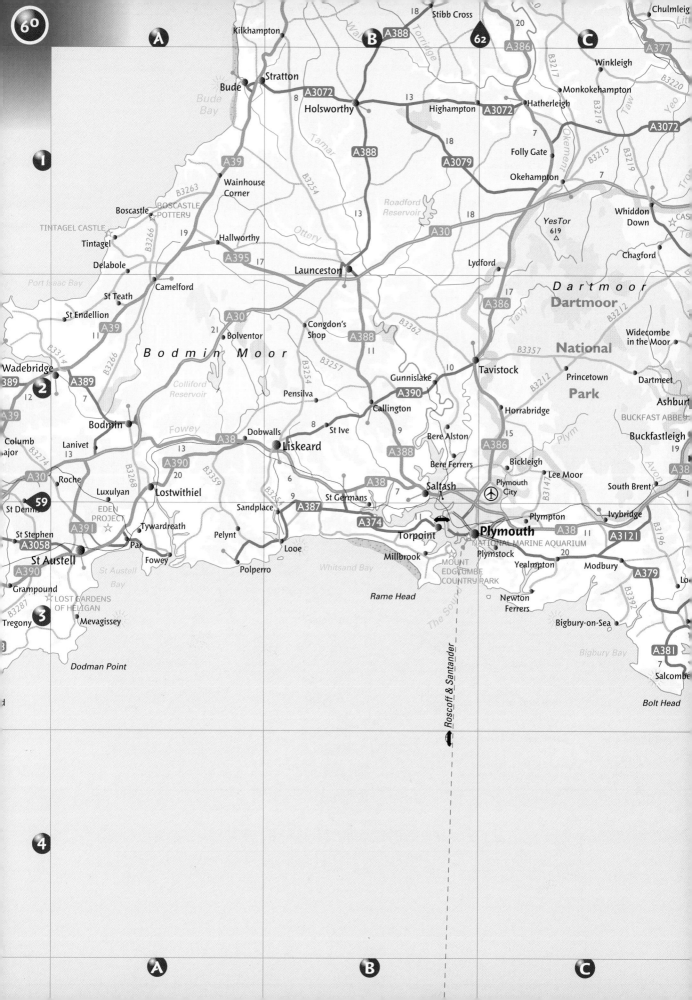

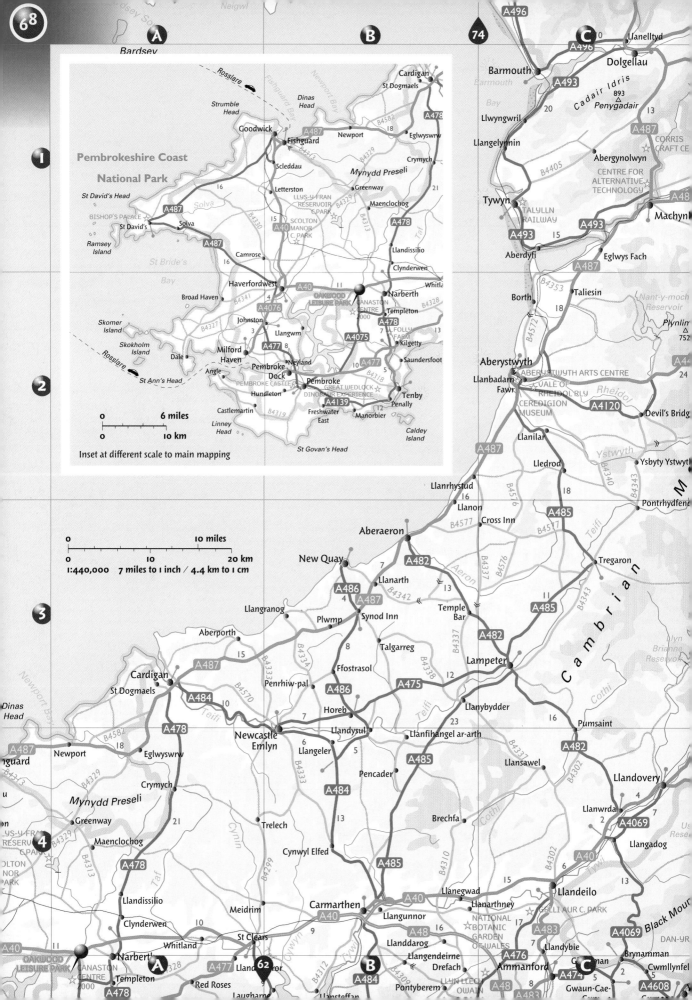

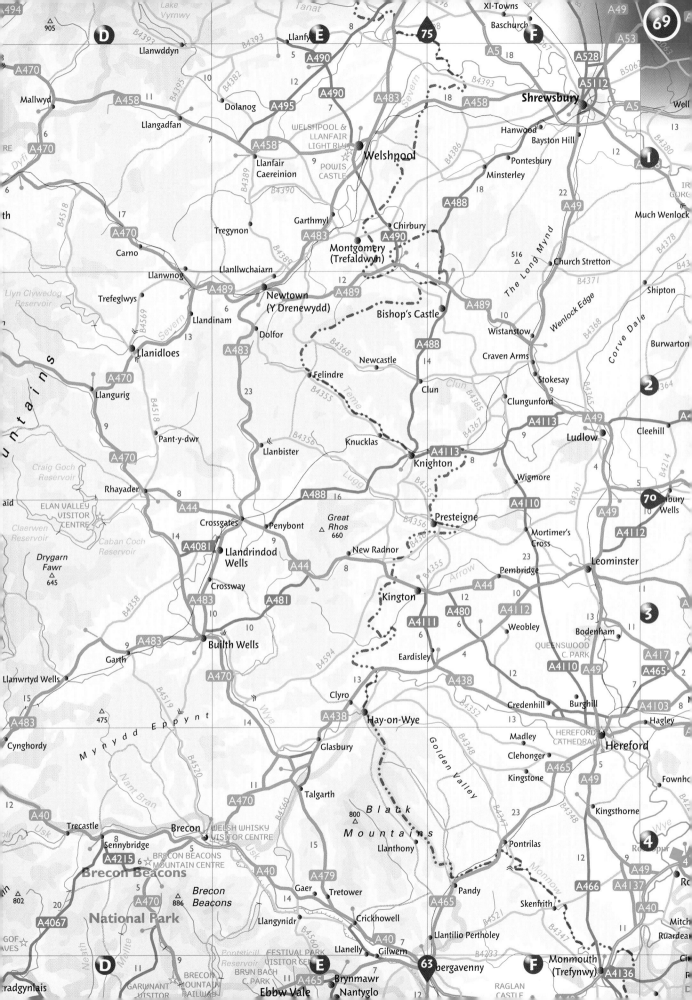

Breckland

Larling 13   Banham   B1134   Bungay   Carlton Colville
                                                                                              A12
     D   East Harling   A143   79   A145   F   Kessingland
                                                          Harleston   14   Homersfield   12
Thetford   B1123   A144
        A1066   South Lopham   Metfield   Brampton
Little Ouse   Roydon   Diss   Halesworth   A12
Barningham   Hopton A143 Scole   Fressingfield   Blyth   Reydon
                   Rickinghall Botesdale   B1387   Southwold
  A1088   Eye   Walberswick
  10   Stanton   15   Stradbroke   I
            Ixworth   Stoke Ash   Brundish   Westleton
  A143   Finningham   13   Dennington   A1120   Yoxford
        Great Barton   Norton   Framlingham 19   B1119   A12 4   Saxmundham
  7   12 Elmswell   Leiston
  A14   14   A140 Debenham   11
        Stowmarket   A1120 Earl Stonham   A1094   Thorpeness
  13   8   Otley   Aldeburgh
  A134   Needham Market   7 Coddenham   Wickham   Tunstall
  A1141   B1115   Market   B1078   Orford
  Lavenham   20   Monks Eleigh B1078 A14   6   A1152   Orford Ness
  Long Melford   4   Bramford   Claydon 3 Rushmere   Melton
  A1141   9   Ipswich St Andrew A12 Woodbridge   Hollesley Bay
  Hadleigh A1071   Kesgrave 8 Martlesham
  Great Cornard A12 A137 A14 Kirton   Bawdsey
  Stoke-by- 18 Capel St Mary 12
  A134 Nayland Holbrook   Old Felixstowe
  Bures 15 Dedham East Bergholt A14 MANNINGS AMUSEMENT PARK
  Great Horkesley Brantham Shotley Gate Felixstowe
  Earls Colne Lawford Manningtree Landguard Point
  A12 A137 New Mistley Harwich Esbjerg, Hamburg & Hoek van Holland
  West Bergholt Ardleigh A120 Little Oakley
  A1124 Mile End 19 The Naze
  Marks Tey BANANAS Colchester A120 Thorpe-le-Soken Walton on the Naze
  Coggeshall Stanway COLCHESTER ZOO A133 Wivenhoe CLACTON Frinton-on-Sea
  A12 Layer de Alresford Little Holland-on-Sea
  la Haye Brightlingsea Clacton Clacton-on-Sea
  Tiptree St Osyth Jaywick
  Tolleshunt D'Arcy Mersea Island West Mersea
  Heybridge Tollesbury Sales Point
  Maldon Bradwell Waterside Blackwater
  Latchingdon Southminster
  B1018 Crouch
  Burnham-on-Crouch Foulness Point
  Rochford Great Wakering
  A1159 KIDS KINGDOM
  Southend-on-Sea PETER PANS PLAYGROUND
  Shoeburyness

0   10 miles
0   10   20 km
1:440,000   7 miles to 1 inch / 4.4 km to 1 cm

D   E   F

1

0   10 miles

0   10   20 km
1:440,000   7 miles to 1 inch / 4.4 km to 1 cm

2

Blakeney Point

Blakeney A149 19 Sheringham
Wells-next-the-Sea   NORTH NORFOLK RLY   Cromer
arket   *B1156*   A148   8
          Letheringsett   Holt   Roughton   Mundesley
9   A140
21   10   Thorpe Market
B1355   Briston   *B1354*   A149   *B1145*   Happisburgh
A148   Saxthorpe   BLICKLING   North   *B1159*
Fakenham   PENSTHORPE WATERFOWL   HALL   Walsham
hton   PARK   Aylsham   BURE VALLEY   6   Stalham
A1065   *B1146*   Guist   A1067   Cawston   RAILWAY   Low   A149   West Somerton
B1145   25 *B1145*   Reepham   A140   *Bure*   Street   WROXHAM   Martham
North Elmham   Bawdeswell   11   Horstead   Coltishall   BARNS   19   Hemsby
14   *B1147*   Attlebridge   A149   Hoveton   A1062   Ormesby St Margaret
Swanton   Horsford   Horning   The   A149
Morley   *Wensum*   Spixworth   Rackheath   Broads   A1064   Caister-on-Sea
East Dereham   Taverham   Norwich ✈   Salhouse   Billockby   PLEASURE
11   A47   Drayton   A1151   Little   BEACH
A47   16   Sprowston   Plumstead
Necton   A1075   A47 A1074   NORWICH 18   Brundall   Acle   A47   Great
          CATHEDRAL   Yarmouth
9   10   Hethersett   Norwich   Thorpe   SEA-LIFE
ham Toney   Kimberley   *B1172*   St Andrew   Bradwell   CENTRE
Hingham   Cringleford   A146   17   Thurton   A143   A12
Watton   14   Stoke Holy Cross   Loddon   14   Hopton   NEW
A1075   Wymondham   Mulbarton   *B1332*   Brooke   *B1074*   10 Corton   PLEASUREWOOD
B1108   *B1077*   Great Ellingham   Hales   *B1136*   Haddiscoe   Oulton   HILLS
13   A11   Attleborough   Hempnall   Woodton   7   A1117
SNETTERTON   *B1113*   *B1527*   *B1332*   Beccles   A146   Lowestoft
Larling   13   Banham   Long Stratton   9   *B1127*   Carlton Colville
Breckland   *B1111*   *B1134*   20   Homersfield   A143   A45   A12
34   East Harling   A140   Harleston   14   9   Kessingland
Thetford   South Lopham   *B1123*   Metfield   A144   9 Bramp   12
D   19   Diss   E   *B1124*   A12
Little Ouse   Roydon   Scole   73

1

2

3

4

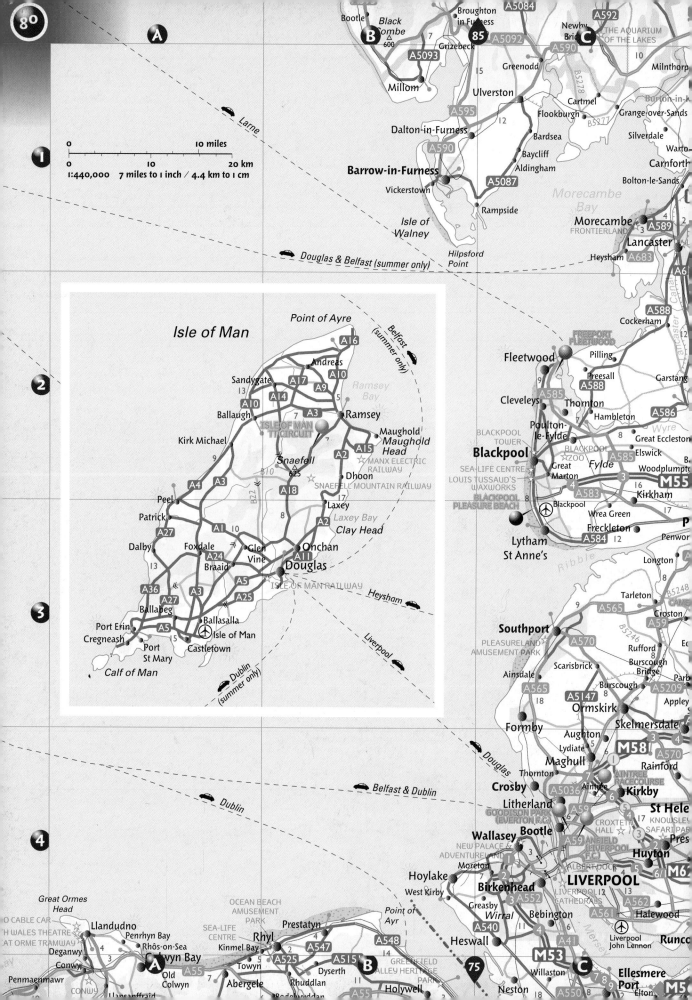

A

B

Bootle
Black Combe
△ 600
7
85
A5084
Broughton in Furness
A5092
Newby Bridge
A5093
Grizebeck
THE AQUARIUM OF THE LAKES
A592
A590
C
Milnthorp
Greenodd
Millom
Ulverston
15
Cartmel
B5278
Flookburgh
Grange-over-Sands
A595
Dalton-in-Furness
Bardsea
12
Silverdale
Warto
A590
Baycliff
B5277
Carnforth

1
0   10 miles
0   10   20 km
1:440,000 7 miles to 1 inch / 4.4 km to 1 cm

Larne

Barrow-in-Furness
A5087
Aldingham
Bolton-le-Sands

Vickerstown
Rampside
Morecambe
Bay
FRONTIERLAND
Morecambe
3
A589
Lancaster
A6

Isle of Walney

Douglas & Belfast (summer only)
Hilpsford Point
Heysham
A683

Isle of Man

Point of Ayre
A16
Belfast (summer only)
Cockerham
A588
FREEPORT FLEETWOOD
Pilling
Garstang

Andreas
A10
Fleetwood
9
Preesall
Sandygate
A17
A9
Cleveleys
A585
Thornton
Hambleton
A586
13
A14
5
A10
Ballaugh
A3
7
Ramsey
Poulton-le-Fylde
Great Eccleston
ISLE OF MAN TT CIRCUIT
BLACKPOOL TOWER
Elswick
Kirk Michael
Maughold
Maughold Head
BLACKPOOL
☆ZOO
Fylde
Woodplumpton
9
Snaefell
△ 625
A15
A2
MANX ELECTRIC RAILWAY
Blackpool
SEA-LIFE CENTRE
LOUIS TUSSAUD'S WAXWORKS
Great Marton
A585
2
B10
Dhoon
SNAEFELL MOUNTAIN RAILWAY
BLACKPOOL PLEASURE BEACH
8
Kirkham
A583
17
Peel
A4
A3
A18
B22
8
Laxey
17
Blackpool
Wrea Green
Patrick
A2
Laxey Bay
Clay Head
A584
12
Freckleton
Penwor
A27
A1
10
Glen Vine
Onchan
Lytham St Anne's
Longton
Dalby
Foxdale
A24
A11
Ribble
Braaid
Douglas
A36
A3
A5
ISLE OF MAN RAILWAY
Tarleton
B5248
A27
A25
Heysham
A565
Croston
A59
Ballabeg
Port Erin
Cregneash
A5
Ballasalla
5
Isle of Man
Southport
A570
PLEASURELAND AMUSEMENT PARK
Rufford
Burscough Bridge
3
Port St Mary
Castletown
Liverpool
Ainsdale
Scarisbrick
Burscough
A5209
Parb
Calf of Man
Dublin (summer only)
A565
A5147
18
Ormskirk
Appley

Formby
Skelmersdale
3
4
A570
Aughton
M58

Douglas
Lydiate
Maghull
Rainford
Belfast & Dublin
Crosby
AINTREE RACECOURSE
Aintree
7
Kirkby
Dublin
Litherland
A5036
6
St Hele
4
GOODISON PARK (EVERTON F.C.)
A59
CROXTETH HALL
KNOWSLEY SAFARI PARK
17
Pres
Great Ormes Head
OCEAN BEACH AMUSEMENT PARK
Point of Ayr
Wallasey
Bootle
ANFIELD (LIVERPOOL F.C.)
Huyton
M6
O CABLE CAR
H WALES THEATRE
AT ORME TRAMWAY
Llandudno
SEA-LIFE CENTRE
Prestatyn
NEW PALACE & ADVENTURELAND
Moreton
ALBERT DOCK
LIVERPOOL
6/
Penrhyn Bay
Rhyl
A548
Hoylake
Birkenhead
LIVERPOOL CATHEDRALS
12
A562
Deganwy
Rhôs-on-Sea
Kinmel Bay
West Kirby
Greasby
Wirral
Bebington
A561
Halewood
Conwy
A
A55
A525
A547
B
14
A540
Heswall
A41
Liverpool John Lennon
Runco
Penmaenmawr
Old Colwyn
Towyn
Dyserth
Rhuddlan
A515
75
GREENFIELD VALLEY HERITAGE PARK
Willaston
C
7
M53
Ellesmere Port
CONWY
Abergele
A55
11
Holywell
Neston
A550
Elton
M5

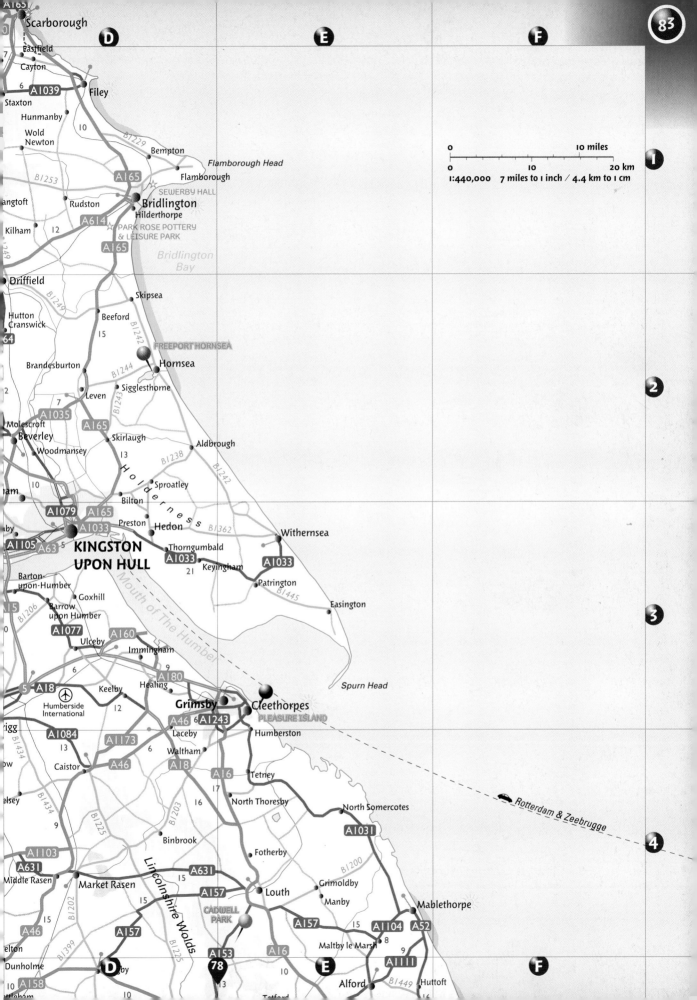

Scarborough

D **E** **F**

Eastfield
Cayton
6 A1039 Filey
Staxton
Hunmanby
Wold
Newton 10
B1229
Bempton
Flamborough Head
B1253 A165
Flamborough
SEWERBY HALL
angtoft Rudston
Bridlington
A614 Hilderthorpe
PARK ROSE POTTERY
Kilham 12 & LEISURE PARK
A165
Bridlington
Bay

1

o   10 miles
o   10   20 km
1:440,000 7 miles to 1 inch / 4.4 km to 1 cm

Driffield
B1249
Skipsea
Hutton
Cranswick
Beeford
64 15 B1242
Brandesburton FREEPORT HORNSEA
B1244 Hornsea
2 Leven Sigglesthorne
7 B1243
A1035
Molescroft A165
Beverley Skirlaugh
Woodmansey Aldbrough
13 B1238
B1242
Sproatley
10 Bilton
A1079 A165
ham A1033 Preston Hedon B1362
A1105 A63 5 **KINGSTON** Withernsea
UPON HULL Thorngumbald A1033
A1033 21 Keyingham
Barton- Patrington
upon-Humber Goxhill B1445
15 B1206 Barrow Easington
upon Humber
A1077
Ulceby Spurn Head
A160
Immingham
6 A180
5 A18 9
Keelby Healing
Humberside
International 12
Grimsby
A46 6 A1243 Cleethorpes
A1084 A1173 Laceby PLEASURE ISLAND
13 6 Waltham Humberston
Caistor A46 A18
A16
Tetney
17
B1434 16 North Thoresby
B1203 North Somercotes
B1225 9 Binbrook A1031
A1103 Fotherby
A631 B1200
Middle Rasen A631 Grimoldby
Market Rasen 15 A157 Louth Manby
15 A157
B1202 CADWELL A157 15 A1104 A52
A46 A157 PARK A16 Mablethorpe
B1399 Maltby le Marsh 8
A153 A1111
D by **78** 9
Dunholme **E** Alford Huttoft
A158 10 B1449 **F**

Holderness
Mouth of The Humber
Lincolnshire Wolds
Rotterdam & Zeebrugge

2

3

4

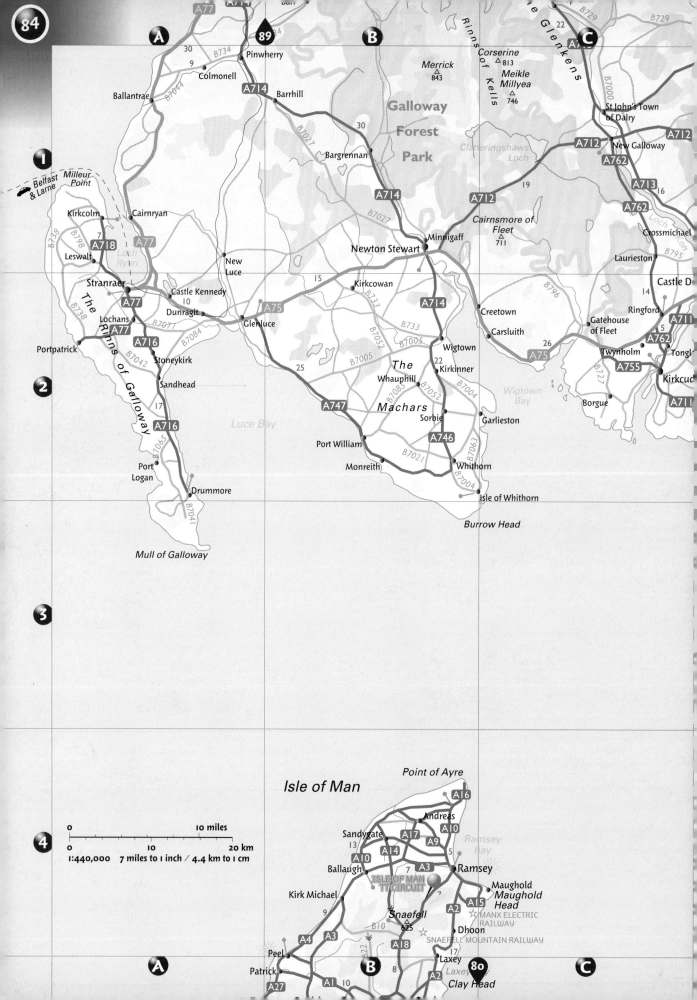

A   **B**   **C**

1

Belfast & Larne
Milleur Point

Kirkcolm
Cairnryan
B798
B738
7
A718
Leswalt
Loch Ryan
A77
Stranraer
A77
Lochans
A77
A716
Portpatrick
Stoneykirk
B7042
B7077
B7084
Sandhead
The Rinns of Galloway
B738
17
A716
Port Logan
B7065
Drummore
B7041

2

Mull of Galloway

Pinwherry
B734
30
9
Colmonell
A77
Ballantrae
B7044
A714
Barrhill
B7027
Bargrennan
30
B7027
A714
19
New Luce
Castle Kennedy
10
Dunragit
Glenluce
A75
15
25
Kirkcowan
B733
B7052
B733
B7005
A747
A714
Newton Stewart
Minnigaff
Creetown
Carsluith
A75
Wigtown
22
Kirkinner
The Machars
B7083
B7052
Whauphill
Sorbie
A746
Garlieston
B7063
Port William
B7021
Monreith
Whithorn
B7004
Isle of Whithorn
Burrow Head
Luce Bay
Wigtown Bay

Galloway Forest Park
Merrick
843
Corserine
813
Meikle Millyea
746
Rinns of Kells
Clatteringshaws Loch
Cairnsmore of Fleet
711
A712
A712
A712
A762
A762
A713
16
B7000
St John's Town of Dalry
New Galloway
The Glenkens
22
B729
B729
Crossmichael
B795
B796
Laurieston
Castle D
14
Ringford
Gatehouse of Fleet
A711
A762
5
Twynholm
A755
Borgue
B727
Kirkcud
A711
Tongl
26

89

80

3

4

Isle of Man

Point of Ayre
A16
Andreas
A10
Sandygate
A17
A9
13
A10
A14
5
Ramsey Bay
7
A3
Ballaugh
A10
Ramsey
Kirk Michael
ISLE OF MAN TT CIRCUIT
Maughold
Maughold Head
9
A2
A15
Snaefell
625
Dhoon
B10
A4
A3
A18
17
Peel
Laxey
Patrick
A27
A1
10
8
A2
Laxey
Clay Head
MANX ELECTRIC RAILWAY
SNAEFELL MOUNTAIN RAILWAY

0 ——————— 10 miles
0 ———— 10 ———— 20 km
1:440,000   7 miles to 1 inch / 4.4 km to 1 cm

A   **B**   **C**

Ellington
Lynemouth
A189
QUEEN ELIZABETH II
COUNTRY PARK **D**
A196 Newbiggin-by-the-Sea
WANSBECK C. PARK

E

F

Amsterdam, Bergen, Göteborg, Haugesund, Kristiansand & Stavanger

1

A189 Blyth
PLESSEY
ODS C. PARK
Cramlington
Seaton Sluice
16 Seaton Delaval
Seghill
A19 Whitley Bay
orth Shiremoor
ROYAL QUAYS Tynemouth
Longbenton North Shields
A1058 Wallsend South Shields
TELEWEST
ARENA Jarrow SOUTH SHIELDS
MUSEUM & ART
Hebburn A183 GALLERY
Felling Cleadon
A194 Boldon
head A19 STADIUM OF LIGHT
A1018 (SUNDERLAND F.C.)
65 A1231 A183 **Sunderland**
ey
64 Washington
A182 A690 A1018
Chester-le-Street
67 Bournmoor
Houghton Hetton-
le Spring le-Hole Seaham
10 Murton
Haswell South Hetton
A62 A182 Easington Colliery
Durham Sherburn Easington
Thornley Horden
CATHEDRAL Peterlee
67 Bowburn A181 Wheatley Blackhall Colliery
urham 6 11 Hill 10
ymoor Wingate A1086
5
Trimdon A179
Ferryhill Fishburn 12
A19 **Hartlepool**
n A1(M) Tees
Chilton 60 Sedgefield 7 Bay
Newton A177 A689 A178
Aycliffe A689
Billingham RIVERSIDE STADIUM
cliffe (MIDDLESBROUGH F.C.) Redcar
59 8 A1085
7 South Marske-by-the-Sea
Stockton-on-Tees Bank 8 Saltburn-by-the-Sea
8 **Middlesbrough** 7 Brotton
58 Eston Skelton
12 A66 Thornaby-on-Tees 6 Loftus
Eaglescliffe B1269 Hinderwell
A67 STEWART PARK Guisborough 16
C. PARK Roseberry A174
Teesside Topping Sandsend
International Yarm △ 22 Whitby
Egglescliffe 320 ST MARY'S
urworth- A172 7 High
on-Tees Great Ayton B1416 Hawsker
Hutton Stokesley Danby A171
A67 Rudby Castleton Sleights Robin
B1264 13 Great Egton Hood's Bay
A19 Broughton 8 NORTH 20
A172 C l e v e l a n d H i l l s YORKSHIRE MOORS
RAILWAY
19 Round Hill Staintondale
North △ **North York Moors** A171
Cowton 454 Cloughton
orton A67 Rosedale Abbey 20 Burniston
erick 15 **North York Moors** Hackness
Brompton A169
A684 **National Park** Scalby
Northallerton 7 Gillamoor NORTH YORKSHIRE A165
Lockton MOORS RWY North Riding
A168 Knayton Kirkbymoorside Forest Park Sca
Leeming A170 Wrelton
A167 Boltby Helmsley 13 Pickering FLAMINGO LAND
10 12 Sproxton **82** F
D Thirsk A170 Vale of Pickering Thornton 17
Sowerby E Dale Snainton Seamer 7
B6267 Wass Ocwaldkirk Cayto

2

0 ────────── 10 miles
0 ─────── 10 ─────── 20 km
1:440,000 7 miles to 1 inch / 4.4 km to 1 cm

3

4

THE DESIGNER ROOM

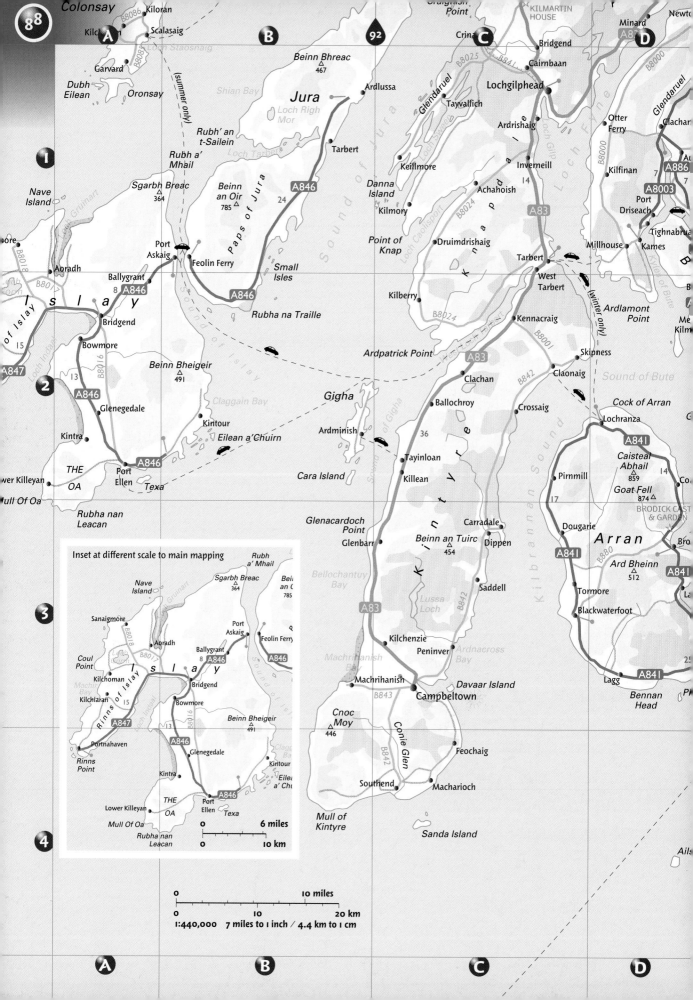

Colonsay

Kiloran
Kilch.. Scalasaig
A
Garvard
Dubh
Eilean
Oronsay

B
Beinn Bhreac
467

92

Craignish
Point
KILMARTIN
HOUSE
Minard
Newto..

Crina..
C
Bridgend
Cairnbaan

Lochgilphead
D
A8...
Glendaruel

Shian Bay

Jura
Loch Righ
Mor

Ardlussa
Glendaruel

Glendaruel
Tayvallich
Ardrishaig
Otter
Ferry
Clachan..
Glendaruel

Rubh' an
t-Sailein
Loch Tarbert

Tarbert
Keillmore
Inverneill
14
Kilfinan
A886
7
A8003

1
Nave
Island
Sgarbh Breac
364
Beinn
an Oir
785 △
24
Danna
Island
Kilmory
Achahoish
A83
Port
Driseach
Tighnabrua..
Kames

..ore
Aoradh
Port
Askaig
Feolin Ferry
A846
A846
Small
Isles
Point of
Knap
Druimdrishaig
Tarbert
Millhouse

I
s
l
a
y
Ballygrant
8 A846
Bridgend
Rubha na Traille
Kilberry
B8024
West
Tarbert
Ardlamont
Point
Me..
Kilm..

of Islay
15
Bowmore
Beinn Bheigeir
491 △
Ardpatrick Point
A83
Kennacraig
(winter only)
Sound of Bute

A847
2
A846
Glenegedale
Claggain Bay
Gigha
Clachan
B842
Skipness
Claonaig

Kintra
Kintour
Eilean a'Chuirn
Ardminish
Ballochroy
Crossaig
Lochranza
A841
Cock of Arran

THE
OA
Port
Ellen
A846
Texa
Cara Island
Tayinloan
Killean
36
Pirnmill
Caisteal
Abhail
859 △
14
Co..
BRODICK CAS..
& GARDEN

.wer Killeyan
Rubha nan
Leacan
Mull Of Oa
Glenacardoch
Point
Glenbarr
Beinn an Tuirc
454
Carradale
Dippen
Goat Fell
874 △
A r r a n
Dougarie
Bro..

Inset at different scale to main mapping
Rubh
a' Mhail
Bein
an C..
785
Saddell
A841
B880
Ard Bheinn
512 △
A841
Tormore

Nave
Island
Sgarbh Breac
364
Kilchenzie
Peninver
Ardnacross
Bay
Blackwaterfoot

Sanaigmore
Port
Askaig
Ballygrant
8 A846
Feolin Ferry
A846
A83
Machrihanish
Bay
Lussa
Loch
B842

Coul
Point
I s l a y
Aoradh
Bridgend
Kilchoman
Bowmore
Machrihanish
B843
Davaar Island
Campbeltown
A841
Lagg
Bennan
Head
25..

Kilchiaran
15
B8016
Beinn Bheigeir
491 △
Cnoc
Moy
446

Rinns of Islay
A847
A846
13
Glenegedale
Kintour
Eilea..
a' Ch..

Portnahaven
Conie Glen
B842
Feochaig

Rinns
Point
Kintra
THE
OA
Port
Ellen
A846
Texa
Southend
Macharioch

Lower Killeyan
Mull Of Oa
Rubha nan
Leacan
0   6 miles
0   10 km
Mull of
Kintyre
Sanda Island
Ailsa..

0   10 miles
0   10   20 km
1:440,000 7 miles to 1 inch / 4.4 km to 1 cm

A
B
C
D

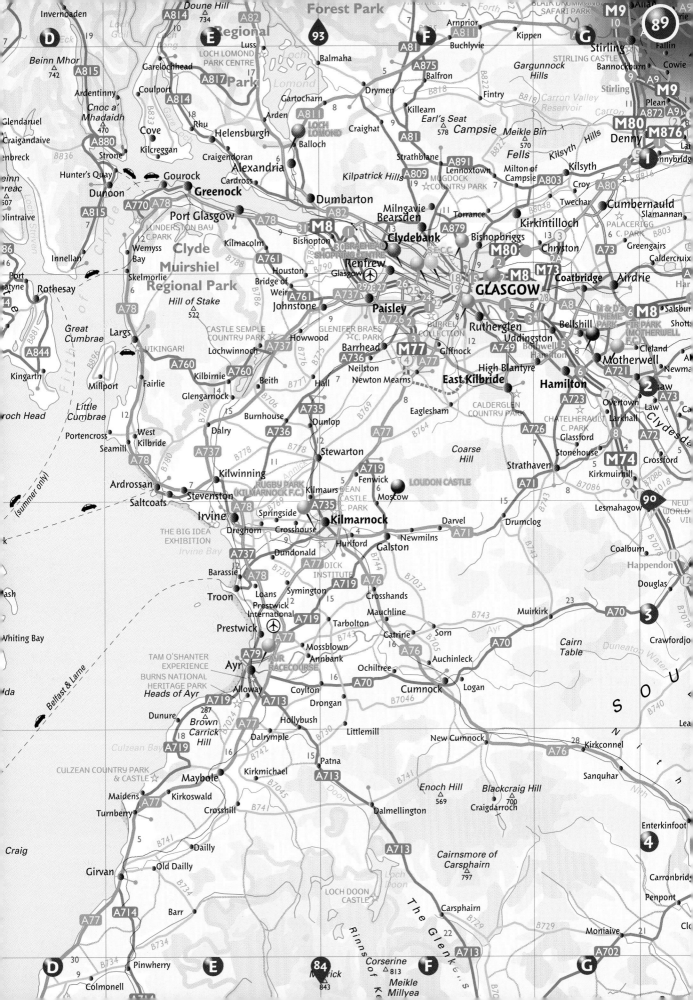

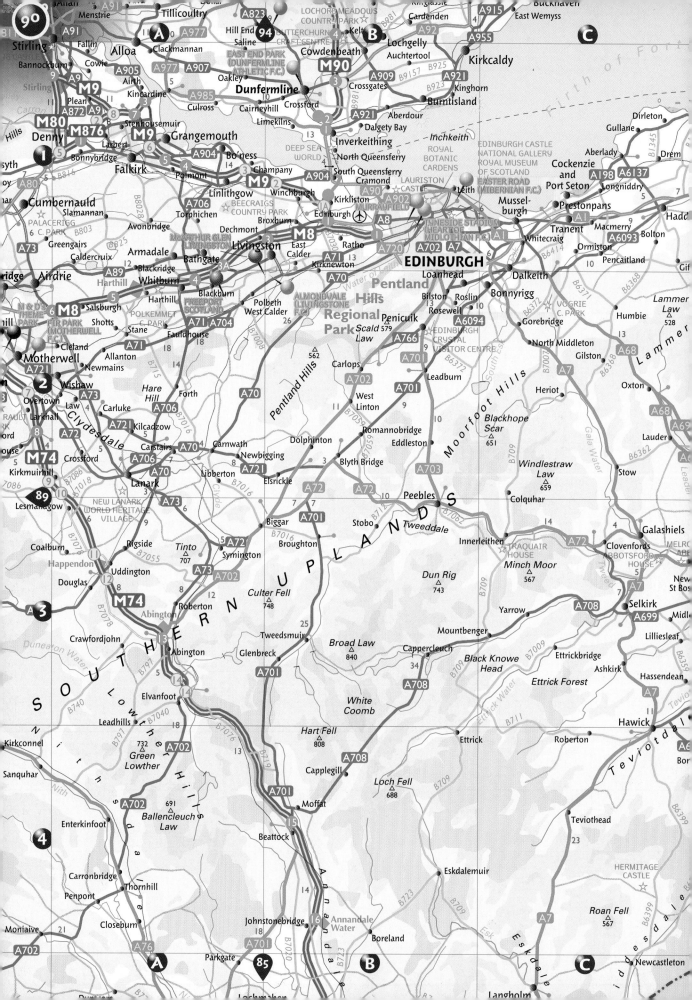

A

B **Rum (Rhum)** 96 C

Kinlo

Aird of Sleat

Point of Slea

Morar

A830

Ari

18

Askival
812

Rubha nam
Meirleach

Cleadale

Eigg

An Sgurr
393

Galmisdale

Eilean
nan Each

Eilean
Shona

Sound of Arisaig

Loch na

Ro

INNER HEBRIDES

Muck

1

Lochboisdale

Castlebay

Ockle

Ardtoe

B804

Acharacle

Point of
Ardnamurchan

Achosnich

A r d n a m u r c h a n

B8007

Eilean Mor

Sorisdale

B8072

Coll

12

Clabhach

Arinagour

B8070

Loch
Eatharna

Ardmore Point

Kilchoan

Ben Hiant
528

Glenbeg

B8007

Glenborrodale

Loch

2

Gunna

Crossapol
Bay

Caliach
Point

Calgary

Dervaig

Tobermory

Drimnin

Mor

Loch
Arienas

B8073

Loch
Frisa

Killundine

A848

Fiunary

B8049

Hough Bay

B8068

B8069

Caolas

Kilninian

Calgary Bay

Loch Tuath

Salen

A849

Fish

Tiree

Scarinish

B8068

Hynish Bay

Treshnish Isles

Gometra

Lagganulva

B8073

B8035

23

Knock

Dun da
Ghaoith
766

Barrapoll

Balephuil

Balemartine

Ulva

Little
Colonsay

Staffa

Balnahard

Loch Na Keal

Loch
Ba

M u l l

3

Ben More
966

Glen More

A849

Ben Buie
717

Loch Buie

ÌONA ABBEY
Baile Mòr ☆

Iona

Fionnphort

Sound of Iona

Bunessan

A849

35

Pennyghael

Carsaig

R o s s   o f   M u l l

Soa Island

Ardchiavaig

Malcolm's
Point

Firth

0		10 miles
0	10	20 km

1:440,000   7 miles to 1 inch / 4.4 km to 1 cm

Garvellachs

4

Scarba

C
S

Kiloran Bay

Rubh' a'Geodha

Colonsay

Kiloran

B8086

Kilchattan

Scalasaig

A

Garvard

B

B8085

88

C Beinn Bhreac
467

Aird Asaig

Tarbert (An Tairbeart)

A859

Caolas Scalpaigh

Scalpay (Eilean Scalpaigh)

SOUTH HARRIS
ann a Deas
Heara

25

Roghadal
enish Point

103

Shiant Islands

B

Greenstone Point

Rubha Reidh

Cove

Melvaig

Poolewe

B8021

B8057

Gairloch

Gair Loch

Port Henderson

Redpoint

B8056

Rubha Hunish

Kilmaluag

A855

19

Balgown

Staffin

Staffin Bay

1

Little Minch

Lochmaddy
Vaternish Point

Idrigil

Uig

Culnaknock

A87

Trotternish

Lower Diabaig

Fearnmore

Inveralligan

Beinn

Loch Torridon

2

Ben Geary
284

Lusta

Loch Snizort

B886

13

A855

The Storr
719

Rona

Sound of Raasay

Shieldaig

Dunvegan Head

Boreraig

Loch Dunvegan

14

Kensaleyre

A896

Milovaig

6

A850

DUNVEGAN CASTLE

Bernisdale

Carbost

Borve

Brochel

Beinn Bhan
896

18

Loch

102

B884

Dunvegan

Roskhill

B885

4

Portree

Raasay

Applecross

Loch Kishorn

Healabhal Bheag
488

8

Skye

9

Oskaig

Clachan

Toscaig

3

Bracadale

A863

B8009

Portnalong

Carbost

Talisker

B883

A87

Peinchorran

Sconser

Crowlin Islands

Inner Sound

Duirinish

6

A8

Kyle of Lochalsh

Balmacara

Loch Alsh

A

13

Sligachan

11

Luib

Scalpay

A87

Kyleakin

9

Beinn Bhreac
445

Cuillin Hills

Bla Bheinn (Blaven)
928

Broadford

A87

6

Breakish

Glenbrittle

Sgurr Alasdair
993

Torrin

A851

Kylerhea

Glenelg

Loch Brittle

Cuillin Sound

B8083

Beinn na Seamraig
561

Beinn Sgrithe
981

4

Soay

Loch Scavaig

Elgol

Loch Eishort

17

Sleat

Loch Hourn

Arni

Canna

Sound of Canna

Kilmory

Clan Donald Centre

Teangue

A851

Ladhar Bheinn
1020

Knoyda

Ardvasar

Aird of Sleat

Meall Bu
946

Rum (Rhum)

Kinloch

A

92

Askival
812

Point of Sleat

B

Sound of Sleat

Mallaig

C

Morar

Bracora

Loch Nevis

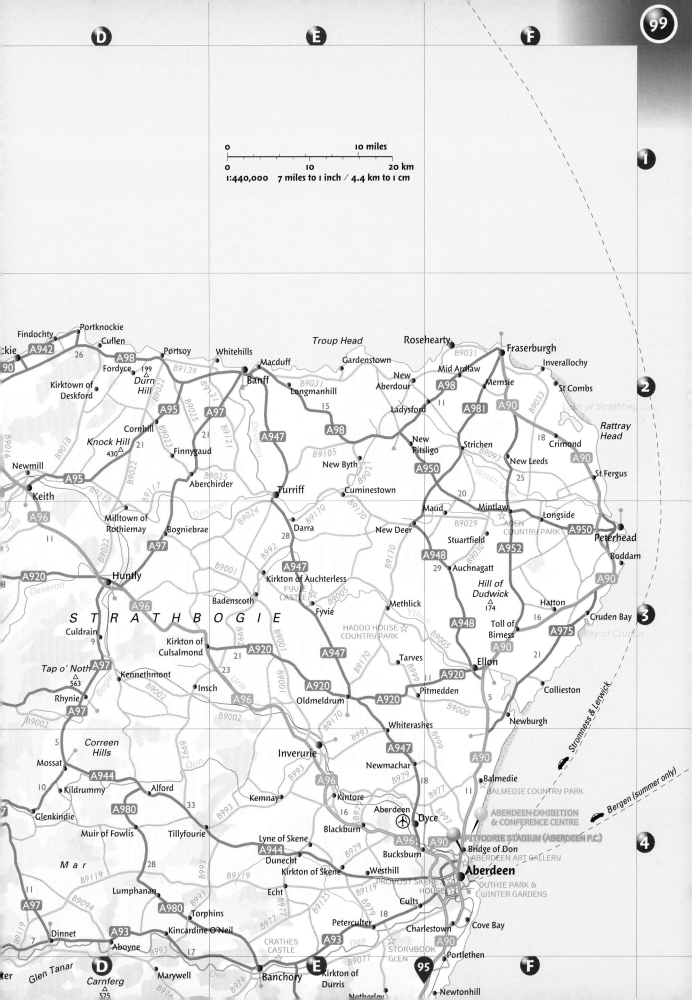

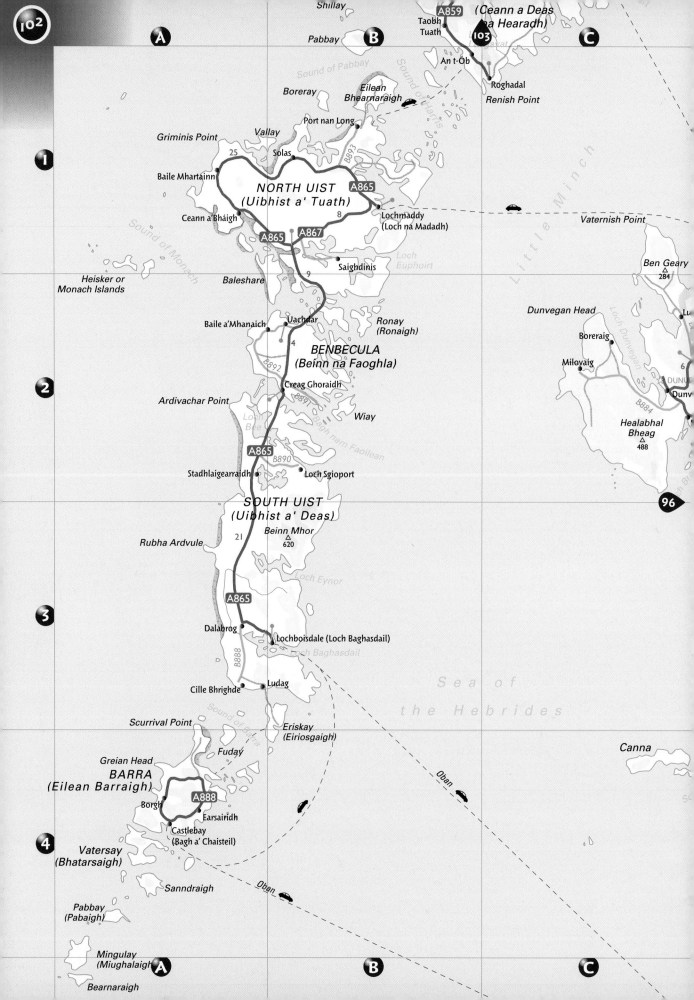

Rubha Robhanais

Eoropaidh
Tabost
Port Nis
Sgiogarstaigh
Dail Bho
Thuath

A857
15

ISLE OF LEWIS
(Eilean Leodhais)

Muirneag
248
Tolastadh Úr
Tolsta Head

Arnol
Barabhas

Siabost
Bragar

A858

Carlabhagh

Beinn
Mholach
292

A857
11

Griais

Tolastadh
a'Chaolais

Breascleit
Calanais

*Great
Bernera*

Stornoway
(Steornabhagh)

Tunga

Newmarket

*Loch a'
Tuath*

Rubha an t-Siumpain

Port nan Giúran

Siulaisiadar

An Rubha

Miabhig

Timsgearraidh

Crulabhig

Gearraidh na h-Aibhne

A858

A866

*West
Loch Roag*

Einacleit

Mealisval
574

Breanais

*Loch
Suainaval*

Achadh
Mór

A859
13

12

Crosbost

Baile Ailein

Cearsiadar

Grabhair

*Mealasta
Island*

NORTH HARRIS
(Ceann a Tuath na Hearadh)

Airidh
a'Bhruaich

B8060

Kebock Head

*Loch
Langavat*
21

Leumrabhagh

*Loch
Resort*

A859

Scarp

Huisinis

Tirga Mor
679

A859

Beinn
Mhór
572

*Loch
Shell*

Abhainnsuidhe

B887

Clishham
799

A859

*Loch
Claidh*

Ullapool

*Taransay
(Taransaigh)*

Aird
Asaig

Tarbert
(An Tairbeart)

Shiant Islands

A859

Rubha Re

**SOUTH
HARRIS**
**(Ceann a Deas
na Hearadh)**

Caolas Scalpaigh

25

*Scalpay
(Eilean Scalpaigh)*

Toe Head

A859

Taobh
Tuath

*Loch
Langavat*

An t-Ób

Me

Roghadal
Renish Point

Rubha Hunish

Kilmaluag

Port He

A855
19

Staffin Bay

Balgown

Staffin

102

Redpoi

*Lochmaddy
(Loch na Madadh)*

Vaternish Point

Idrigil
Uig

Culnaknock

Ben Geary
284

A87
96

Trotternish

Fearnmore

Rona

1:440,000 7 miles to 1 inch / 4.4 km to 1 cm

0 ——— 10 miles ——— 20 km

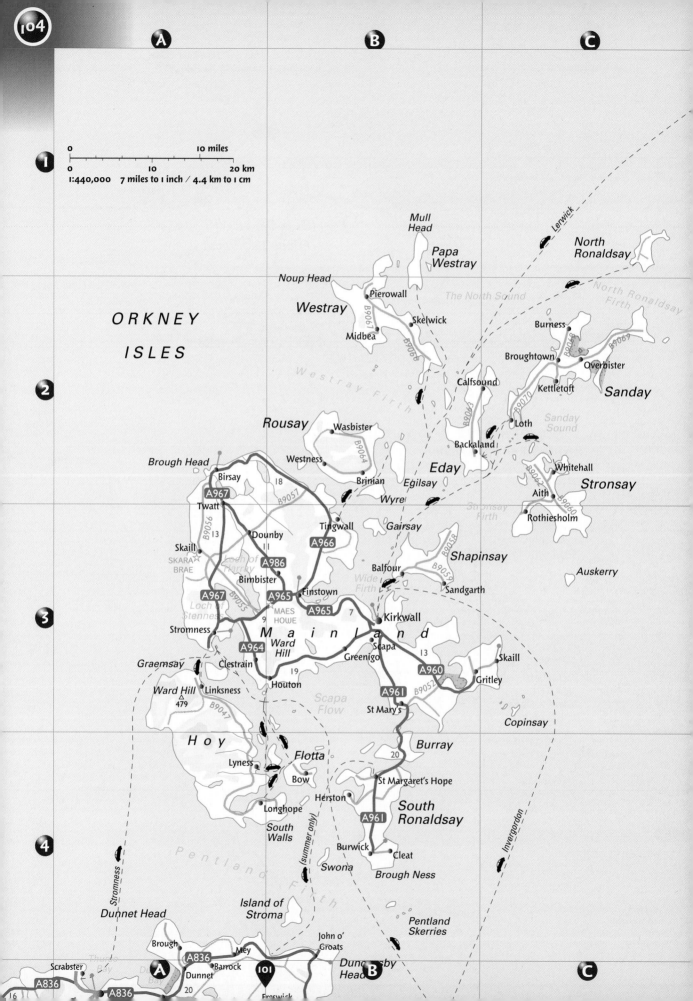

A B C

1

0 ———— 10 miles
0 ———— 10 ———— 20 km
1:440,000   7 miles to 1 inch / 4.4 km to 1 cm

ORKNEY
ISLES

Mull
Head

Papa
Westray

Noup Head

Lerwick

North
Ronaldsay

Pierowall

The North Sound

Skelwick

Westray

Burness

North Ronaldsay
Firth

B9066

B9065

Midbea

B9069

Broughtown

Overbister

2

Westray Firth

Calfsound

Kettletoft

Sanday

Rousay

B9063

Loth

Sanday
Sound

Wasbister

B9064

Eday

Backaland

Westness

Whitehall

Brough Head

Brinian

Egilsay

Aith

Stronsay

Birsay

Wyre

B9062

B9060

A967

Twatt

18

B9057

Gairsay

Rothiesholm

13

Dounby

Tingwall

Shapinsay

B9056

11

Stronsay
Firth

Skaill

A986

A966

Balfour

B9058

Auskerry

SKARA
BRAE

Loch of
Harray

Bimbister

B9059

Shapinsay

A967

Finstown

A965

B9055

3

Stromness

MAES
HOWE

Loch of
Stenness

A965

7

Kirkwall

Sandgarth

Mainland

Ward
Hill

A964

Greenigo

Scapa

13

Skaill

Clestrain

19

Gritley

A960

Graemsay

Houton

St Mary's

B9052

Ward Hill
△
479

A961

Copinsay

B9047

Linksness

Scapa
Flow

Hoy

Burray

Lyness

Flotta

20

Invergordon

Bow

St Margaret's Hope

Longhope

Herston

South
Ronaldsay

South
Walls

A961

4

Stromness

(summer only)

Burwick

Cleat

Pentland Firth

Swona

Brough Ness

Dunnet Head

Island of
Stroma

Pentland
Skerries

Brough

John o'
Groats

Scrabster

A836

Mey

Dunnet

Barrock

Dunnesby
Head

Thurso
Bay

A836

101

A B C

16

A836

SHETLAND
ISLES

Herma
Ness

Unst

Valsgarth Norwick
Haroldswick
Baltasound
10
A968

Cullivoe
Belmont
Gutcher
Sellafirth
A968

Uyeasound

Fetlar

Oddsta Houbie
B9088
Funzie

Point of
Fethaland

Isbister

The Faither

Yell

Mid Yell
Hascosay

A968

Ronas
△Hill
450
Collafirth

Ollaberry
Urafirth
B9078
Esha Ness
Stenness
Hillswick

A970

A970
17

Otterswick
West Yell
A968
B9081

Hamnavoe
Ulsta
Burravoe
B9081

Toft

St. Magnus
Bay

B9076
10

A968

Brae

Out Skerries

**Muckle
Roe**

Hillside
Voe
Laxo
B9071
B9071

Vidlin
Brough
Skaw
Whalsay
Isbister
Symbister

*Papa
Stour*

M
a
i
n
l
a
n
d

A970
B9075

Dury Voe

South
Nesting Bay

Sandness
A971
Aith
B9075
20

Bridge
of Walls
Bixter
Setter
Heglibister

Girlsta

B9071
Walls

Garderhouse

Culswick

B9074
Veensgarth

Lerwick

*Isle of
Ness*

Scalloway

Bressay

Hamnavoe

Bergen, Torshavn & Seydisfjordur
(all summer only)

Easter
Quarff

**West
Burra**

A970

Cunningsburgh

Sandwick

Mousa

25

Levenwick

B9122

A970

Scousburgh

Boddam

Aberdeen & Stromness

Toab
JARLSHOF
Grutness
Sumburgh

Sumburgh

Ham
Foula

D   E   F

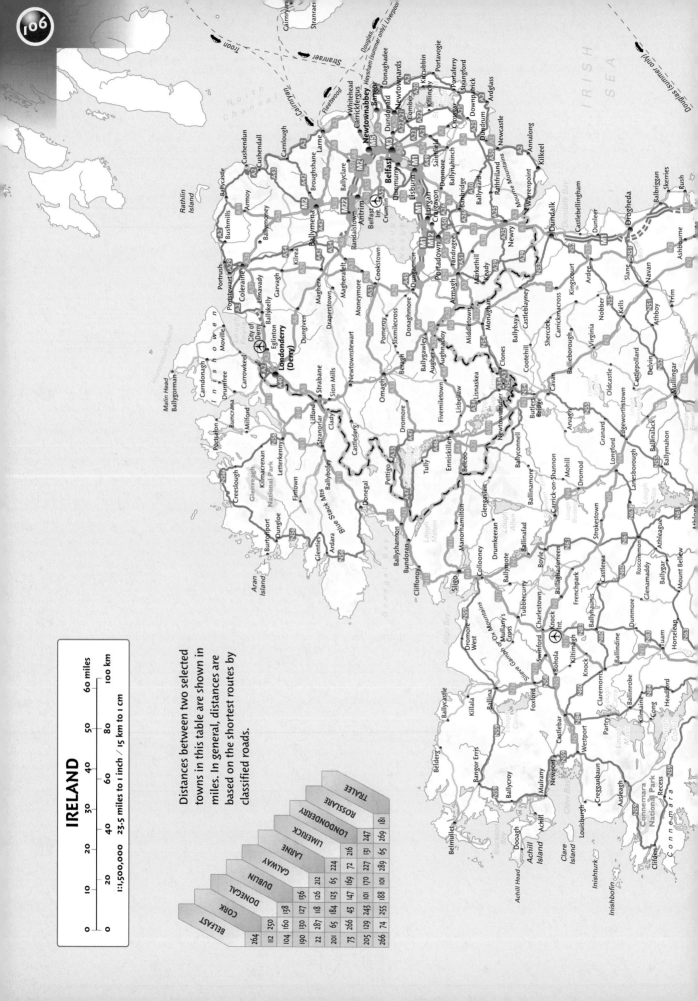

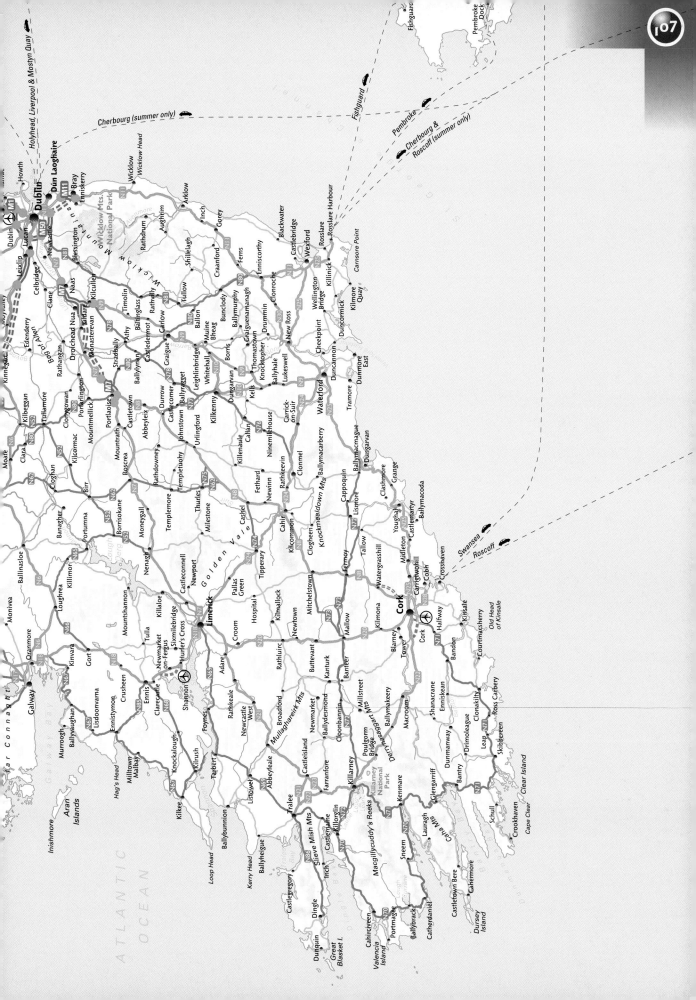

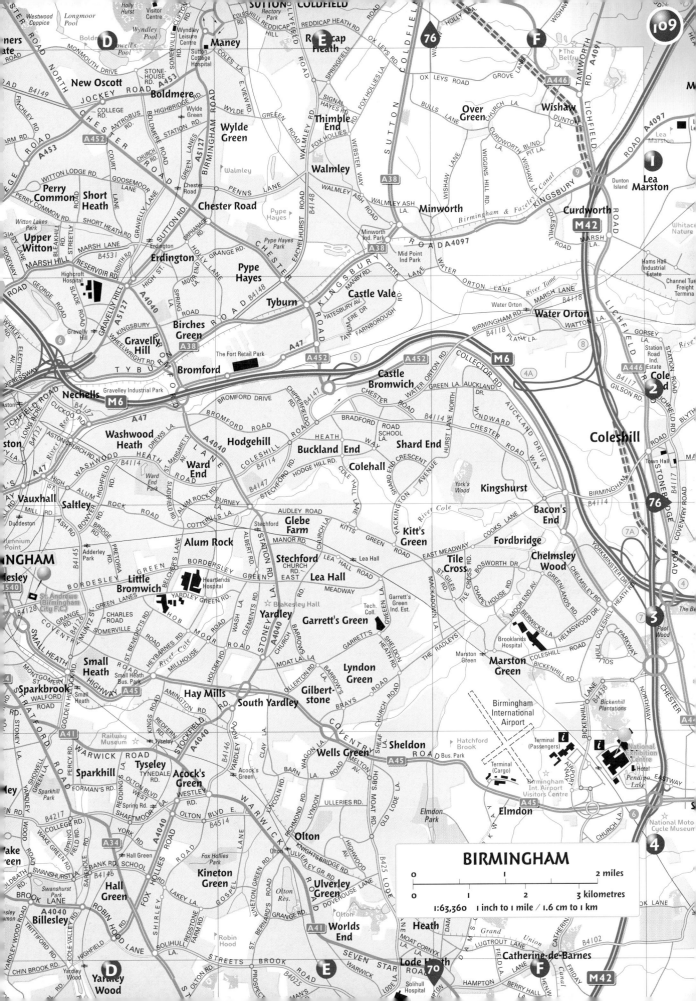

BIRMINGHAM

| 0 | | 1 | | 2 miles |
| 0 | 1 | | 2 | 3 kilometres |

1:63,360   1 inch to 1 mile / 1.6 cm to 1 km

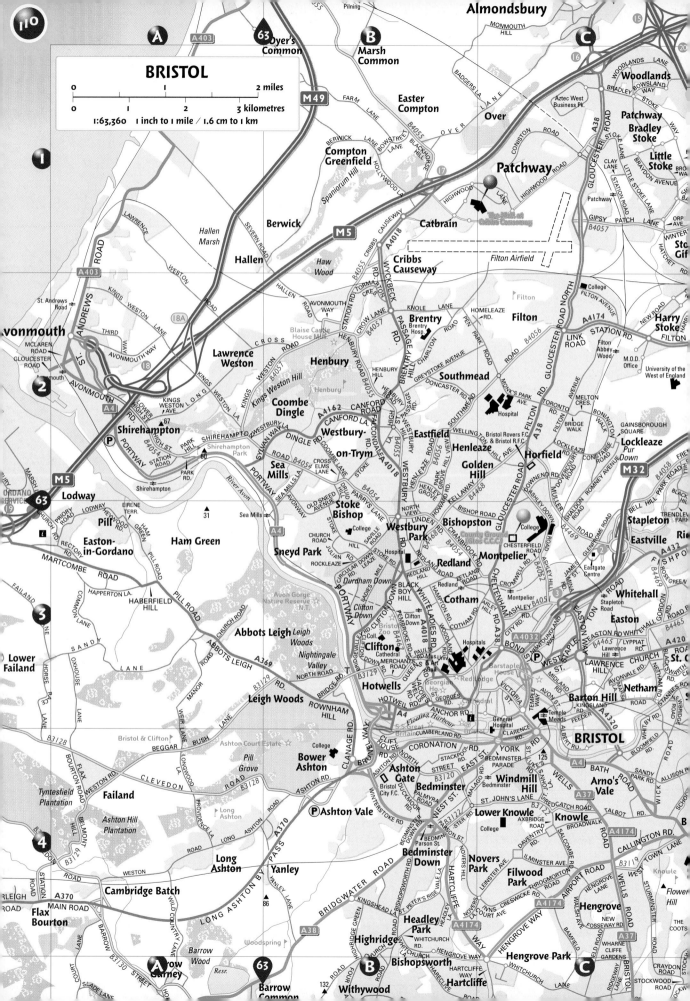

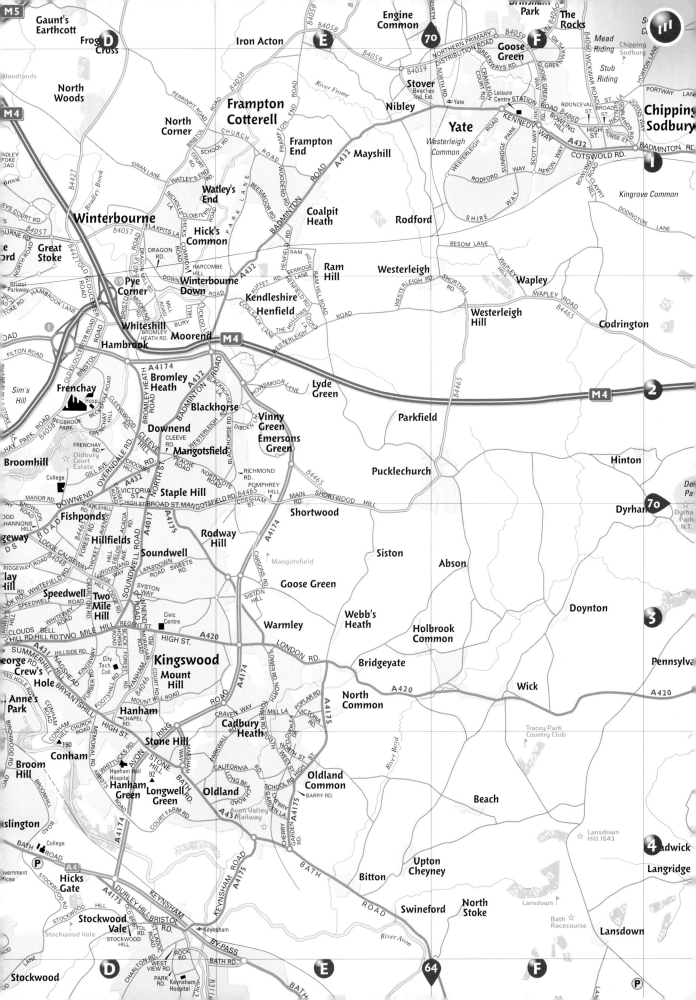

CARDIFF & NEWPORT

0 — 1 — 2 miles

0 — 1 — 2 — 3 kilometres

1:63,360   1 inch to 1 mile / 1.6 cm to 1 km

BRISTOL CHANNEL

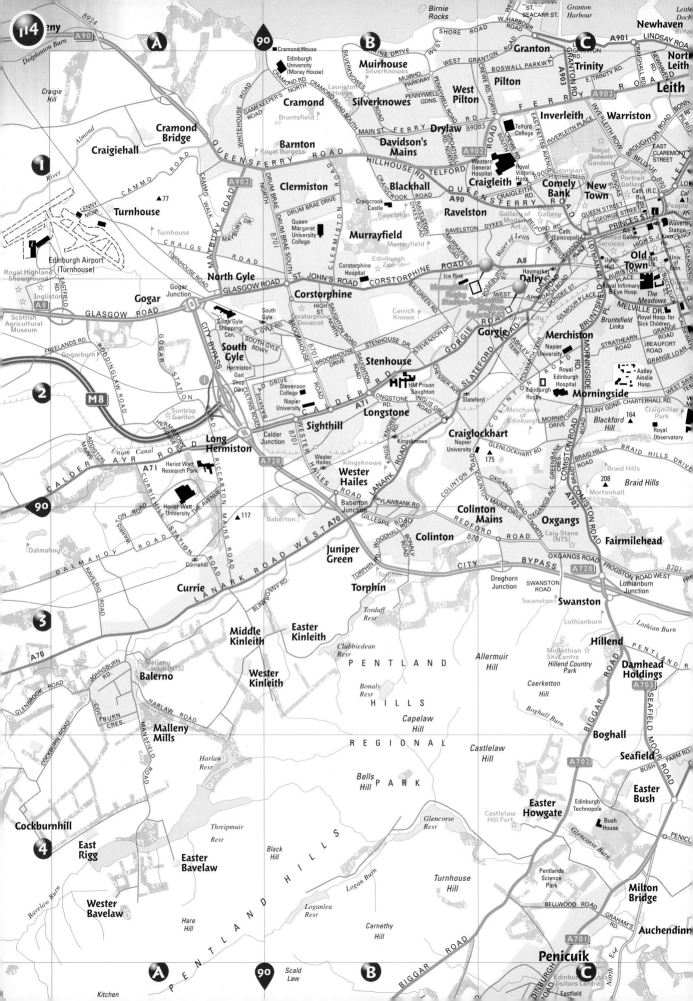

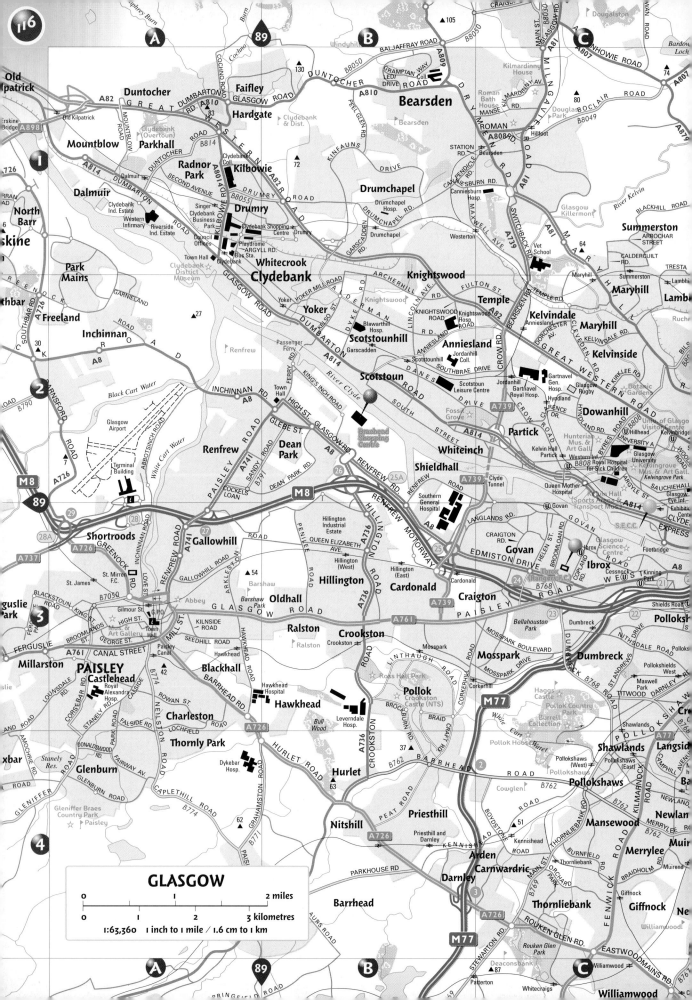

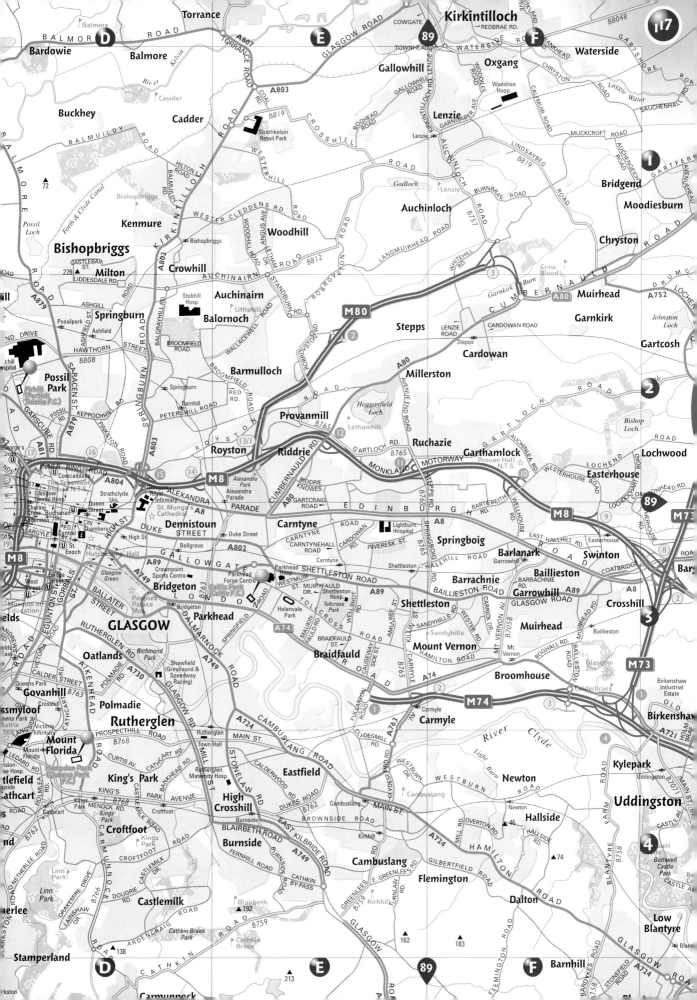

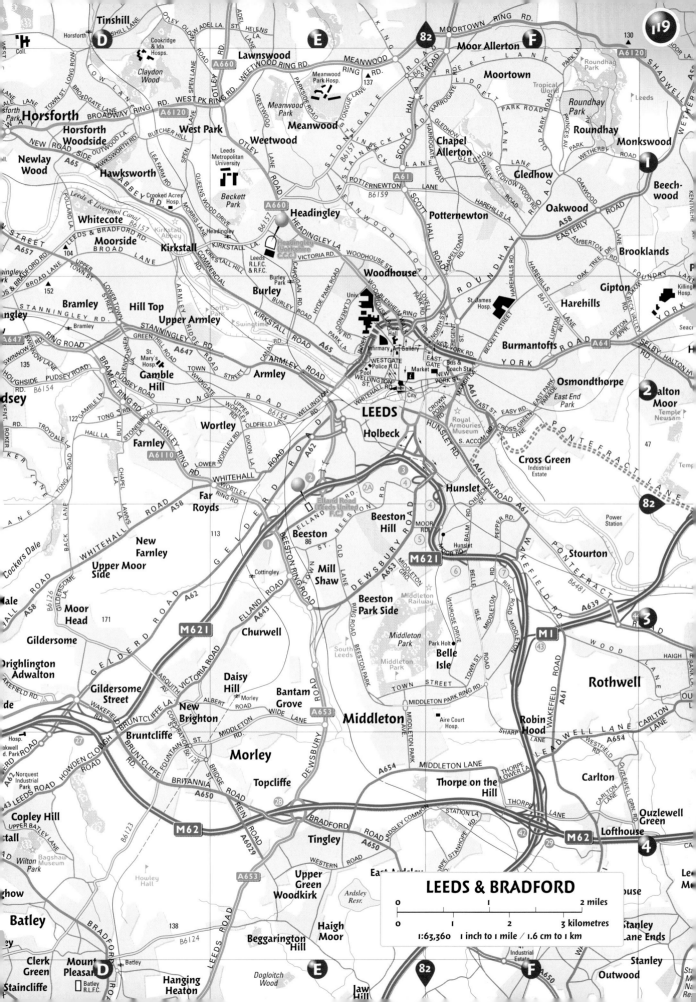

LEEDS & BRADFORD

0   1   2 miles

0   1   2   3 kilometres

1:63,360   1 inch to 1 mile / 1.6 cm to 1 km

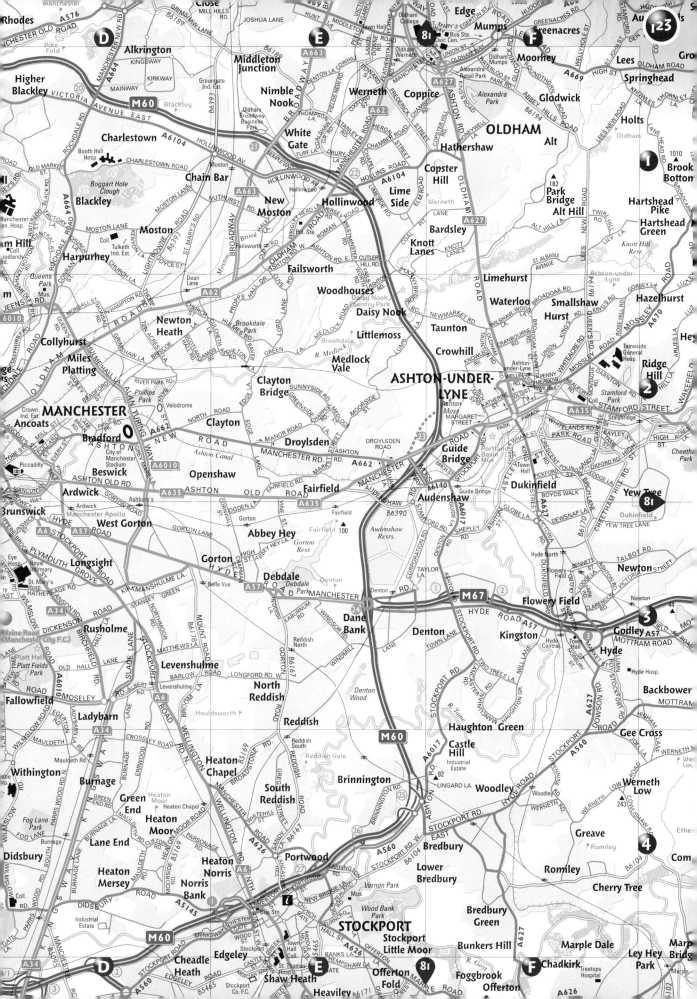

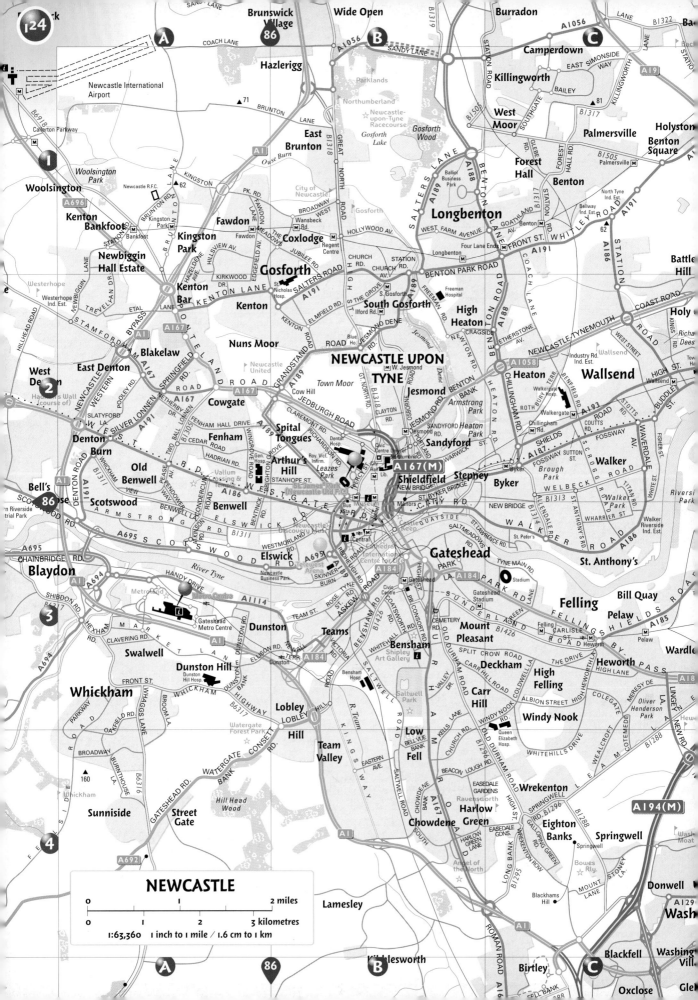

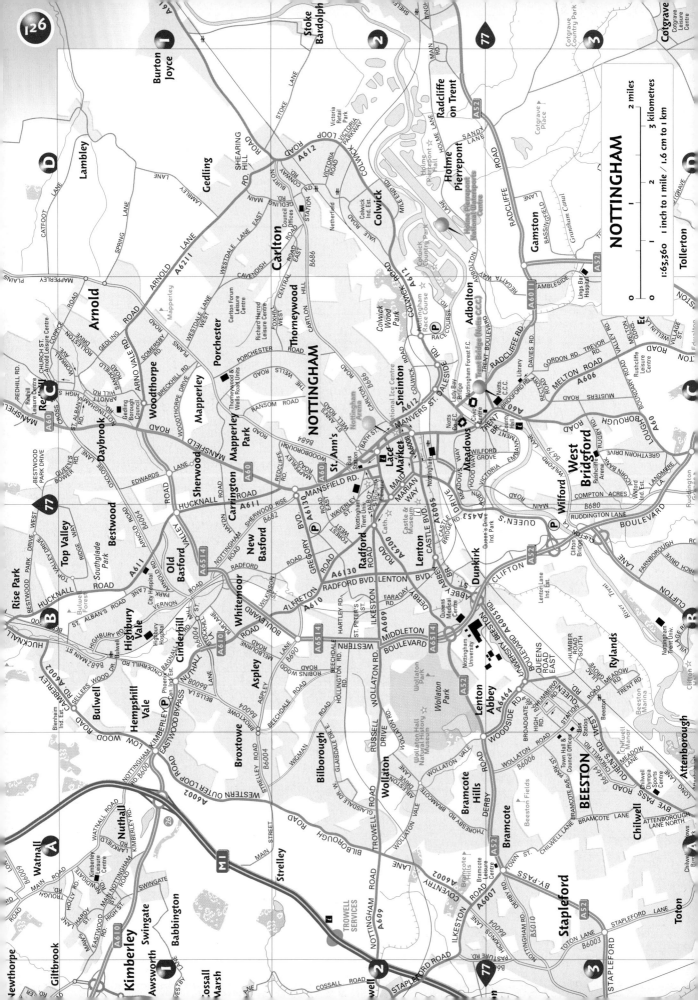

NOTTINGHAM

1:63,360   1 inch to 1 mile / 1.6 cm to 1 km

0   1   2 miles

0   1   2   3 kilometres

3 kilometres

Newthorpe   Giltbrook   Watnall   Awsworth   Swingate   Kimberley   Babbington   Cossall Marsh   Cossall   Strelley   Nuthall   Bilborough   Wollaton   Bramcote Hills   Bramcote   Chilwell   Stapleford   Toton   Attenborough   Rylands   BEESTON   Lenton Abbey   Dunkirk   Wilford   West Bridgford   Gamston   Tollerton   Cotgrave

Rise Park   Top Valley   Bestwood   Old Basford   New Basford   Whitemoor   Aspley   Bilborough   Hucknall   Bulwell   Hempshill Vale   Broxtowe   Cinderhill   Highbury Vale

Arnold   Daybrook   Woodthorpe   Mapperley   Sherwood   Carlton   Thorneywood   Sneinton   Colwick   Adbolton   Holme Pierrepont   Radcliffe on Trent

Lambley   Gedling   Porchester   Mapperley Park   Carlington   St Ann's   Meadows

NOTTINGHAM   Lenton   Radford   Lace Market   Maid Marian Way

Burton Joyce   Stoke Bardolph

Trent Bridge (Notts CCC)

PORTSMOUTH

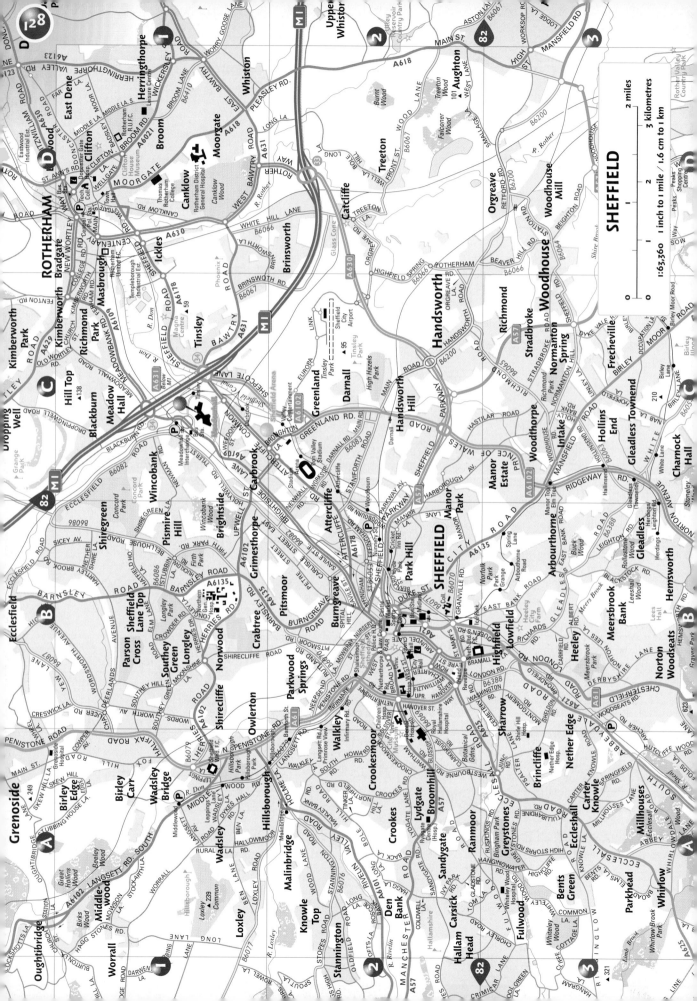

SOUTHAMPTON

129

LONDON-WEST

1:63,360 1 inch to 1 mile / 1.6 cm to 1 km

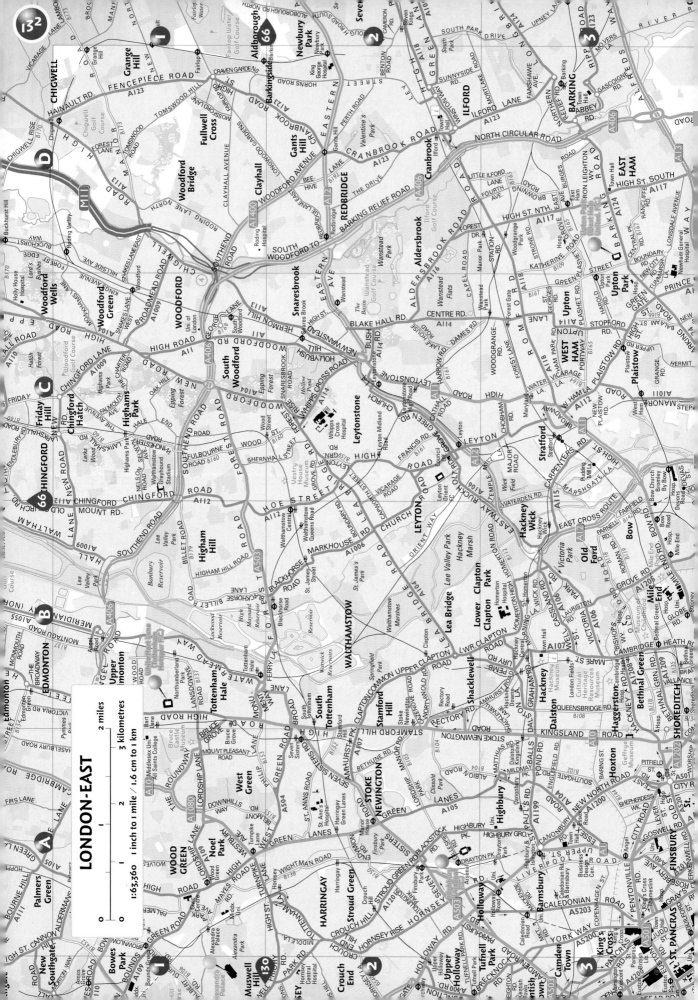

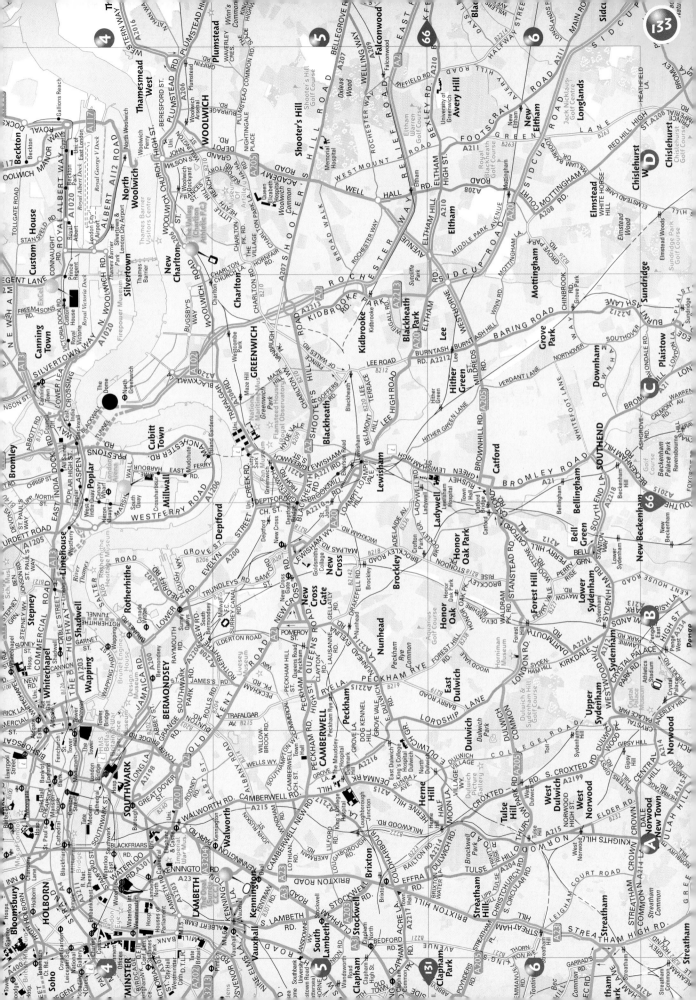

133

CENTRAL LONDON   1:10,000   6.3 inches to 1 mile / 10 cm to 1 km

CENTRAL LONDON

1:10,000   6.3 inches to 1 mile / 10 cm to 1 km

0   1/4   1/2 mile

0   1/4   1/2   3/4   1 km

ABERDEEN

WEB-SITE www.aberdeencity.gov.uk

LOCAL RADIO
BBC RADIO SCOTLAND 93.9 FM & 810 AM
NORTHSOUND 1 96.9 FM, NORTHSOUND 2 1035 AM

ABERDEEN

[Map of Aberdeen with grid columns 1, 2, 3 and rows A, B, C. Labels include:]

Rosehill Dri, A9012, Hilton Street, A978, Clifton Rd., A96, Cairncry Road, Back Hilton Road, Ashgrove Road, Bedford Road, College Bounds, King's College, Chris Anderson Stadium, Linksfield Road, Golf Road, Golf Course, Ashgrove Rd. W., Westburn Drive, Cornhill, Westburn Indoor Tennis Centre, Berryden Road, Powis Terrace, Leslie Ter., Holland Street, George St., Sunnybank Road, Spital, King's Crescent, Pittodrie St., Pittodrie Aberdeen F.C., Royal Infirmary, Children's Hospital, Westburn Park, Road, Royal Cornhill Hospital, Hutcheon Street, Powis Pl., Causeway, Nelson St., West North St., King Street, Fire Station, Seaforth Road, Urquhart Road, City Hospital, Satrosphere, A944, Westburn Road, Victoria Park, Mid Stocket Road, Rosemount, Jonah's Journeys, Esslemont Ave., Skene Square, P.O., Mount Street, Baker Street, Loch Street, Maberly St., Aberdeen Coll., Spring Gdns., Robert Gordon University, Art Gallery, Library, His Majesty's Theatre, Schoolhill, Bon Accord Centre, Marischal College, Municipal Bldgs., P.O., St Andrew's Cathedral, Lemon Tree, Commerce St., Park Road, Constitution Street, Beach Boulevard, Beechgrove Terrace, Whitehall Rd., Fountainhall Road, Albert St., Place, Skene St., Rose St., Chapel St., St Mary's Cathedral, Kirk of St Nicholas, Music Hall, Trinity Centre, Market, Maritime Museum, Regent Quay, Ferry Terminal, Victoria Dock, Forest Road, Desswood Place, Carden Place, Albyn Place, Union Street, Langstane, Bon-Accord St., Crown St., Guild St., College St., P.O., Bus Station Aberdeen, Market Street, Blaikie's Quay, Commercial Quay, Fish Markets, Albert Basin, Albert Quay, Queens Road, St. Swithin St., B9119, Ashley Rd., Union Grove, Bon Accord Park, Cinema, Willowbank Rd., Springbank Ter., Albury Road, Rec. Grd., Palmerston Road, North Esplanade W., Victoria Bri., Dee, Cromwell Rd., Forest Avenue, P.O., Great Western Road, Holburn St., Southern Rd., Cemetery, Hardgate, Fonthill, Road, Bon-Accord St., Ferryhill Rd., Crown Street, P.O., River Dee, A93, Great Southern Road, Seaforth Road

N 0 500 yds / 0 500m

INDEX TO STREET NAMES

Apparently, the best time to see 'the Granite City', is just after it's rained, 'When it sparkles like a jewel'! Hmm! Anyway, oil made Aberdeen the affluent place it is today, with a cosmopolitan population that want fun! Consequently, there are more **pubs and clubs** per person here than in any other Scottish city! A couple of the largest clubs attract really well known DJs, and there's 70s retro, folk nights, indie, everything! Now, **shops, shops, shops!** There are seven shopping malls here, all the big names; hand made Scottish goods, luverly jewellery and speciality shops. Try Royal Deeside for more 'exclusive' stuff. International **ballet, theatre and opera** companies perform at His Majesty's Theatre, and there are concert halls featuring every type of musical genre (posh word!). Try The Lemon Tree for more contemporary **entertainment** including stand-up **comedy**, and there are **festivals** throughout the year too. Several **cinemas** and excellent well-funded **museums and art galleries**, a **Planetarium** and '**Satrosphere**' are good for wet days (after which you can go 'ahhh' at the sparkling architecture! – which **is** pretty impressive by the way). With all this to do, it's easy to forget that Aberdeen has a **beach** (reputedly the best of any British city), miles of clean golden sand; you can even **windsurf!** Stay longer and do 'outdoorsy' stuff in the magnificent surrounding countryside – **skiing?** Yep, that too!

TOURIST INFORMATION ☎ 01224 632727
ST. NICHOLAS HOUSE, BROAD STREET, ABERDEEN, AB9 1DE

HOSPITAL A & E ☎ 01224 681818
ABERDEEN ROYAL INFIRMARY, FORESTERHILL, ABERDEEN, AB25 2ZN

Area Code 01225

Bath and N.E. Somerset

BATH

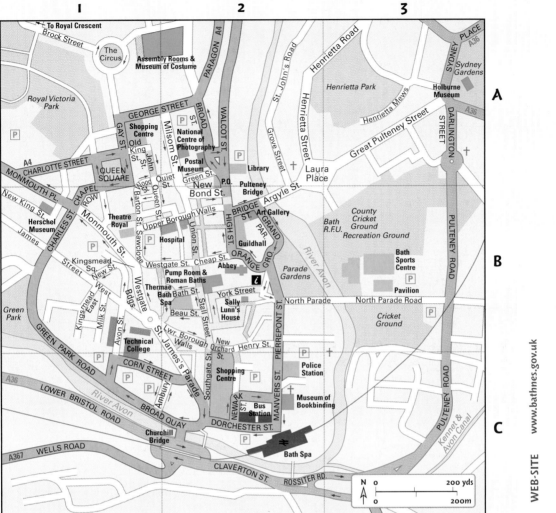

To Royal Crescent — Brock Street — The Circus — Assembly Rooms & Museum of Costume — Royal Victoria Park — George Street — Shopping Centre — National Centre of Photography — Postal Museum — Library — Laura Place — Holburne Museum — Henrietta Park — Sydney Gardens — Henrietta Road — Henrietta Mews — Great Pulteney Street — Charlotte Street — Queen Square — Herschel Museum — Theatre Royal — Upper Borough Walls — New Bond St. — Pulteney Bridge — Argyle St. — Art Gallery — Bath R.F.U. — County Cricket Ground Recreation Ground — Hospital — Guildhall — Westgate St. — Cheap St. — Abbey — Pump Room & Roman Baths — Thermae Bath Spa — Bath St. — York Street — Sally Lunn's House — Parade Gardens — North Parade — North Parade Road — Bath Sports Centre — Pavilion — Cricket Ground — Green Park — Technical College — New Orchard St. — Henry St. — Police Station — Shopping Centre — Museum of Bookbinding — Bus Station — Churchill Bridge — Dorchester St. — Bath Spa — Claverton St. — Rossiter Rd. — Wells Road — Lower Bristol Road — River Avon — Green Park Road — Broad Quay — Kennet & Avon Canal — Pulteney Road — Darlington Street — Sydney Place

N 0 200 yds / 0 200m

WEB-SITE www.bathnes.gov.uk

LOCAL RADIO BBC RADIO BRISTOL 1548 AM & 104.6 FM — CLASSIC GOLD 1260 AM, 103 GWR FM 103 FM

INDEX TO STREET NAMES

'What did the Romans ever do for us?' Well, they converted a Celtic pig wallow into the only hot spring bathing emporium in the country. You can now enjoy this legacy at the new **Thermae Bath Spa,** near to the original **Roman Baths** (see Roman graffiti!), which includes an open-air thermal rooftop pool! Then came the Georgians, who gave Bath the 'posh' atmosphere it has today. The elegant architecture houses countless **museums, theatres and art galleries** but more importantly **SHOPS!** Retail therapy doesn't get any better! Bath has everything from all the better High Street names, yummy small independent gift shops and very exclusive designer stuff, to the 'Bohemian' Walcot Street – funky, less expensive goodies, with an excellent flea market on Saturdays. For **eating,** 'do lunch'. It's much cheaper than evening meals – fill the gaps with tea and buns! There's everything from Michelin stars to take-aways, 'real ale' pubs to shiny new bars. Other things to do? **Music, literary and film festivals** are good, or try **punting** on the Avon. The **Bath walking tour** is reputedly hysterical rather than historical – say no more! **Nightlife?** There's free music somewhere every night of the week. For theatre and ballet try the Theatre Royal, and for clubbing and gigs, check out 'Venue' magazine. Oh, and the traffic in Bath is a nightmare, so drive to one of the Park 'n Rides and bus in.

TOURIST INFORMATION ☎ 01225 477101
ABBEY CAMBERS, ABBEY CHURCHYARD,
BATH, BA1 1LY

HOSPITAL A & E ☎ 01225 428331
ROYAL UNITED HOSPITAL, COMBE PARK,
BATH, BA1 3NG

BELFAST

WEB-SITE www.belfastcity.gov.uk

LOCAL RADIO
BBC RADIO ULSTER 92·4·95·4 FM
CITY BEAT 96·7 FM, COOL FM 97·4 FM

INDEX TO STREET NAMES

With a new lease of life, Belfast is buzzing. So to really enjoy the 'craic', get a copy of 'That's Entertainment' or the 'Big List'. The main frolicsome **'club 'n pub'** areas are in Victoria Street and 'The Golden Mile' (the road leading to the University – which contains an original **Victorian 'gin palace'!**). **Live music** includes traditional Irish (try Kelly's Cellars), to classical, and clubs play everything from 70s retro to hip-hop and beyond! Remember that Sundays here are quiet! **Cultural** events abound, from productions at the Grand Opera House (1894) to those in the new Waterfront Hall. There are also **theatres** and loads of **art galleries**, **museums** and **festivals**. Now this might sound rather macabre, but if you're in the mood, taxis and buses will take you round the (in)famous **political murals** in West Belfast. They are spectacular works of art however and they are ever changing – the first Loyalist one recorded was painted in 1908, they're well worth a visit. Lightening up, 'new' Belfast has, over the last few years, seen a flourishing of **eating** emporiums. Modern Irish and European mostly, but some good Eastern restaurants are also appearing, try 'The Golden Mile' again. **Shopping** is mainly north from City Hall, and there's all sorts of shops. Then to finish off, you've just got to see Goliath and Samson! the World's second and third largest cranes in the Harland & Wolff shipyard of East Belfast.

TOURIST INFORMATION ☎ 028 9024 6609
BELFAST WELCOME CENTRE, 47 DONEGALL PLACE,
BELFAST BT1 5AD

HOSPITAL A & E ☎ 028 9032 9241
BELFAST CITY HOSPITAL, 51 LISBURN STREET,
BELFAST BT9 7AB

Area Code 0121

West Midlands

BIRMINGHAM

www.birmingham.gov.uk

WEB-SITE

BBC RADIO WM 95.6 FM
RADIO XL 1296 AM, BRMB 96.4 FM, HEART FM 100.7 FM,
GALAXY 102.2 FM

LOCAL RADIO

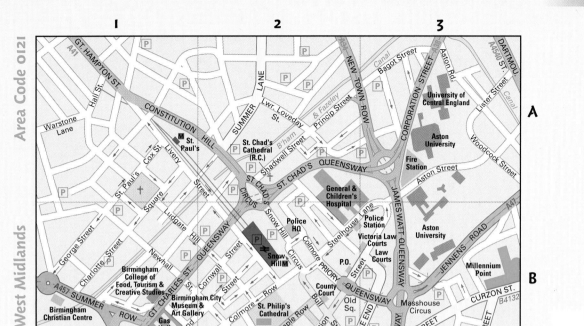

INDEX TO STREET NAMES

Welcome to exotic, cosmopolitan 'Brum'! Britain's second largest city has evolved from its industrial beginnings to one of the best multi-cultural/entertainment places to be. For **shopping**, the city centre has all the big shops, with the new Bullring development opening in stages with final completion in Autumn 2003 – it will be mega! There are also small boutiques and individual outlets – try New Street for a start. Take your trembling credit card to the **Mailbox Complex** for designer threads, then don't go to the **Jewellery Quarter**, too much temptation – oh, just a quick look then! Take the weight off your feet in **Brindley Place**, a revitalised canalside area, more shops and good **food** – and hot **night spot**. Then travel a few miles south west and make yourself sick on samples at **Cadbury World** – pretend to be interested in the tour as well if you like! (Book first). Back for a famous **Balti**, and for a good one, head for **Sparkhill** or **Balsall Heath** – incredibly good value. Most other tastes are also catered for, Oriental, in Chinatown (no!), and try the Broad Street area for choice. This is also one of the best areas for **pubs** and **clubs** (some of the best are in Birmingham – pick up 'What's On'), not to mention the **Symphony Hall**! There are many **art galleries** (Pre-Raphaelite to contemporary), **museums, theatres** and **cinemas**, and look out for huge concerts at the **NEC**.

TOURIST INFORMATION ☎ 0121 643 2514
2 CITY ARCADE, BIRMINGHAM,
WEST MIDLANDS, B2 4TX

HOSPITAL A & E ☎ 0121 554 3801
CITY HOSPITAL, DUDLEY ROAD,
BIRMINGHAM, B18 7QH

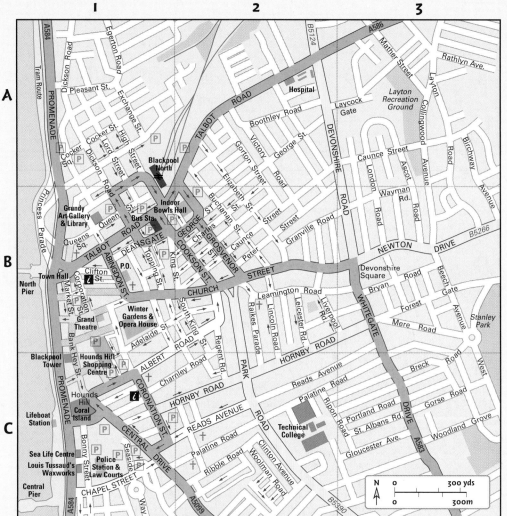

Area Code 01253

BLACKPOOL

WEB-SITE www.blackpool.gov.uk

LOCAL RADIO BBC RADIO LANCASHIRE 104.5 FM
MAGIC 999 AM, RADIO WAVE 96.5 FM, ROCK FM 97.4 FM

INDEX TO STREET NAMES

Get candyfloss all round your face, go on a **boating lake** and do **crazy golf** on one of the five greens! There is a superb **beach**, seven miles of soft golden sand (bucket and spade are compulsory, whatever your age!), and there are apparently "forty acres of fun and thrill rides" (which includes **'The Big One'** –the World's fastest roller coaster ride!). If it's wet (never!), Blackpool can cope, there's the **Sea Life Centre**, with the largest shark display in Europe, **ten-pin bowling**, **Blackpool Tower** (including a circus and ballroom dancing – get your frocks on girls!), **tram rides**, **cinemas**, **waxworks** and shows on the **pier(s)**. **Eating?** Fish, chips 'n sand to upmarket seafood. After dark, there are **pubs** and **nightclubs**, around 15 of the latter along the promenade and on the North pier; it's also one of the most popular gay resorts in the country. From September to November there are the **Blackpool Illuminations,** six miles of light bulbs in the shape of film stars, tea pots etc. even the Tower and trams are lit up! **Shopping** ranges from the major retail stores and shopping centres to the wonderful, traditional seaside shops, where you can buy that perfect present – a bronze plastic Viking with removable axe, or something tasteful covered in tiny seashells!

TOURIST INFORMATION ☎ 01253 478222
1 CLIFTON STREET,
BLACKPOOL, FY1 1LY

HOSPITAL A & E ☎ 01253 300000
VICTORIA HOSPITAL, WHINNEY HEYS ROAD,
BLACKPOOL, FY3 8NR

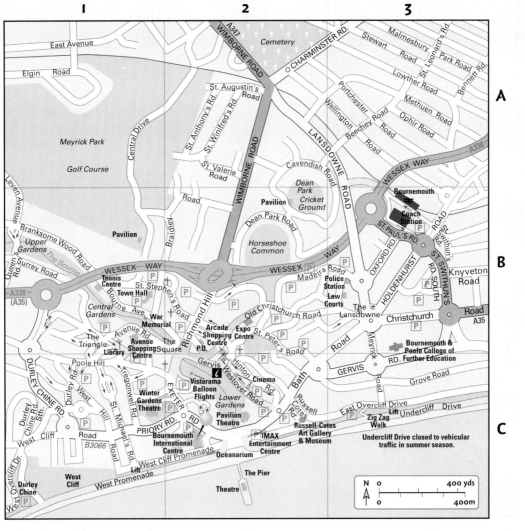

Area Code 01202

BOURNEMOUTH

WEB-SITE www.bournemouth.gov.uk

LOCAL RADIO — BBC RADIO SOLENT FOR DORSET 103.8 FM, CLASSIC GOLD 828 AM, 2CR FM 102.3 FM, FIRE 107.6 FM

INDEX TO STREET NAMES

'The next coolest city on the planet,' to quote Harpers and Queen! Bournemouth has a thriving **club** scene, claiming to be the best place on the south coast to **party**. It's popular for those 'fun' hen and stag do's! and it's also on the 'must visit' list of young Europeans. The seven miles of sand, is cleaned and sifted every morning! Then patrolled by 'Baywatch' style lifeguards...now that's got to be worth a look! You can hang out with the crowds near the pier or **sunbathe**. For the more energetic, there's **jet skiing, water skiing, paragliding or windsurfing** – just like the Med really! **Shopping** is pretty good, with big department stores, High Street names, trendy boutiques, shopping centres and Victorian arcades, as well as the essential seaside rock shops. If you fancy a good view of the area and don't pass out standing on a beer mat, then try an ascent in the **Vistarama tethered balloon** – you can't miss it! For wet days there's the **Oceanarium** or the fascinating **Russell-Cotes Art Gallery**. There are plenty of **theatres, concert halls** and the **Bournemouth International Centre** for everything from stand-up comedy to classical performances, and **eating** is a pleasure, English to Lebanese. Finally, visit St. Peter's graveyard and see the grave of **Mary Shelley** (of Frankenstein fame), she's buried here with the heart of her husband – wonder what she had in mind – da da daaaaaa!

TOURIST INFORMATION ☎ **0906 802 0234**
WESTOVER ROAD,
BOURNEMOUTH, BH1 2BU

HOSPITAL A & E ☎ **01202 303626**
ROYAL BOURNEMOUTH HOSPITAL,
CASTLE LANE EAST, BOURNEMOUTH, BH7 7DW

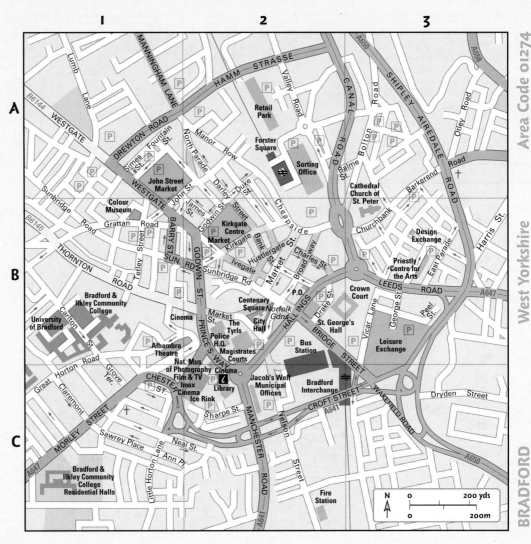

Area Code 01274

West Yorkshire

BRADFORD

WEB-SITE www.bradford.gov.uk

LOCAL RADIO BBC RADIO LEEDS 102.7 FM, WEST YORKS CLASSIC GOLD 1278 AM, THE PULSE 97.5 FM, SUNRISE RADIO 103.2 FM,

INDEX TO STREET NAMES

Let's start with **food!** You can't come to the **'curry capital'** of Britain, without trying one of the 200 or so superb **Asian restaurants!** (Log on to www.bradfordcurryguide.co.uk) - but remember, some **do not** allow alcohol. If you can't take the heat, there's plenty of **pub grub** (lightweight!), as well as international cuisine from Tapas to Italian. There are lots of **bars** and **clubs** where you can dance the night away, try the West End quarter; it's a veritable 'hot spot'! **Shopping** in Bradford is great! You must visit the **Bombay Stores** on Shearbridge Road; it's a huge Aladdin's cave, with stunning silks and satins rubbing shoulders with Asian cooking appliances! For 'upmarket' shopping, go to Darley Street and North Parade, the restored Venetian-Gothic Wool Exchange is now a retail centre, and all the High Street names are around the pedestrianised Broadway and Kirkgate areas. Top of the list for places to go must be the **National Museum of Photography, Film & Television**, superb! It also houses three cinemas, including a 3D IMAX – one day isn't enough! The new **Leisure Exchange** has a 16-screen cinema and Hollywood Bowl. **David Hockney's** work can be seen in the **1853 Gallery** at **Salts Mill** a few miles north, and there are many other **art galleries, museums** and **theatres** to amuse you. If you're here in summer, catch Europe's biggest Asian Festival – the spectacular **Mela!**

TOURIST INFORMATION ☎ 01274 753678
CENTRAL LIBRARY, PRINCES WAY,
BRADFORD, W.YORKS, BD1 1NN

HOSPITAL A & E ☎ 01274 542200
BRADFORD ROYAL INFIRMARY, DUCKWORTH LANE,
BRADFORD, BD9 6RJ

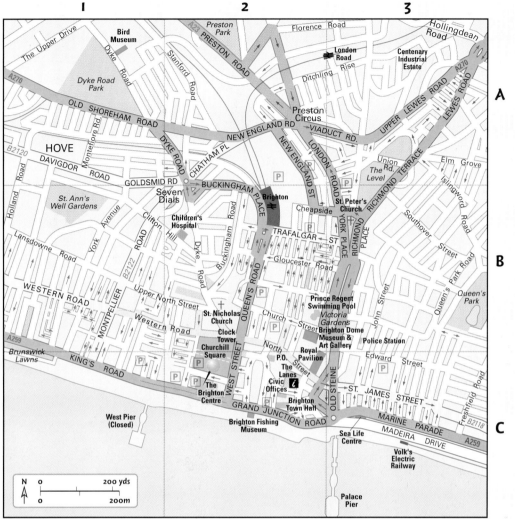

Area Code 01273

Brighton & Hove

BRIGHTON

www.brighton-hove.gov.uk

WEB-SITE

BBC SOUTHERN COUNTIES RADIO 95.3 FM
CAPITAL GOLD 1323 AM, SOUTHERN FM 103.5

LOCAL RADIO

INDEX TO STREET NAMES

Fun, Brighton rock, everything! Pick up 'Insight', 'Source', 'What's On' and 'Gscene', then head for the **North Laine** area, grab a coffee in one of the many **bistros** or **cafés** and read. The following is a very brief resume. There are more than 180 **restaurants** here, **The Lanes** for most tastes, and lots for you real foodies - there are even **all-night cafés**! **Pubs and wine bars** (trad to chic) are too numerous to mention, you'll find **pre-club bars** in The Lanes, and there are over 40 **nightclubs** (it's Fatboy Slim's hometown - try West Street and Kings Road Arches). There is a huge **Arts scene** with digital arts exhibitions to contemporary and classical paintings. **Live music** includes the **Brighton Philharmonic Orchestra** to major rock and pop gigs in the **Brighton Centre**. The **Brighton Festival** in May is the largest arts festival outside Edinburgh, coinciding with the **Fringe Festival** and the **Essential Music Festival**. Then **Gay Pride** in August really 'camps it up'! (A bright spot on the pink map!). You could spend weeks and a year's dosh in the **shops**, the **North Laine** area is the nearest you'll get to the Kasbah! New Age, second-hand and other funky stuff – you can even barter! Also try the **markets**. **Churchill Square** houses High Street names and lots more. **The Lanes** has more individual shops, then **Brighton Marina** has Factory outlets. Palace Pier is compulsory seaside tackville, while you'll need a hard hat to tour **West Pier**! Go round the onion-domed **Royal Pavilion**. With lots of **theatres**, **cinemas** and **museums** and even **nude bathing** on part of the pebbly beach – ouch! What more could you want!

TOURIST INFORMATION ☎ 0906 711 2255
10 BARTHOLOMEW SQUARE,
BRIGHTON, BN1 1JS

HOSPITAL A & E ☎ 01273 696955
ROYAL SUSSEX COUNTY HOSPITAL, EASTERN ROAD,
BRIGHTON, BN2 5BE

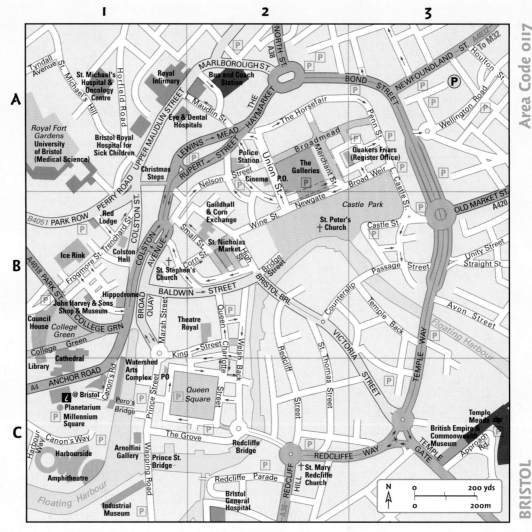

WEB-SITE www.bristol-city.gov.uk

LOCAL RADIO BBC RADIO BRISTOL 94.9 FM BRUNEL CLASSIC GOLD 1260 AM, GWR FM 96.3 FM, GALAXY 101 97.2 FM, STAR 107.3 FM

INDEX TO STREET NAMES

The World's first **bungee jump** was off the Clifton Suspension Bridge, and you can still do it! **Shopping** requires even more stamina! There's Broadmead and The Galleries - over 400 stores – girlie heaven! Hike up to Clifton Village for some window-shopping, expensive little boutiques. Christmas Steps is a must, old streets, and quaint shops. Another hike up Park Street for loads of individual goodies. More? You can always drive out to Cribbs Causeway for chain store bliss! Recently, **clubland** has blossomed, you can glam up or down, there's even a club on a boat! – check out 'The Venue'. Loads of **live music** ranges from jazz to everything else, and several **comedy clubs** stage 'alternative' artists. 'Fer a bit 'o culture' there are **theatres** and **concert halls** staging ballet, West End shows (try the Theatre Royal, the oldest working theatre in Britain) and 'experimental' stuff at The Tobacco Factory. Two art-house **cinemas**, plus your multiplexes and a state of the art IMAX leave you spoilt for choice and that's before you've investigated the huge variety of **restaurants** (try the harbour) and **pubs** (mostly traditional). Watch out for the local tipple – cider, tends to remove bones from legs – be warned! Then there's... museums and the **SS Great Britain** in the Docks, IT heaven at the **@ Bristol** complex, oh and Europe's largest hot air '**Balloon Fiesta**' in August. Have fun!

TOURIST INFORMATION ☎ 0117 926 0767
THE ANNEXE, WILDSCREEN WALK, HARBOURSIDE,
BRISTOL, BS1 5UD

HOSPITAL A & E ☎ 0117 923 0000
BRISTOL ROYAL INFIRMARY,
MARLBOROUGH STREET, BRISTOL, BS2 8HW

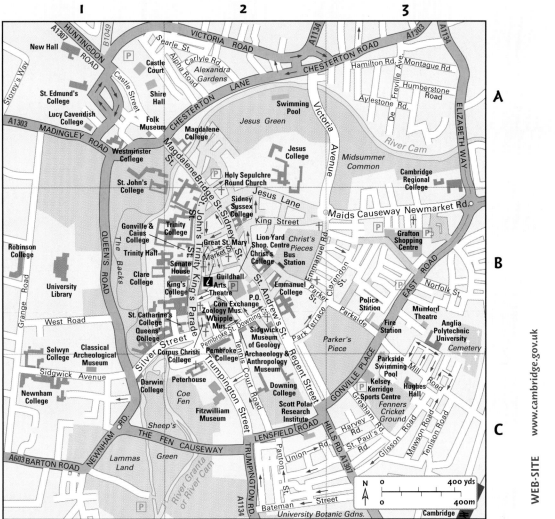

Area Code 01223

Cambridgeshire

CAMBRIDGE

WEB-SITE www.cambridge.gov.uk

LOCAL RADIO — BBC RADIO CAMBRIDGESHIRE 96 FM, Q 103 FM, STAR 107.9 FM

INDEX TO STREET NAMES

Wander round the **grounds** of some of the 31 colleges, pretending to be clever! Then **hire a punt** on the River Cam and put your drowning skills to the test – alternatively, hire a **'chauffer punt'** and enjoy the scenery! The river flows along **'The Backs'** (the lawns and backs of some of the old colleges). **Culture** and **History** ooze out of every stone, visit the **Fitzwilliam Museum**, it has everything from Egyptian mummies to paintings by Picasso. **King's College Choir** sing at evensong most evenings in the amazing **King's College Chapel** – really calming after a hectic day. **Touring the colleges** is like walking through a series of 'University Challenge'! With names like ' Magdalene', 'Jesus' and 'Corpus Christi' – you can go round most of them most of the time. 'Nuff culture? Okay, let's hit the **shops!** Try the Kings Parade/Trinity Street and Bridge Street/Regent Street areas to start. For 'chic', the less financially challenged amongst you could visit Rose Crescent, and if you want funky, go to Sidney Street. Then there's still the huge Grafton Centre, and much more... If you're a **bookworm**, you'll be in heaven – Heffers bookshop alone has six branches here! **Peckish?** Choose from Veggie to fresh seafood, and of course there are cosy teashops! The many traditional **pubs** serve ale and pub fayre. For **entertainment**, there's **mainstream theatre** and **student productions,** and **live music** is abundant. **Nightclubs** are 'hip 'n happenin' with a couple of large discos and several smaller venues. Look out for listings in 'Varsity' and 'What's On'.

TOURIST INFORMATION ☎ **01223 322640**
WHEELER STREET, CAMBRIDGE,
CAMBRIDGESHIRE, CB2 3QB

HOSPITAL A & E ☎ **01223 245151**
ADDENBROOKE'S HOSPITAL, HILLS ROAD,
CAMBRIDGE, CB2 2QQ

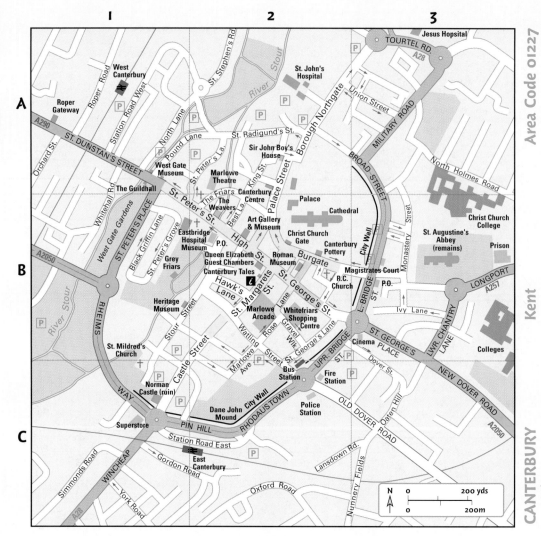

WEB-SITE www.canterbury.gov.uk

LOCAL RADIO BBC RADIO KENT 97.6 FM
INVICTA FM 103.1 FM, 106 CTFM 106 FM

Area Code 01227

Kent

CANTERBURY

INDEX TO STREET NAMES

Remember Chaucer's 'Canterbury Tales' at school? Don't be put off coming here! If you actually enjoyed it, visit the **Canterbury Tales Visitor Centre**, where you can smell the Middle Ages too, and even buy the T-shirt! Stacks of history to see here, from early Christian onwards. Quite a bit of the **city wall** remains and one of the massive fortified gatehouses, the **'West Gate'**. Even if you're not in to all that, a visit to **Canterbury Cathedral** is still a must, it's just stunning (and it is a World Heritage Site and the Mother Church of the Anglican Communion). There's also a **Rupert Bear exhibition** at the **Museum of Canterbury!** The medieval city centre, (quaint, squiffy Tudor buildings) has lots of small, interesting **shops**, as well as some of the bigger High Street names. **Eating and drinking** is a delight, with a selection of pubs and all kinds of food from Anatolian to French and everything in between. **Nightlife** is generally low-key, with a cinema and three **nightclubs** (two in the same building opposite Canterbury East Station). The **Marlowe Theatre** hosts drama, jazz, ballet etc., the **Gulbenkian Theatre** is part of the University and open during 'school terms'! If you're feeling brave, do the **'Ghostly Tour of Old Canterbury'** and if you're rich, you can **hot-air balloon** above the city!

TOURIST INFORMATION ☎ 01227 766567
34 ST. MARGARET'S STREET,
CANTERBURY, KENT, CT1 2TG

HOSPITAL A & E ☎ 01227 766877
KENT & CANTERBURY HOSPITAL, ETHELBERT ROAD,
CANTERBURY, CT1 3NG

Area Code 029

CARDIFF

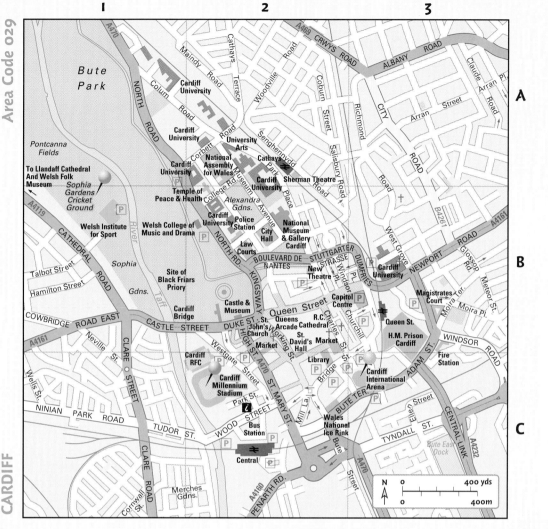

WEB-SITE   www.cardiff.gov.uk

LOCAL RADIO   BBC RADIO WALES 96.8 FM
CAPITAL GOLD 1305 & 1359 AM, RED DRAGON FM 103.2 FM

INDEX TO STREET NAMES

Cardiff is a friendly city, especially on rugby international days, even when Wales are playing England! A visit to the magnificent new **Millennium Stadium** (if you've got match tickets) is unforgettable, if you haven't got a ticket, tough! There's still a **guided tour** though, where you can walk down the players tunnel and imagine the glory! Wales is also famous for music, and **live gigs** are often staged here. You can hear everything from the **Welsh National Opera** to **jazz** at various venues – look in the local papers for dates (especially the South Wales Echo). Several **theatres** offer contemporary and classical drama, and **comedy** is positively rife in Cardiff Bay, where you'll also find a huge **cinema**, several **nightclubs** and cosmo **restaurants**. The club scene is excellent, with top name DJ's; check out 'Buzz' entertainment guide. The choice of **food** is wide, from traditional Welsh to Italian and many curry parlours! We haven't **shopped** yet have we? Well try the many **Victorian Arcades** for funky stuff of all sorts. You can gain Brownie points with your partner by visiting the **Welsh 'lurve' spoon shop** and for modern malls and BIG shops Queen Street is your best bet. **Places to see?** **Cardiff Castle** is central and impressive and do have a look at the **'Animal Wall'** on Castle Street, it's amazing! Another 'must see' is the **National Museum of Wales,** It has the most incredible interactive walk through 'Evolution of Wales' exhibition, and several art galleries, including a large collection of Monet – real ones! Oggy Oggy Oggy!!

TOURIST INFORMATION ☎ 029 2022 7281
CARDIFF VISITOR CENTRE, 16 WOOD STREET, CARDIFF, CF10 1ES

HOSPITAL A & E ☎ 029 2074 7747
CARDIFF UNIVERSITY OF WALES HOSPITAL, HEATH PARK, CARDIFF, CF14 4XW

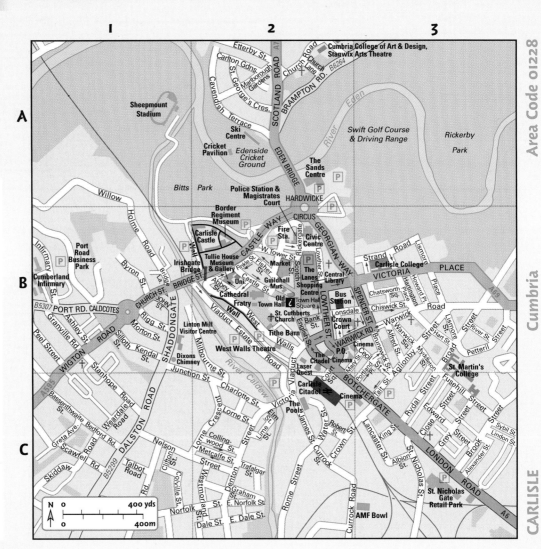

WEB-SITE www.carlisle-city.gov.uk

LOCAL RADIO BBC RADIO CUMBRIA 95.6, 96.1, 104.2 FM CFM RADIO 96.4 FM

Area Code 01228 Cumbria CARLISLE

INDEX TO STREET NAMES

"Oh no, stuff this for a game of soldiers, how long does Hadrian want this wall? 80 miles, I'm off back to Rome!" Luckily, they left an interactive exhibition in the **Tullie House Museum**, which explains all about the wall and what the Romans did for Carlisle! The museum also houses a Wildlife and Geology exhibition and a Fine and Decorative Arts gallery. After the Romans left, Carlisle was left to be scrapped over by the Danes and the Scots, then the Scots lost it to the Normans. Mel Gibson (sorry, **William Wallace!**) was 'repelled' here in 1297, and after a lot of skirmishing, it finally fell to the Duke of Cumberland in the mid 1700s. Talking about Cumberland, the **Cumberland sausage** is alive and well in Carlisle, unless you're veggie, try one! There are also pavement **cafés**, with international cuisine to be found along Warwick Road. For **liquid refreshment,** there are café bars and some traditional pubs, with several **nightclubs** in which to 'strut your stuff' come sundown. **Shopping** varies from High Street shops in **Lanes Shopping Centre**, to regional crafts and a really good Victorian market. **For live music, theatre and ballet,** see what's on at the **Sands Centre**, and for a bit of **culture**, have a look round the **cathedral** and the **castle**. If it's raining and you can cope with the bobble hats, take a trip on a steam train on the **Settle-Carlisle** railway, and if it's August and sunny, go to the **Carlisle Great Fair** – Edinburgh, but smaller!

TOURIST INFORMATION ☎ 01228 625600 OLD TOWN HALL, GREEN MARKET, CARLISLE, CA3 8JH

HOSPITAL A & E ☎ 01228 523444 CUMBERLAND INFIRMARY, NEWTOWN ROAD, CARLISLE, CA2 7HY

Area Code 01242

Gloucestershire

CHELTENHAM

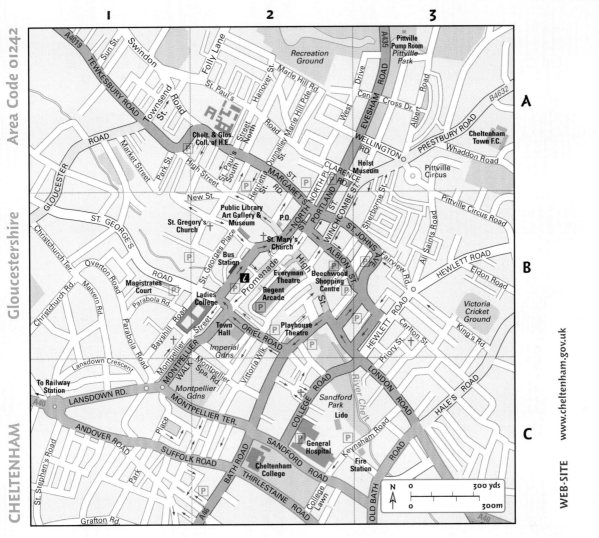

WEB-SITE www.cheltenham.gov.uk

LOCAL RADIO
BBC RADIO GLOUCESTERSHIRE 104.7 FM
CLASSIC GOLD 774 AM, SEVERN SOUND FM 102.4 FM,
STAR 107.5 FM

INDEX TO STREET NAMES

Regency and elegant spring to mind. Talking of springs, 'Take the waters' at **Pittville Pump Rooms** (for free – you'll see why!), the alkaline brew was thought to banish all manner of 'orrible afflictions,' so once you've been cured of your warts, you can go **shopping**, it's such fun! The wide **Promenade** has classy boutiques and individual shops, a short walk south brings you to **Montpellier**, very elegant frock shops, gift shops, wine bars and pavement cafés – who needs Paris! For big High Street names, try the **High Street**! where there are also two smart shopping arcades (Regent and Beechwood). The former has the most amazing **Wishing Fish Clock** – totally bizarre, catch a bubble and make a wish! **Gold Cup** race week (March) gets very festive, especially if an Irish horse wins! To go to the actual races on Gold Cup day, you need to book tickets before Christmas! There are several other mega **festivals,** including **literature** (October), **Jazz** (May), **Fringe** (July), and **Music** (the same two weeks as Fringe week). For **eating**, take your pick, from Vegan to French, and there's a good mix of **theme pubs, trad pubs and wine bars**. The **club scene** is pretty good, with most tastes catered for. **Culture**-wise, there are examples of work by the **Arts and Crafts movement** plus social history at the **Art Gallery & Museum.** **The Everyman Theatre** is like an inside out iced wedding cake! And stages everything from West End shows to panto, while the nearby **Playhouse Theatre** is home to various amateur productions. Holst came from Cheltenham, go to the **Holst Birthplace Museum** and see his piano!

TOURIST INFORMATION ☎ 01242 522878
77 THE PROMENADE, CHELTENHAM,
GLOUCESTERSHIRE, GL50 1PP

HOSPITAL A & E ☎ 01242 222222
CHELTENHAM GENERAL HOSPITAL,
SANDFORD ROAD, CHELTENHAM, GL53 7AN

Area Code 01244

Cheshire

CHESTER

Map labels (clockwise/by grid):

Countess of Chester Hospital (Accident Unit) · Garden Lane · UPPER NORTHGATE · A5116 · A540 · HOOLE ROAD · A56 · Station Road · Chester · Northgate Arena · Fire Sta. · St. Anne Street · Brook Street · Francis St. · City Road · ST. OSWALDS WAY · Bus Station · George Street · Milton Street · HOOLE WAY · Canal Street · Raymond St. · King Charles Tower · King Street · Northgate St. · Cathedral · City Wall · Shropshire · Union · Canal · ST. OSWALDS WAY · THE BARS · BOUGHTON · A51 · Hunter St. · Bus Station · Market · Town Hall · St. Werburgh St. · Frodsham St. · Queen St. · Shopping Precinct · Foregate St. · Dee Lane · CITY WALLS ROAD · Bedward Row · Princess St. · Theatre · Forum Shopping Precinct · Eastgate Street · P.O. · Love St. · UNION ST. · Dee Lane · Guildhall · Broadcasting Museum · St. John St. · Chester Visitors Centre · Grosvenor Park · The Meadows · A548 · Watergate · Bishop Lloyd's House · Commonhall · Shopping Centre · Bridge Street · N'gate St. · VICAR'S LANE · Roman Amphitheatre (remains of) · NICHOLAS ST. · Weaver St. · St. Dewa Roman Experience · White Friars · PEPPER STREET · Souter's La. · The Groves · River Dee · Victoria Crescent · Lower Park Road · Racecourse · City Wall · Black Friars · GROSVENOR ST. · Toy and Doll Museum · Lower Bridge St. · Duke St. · The Groves · Police H.Q. · Nun's Road · Tudor House · Grosvenor Museum · County Hall · Weir · City Wall · GROSVENOR ROAD · The Roodee · Castle and Military Museum · Castle Drive · Old Dee Bridge · Dee Bridge Handbridge · Queens Park Road · A483 · Little Roodee

N 0 200 yds / 0 200m

WEB-SITE www.chestercc.gov.uk

LOCAL RADIO BBC RADIO MERSEYSIDE 95.8 FM / MAGIC 1548 AM, RADIO CITY 96.7 FM

INDEX TO STREET NAMES

Ah **shopping!** A truly unique experience here. The 15th century restored **Chester Cross** (almost flattened in the English Civil War by vandals - young hooligans!), marks the junction of the four main shopping streets. All the post-medieval black and white buildings sport galleried arcades running above the ground floor shops, called **The Rows** – two tier shopping – brilliant! There are the usual High Street names, plus lots of 'traditional' and specialist crafty/gifty/sweety shops. You trip over **eating** emporiums in Chester, with everything from Japanese to Fish 'n Chips and quaint tea shops. It's cheaper to eat lunch than dinner though, and book at weekends for that romantic dinner for two. **Pubs** are abundant and often in medieval buildings (if you're interested!). After dark there are **cinemas, a theatre,** a fair smattering of **clubs** and, believe it or not, one of the largest dance studios in the UK – check out 'What's On This Week'. Thanks to the Romans (again), the city layout is well organised and compact enough to walk round all the sights in a day. It is surrounded by the most complete Roman and Medieval **city wall** in Britain, and you can walk on top of this two mile phenomenon. A visit to the **Grosvenor Museum** is great if you like all things Roman. Other things? Go on a spooky **Ghost Hunter guided walk** in the evening, or relax on a **pleasure boat** on the River Dee. See the **oldest racecourse** in the country and take a piccy of the **Eastgate Clock** – everyone else does!

TOURIST INFORMATION ☎ 01244 402111
TOWN HALL, NORTHGATE STREET,
CHESTER, CHESHIRE, CH1 2HJ

HOSPITAL A & E ☎ 01244 365000
COUNTESS OF CHESTER HOSPITAL, HEALTH PK,
LIVERPOOL ROAD, CHESTER, CH2 1UL

Area Code 01332

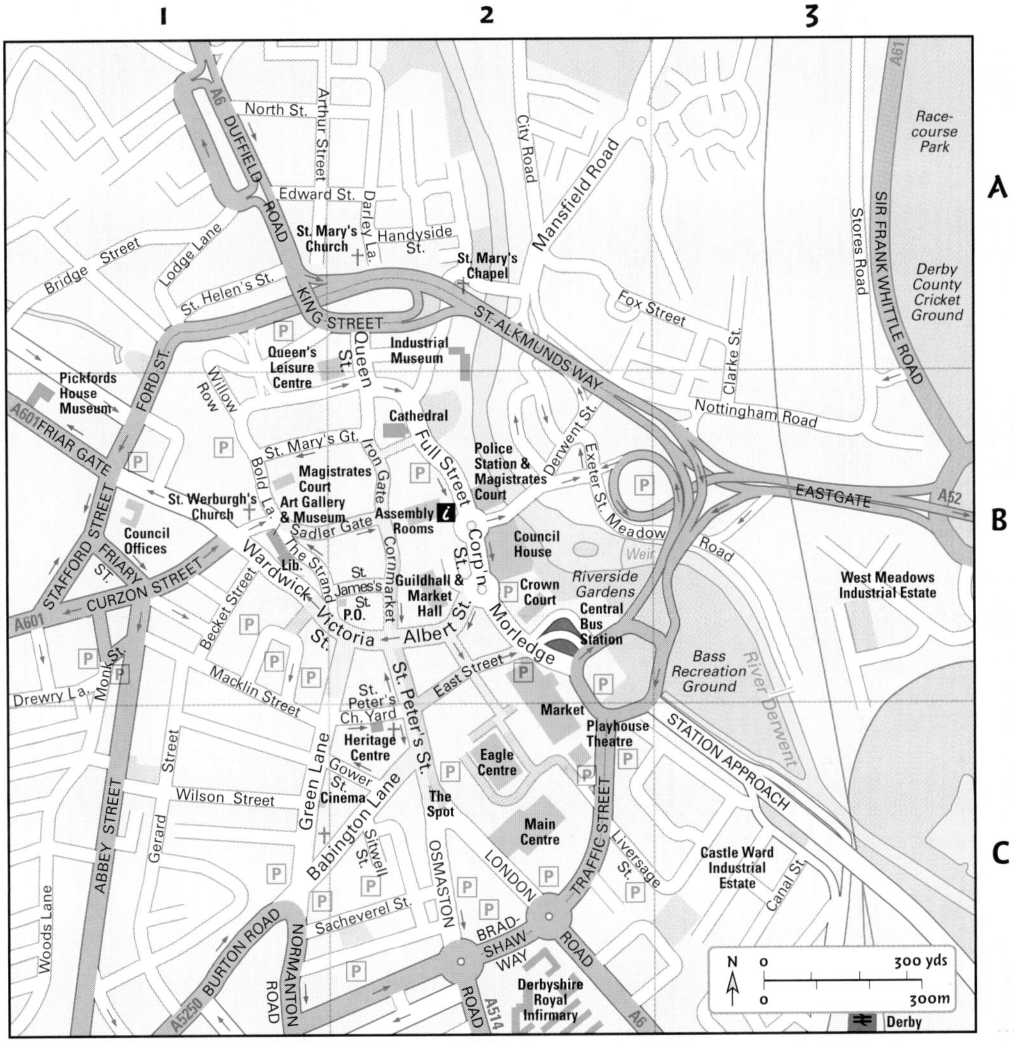

DERBY

WEB-SITE www.derby.gov.uk

LOCAL RADIO BBC RADIO DERBY 104.5 FM CLASSIC GOLD GEM 945 AM, RAM FM 102.8 FM

INDEX TO STREET NAMES

Let's start with **shopping**. Word is that **Sadler Gate** (pretty black 'n white buildings) is your best bet for funky, designer and independent, with **Iron Gate** a close second (these both have decent **bars** and **restaurants** as well by the way). For High Street stuff, the **Eagle Centre** is for you, over 90 shops and several cafés, with an indoor market too. **Victoria Street** and **The Cornmarket** will give you a similar shopping experience, and if you've got a posh friend who's put 'Crown Derby' on the wedding list, you can save a few pennies by visiting the **Royal Crown Derby Porcelain factory shop**. You can buy **ethnic goods** south west of 'The Spot' in the Asian shops – some good **restaurants** here too. Now, **nightlife**...pretty good actually, you can walk down **Ashbourne Road Mile** (visiting one of the many **pubs** on the way!) to the city centre **clubs, bars** and **restaurants** in **Friar Gate** – **London Road** is also good. **Live bands** and **gigs** are frequently found in the **Victoria Inn**, the **Flowerpot** and the **Assembly Rooms** in the **Market Place** (purpose built for entertainment! – also stages plays, opera etc). There are other venues showing plays and comedy, and there's always Derby's **Museum and Art Gallery**, which amongst other things has the bones of a prehistoric hippo! You're right on the edge of the beautiful **Peak District** here, so you outdoorsy types, take yer walking gear, wander along **Dovedale** and stoke up on trad **pub grub**!

TOURIST INFORMATION ☎ 01332 255802
**ASSEMBLY ROOMS, MARKET PLACE,
DERBY, DE1 3AH**

HOSPITAL A & E ☎ 01332 347141
**DERBYSHIRE ROYAL INFIRMARY,
LONDON ROAD, DERBY, DE1 2QY**

WEB-SITE www.dover.gov.uk

LOCAL RADIO BBC RADIO KENT 104.2 FM NEPTUNE RADIO 106.8 FM, INVICTA FM 97 FM

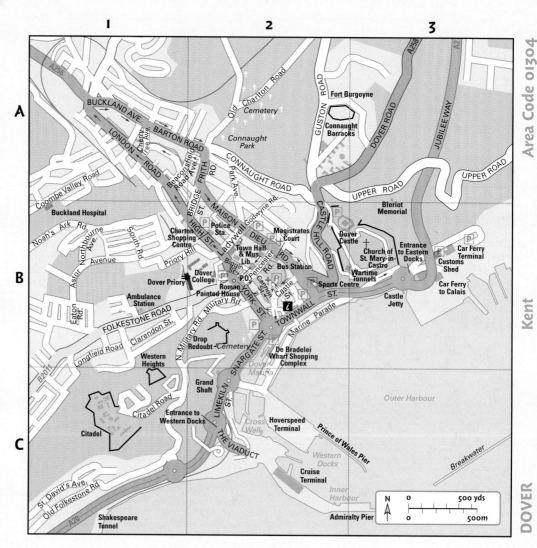

INDEX TO STREET NAMES

Small town, huge port! Make time before the booze cruise to have a look around. On top of the famous **White Cliffs** (of Vera Lynn fame – ask your granny for a song!) stands the massive fortification of **Dover Castle**. Built by the Normans, the outer wall is almost 1.5km (1 mile) in circumference (there's a ruined **Roman lighthouse** inside them), and the central tower has walls up to 7m (about 21 feet) thick! It's well worth the climb and on a clear day you can see 'la France'. Under the castle are tunnels that were the secret command centre for the evacuation of troops from Dunkirk in World War two, there's a fascinating guided tour of them. Also in Dover is the **Roman Painted House**, a hotel for Roman VIP's crossing the channel, the wall paintings are really well preserved. If it's raining, there are several **museums** relating to World War two, and Dover Museum has a **Bronze Age boat** discovered in 1992 – as well as a rather stiff polar bear! Need some **shops**? Well, the largest factory shopping outlet in Kent at De Bradelei Wharf offers discount shopping seven days a week. If the ferry is cancelled there are many **pubs** and some **restaurants** serving decent refreshments, a **cinema** and a couple of **nightclubs**.

TOURIST INFORMATION ☎ 01304 205108 TOWNWALL STREET, DOVER, KENT, CT16 1JR

HOSPITAL A & E ☎ 01227 766877 KENT & CANTERBURY HOSPITAL, ETHELBERT ROAD, CANTERBURY, CT1 3NG

International Code 00 353

DUBLIN

Map labels

WESTERN WAY · National Wax Museum · Dublin Writers Museum · Hugh Lane Gallery · Gate Theatre · James Joyce Centre · McDermott Street · SUMMERHILL · GARDINER ST. MIDDLE · King's Inns · Cinema · Rotunda Hospital · PARNELL SQUARE · Ilac Shopping Centre · Henry St. · Sean MacDermott Street · Talbot Street · Police Station · Sheriff St. Lwr. · Connolly Station · Marlborough St. · St. Mary's Cathedral · General Post Office · Bus Station · Custom House · Brunswick Street North · KING STREET NORTH · Old Jameson Distillery · The Chimney · Ceol-Irish Music Centre · St. Mary's Lane · Mary Street · Jervis Shopping Centre · Hot Press Music Hall of Fame · Four Courts · BACHELORS WK. · Abbey Theatre · EDEN QUAY · CUSTOM HOUSE QUAY · GEORGE'S QUAY · CITY QUAY · Tara Street Station · River Liffey · ARRAN QUAY · INNS QUAY · ORMOND QUAY UPPER · ORMOND QUAY LOWER · ASTON QUAY · BURGH QUAY · Police Station · TOWNSEND STREET · SANDWITH LWR. · USHERS QUAY · MERCHANTS QUAY · WOOD QUAY · ESSEX QUAY · WELLINGTON QUAY · Temple Bar · Bank of Ireland · PEARSE STREET · Dublin's Viking Adventure · DAME STREET · COLLEGE GRN · Trinity College - Book of Kells & The Dublin Experience · Pearse Station · WESTLAND ROW · Christ Church Cathedral · Dvblinia · City Hall · Civic Museum · SUFFOLK ST. · Wicklow St. · NASSAU ST. · Heraldic Museum · CLARE ST. · FENIAN ST. · THOMAS ST. W. · HIGH ST. · Police Station · Dublin Castle · SOUTH GREAT GEORGE'S ST. · Drury St. · William Street · Grafton Arcade · Mansion House · National Library · National Gallery · Leinster House · MERRION SQ. · Francis Street · St. Patrick's Cathedral · Westbury Mall · St. Stephen's Green Shopping Centre · Gaiety Theatre · DAWSON ST. · KILDARE ST. · National Museum · Natural History Museum · Marsh's Library · Police Station · Bishop St. · York Street · ST. STEPHEN'S GREEN · Government Buildings · THE COOMBE · KEVIN ST. UPPER · New Row South · New Bride St. · CUFFE ST. · St. Stephen's Green Park · Newman House Museum · Ardee St.

N 0 400 yds / 0 400 m

WEB-SITE www.dublincity.ie

LOCAL RADIO · RTE RADIO 1 88·8-9 FM · SPIN 103.8 FM, DUBLIN 98 FM

INDEX TO STREET NAMES

A city of EVERYTHING! Shopping, where do you start! The main areas are on Nassau Street (Irish goods), Grafton Street (smaller designer shops and department stores), St. Stephen's Green Centre (anything!), Moore Street (open air market), Temple Bar (smaller shops), O'Connell Street, Henry Street (department stores), The Liberties (antiques) and The Powerscourt Townhouse (nice stuff!). This is a small glimpse, wander around, look out for Irish woolly pully's made from Donegal and Connemara sheep! **Culture.** There is so much in Dublin, check 'In Dublin' mag. or www.visitdublin.com. The range includes opera, classical music, ballet, pop/rock, drama, music hall, pantomime, comedy, Irish dance, art films and mainstream cinema. On **St. Patrick's Day** (17 March), the whole city celebrates! And amongst many other festivals, **Murphy's Unplugged Comedy Festival** takes place in November. **Sport.** If you haven't seen them before, go and see a game of **Gaelic Football** or **Hurling** – mad! **Pubs.** Even if you're tea-total, you have to go to an Irish pub for the atmosphere – they can get a bit 'lively' though, so take care! Many have spontaneous live music! **Clubs.** A fairly recent phenomenon, there is now a selection of top class venues, check out 'In Dublin' and www.wow.ie. Also look out for the vast range of **live music and comedy**. **Other good stuff** - Trinity College (9th century 'Book of Kells'), **National Museum of Ireland, National Gallery of Ireland, Phoenix Park** and the **Guinness Storehouse. Eating.** Traditional Irish and everything else!

TOURIST INFORMATION ☎ 08000 397000
ST ANDREWS CHURCH, SUFFOLK STREET, DUBLIN 2

HOSPITAL A & E ☎ 00 353 1 410 3000
ST JAMES'S HOSPITAL, JAMES'S STREET, DUBLIN 8

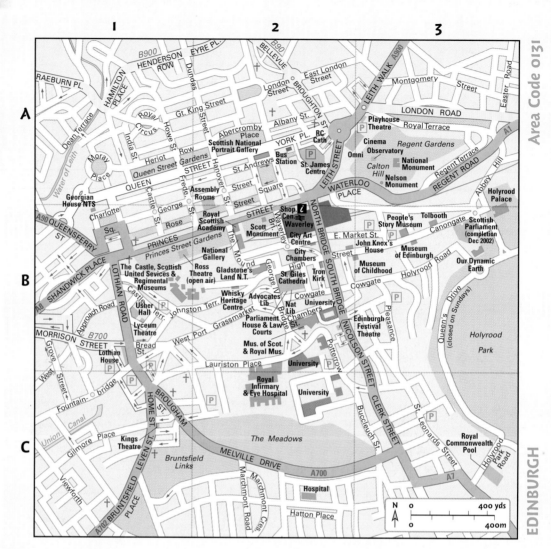

WEB-SITE www.edinburgh.gov.uk

LOCAL RADIO BBC RADIO SCOTLAND 810 AM & 92.4-94.7 FM FORTH 2 1548 AM, FORTH ONE 97.3 FM, REAL RADIO 101.1 FM

INDEX TO STREET NAMES

Bored with New Year? Get rid of those post-Christmas blues with days of fireworks, street parties, music and general mayhem at **Edinburgh's Hogmanay** extravaganza! Or come in August to the famous **Fringe, International, Book, Jazz and Film Festivals**. For drowning in pageantry, there's always the **Military Tattoo!** At the end of May, the **Beltane** (Celtic festival) takes place all night on **Calton Hill** – a bit wild and hippie!! Haggis 'n tatties or Mexican? Whatever your **taste**, Edinburgh probably has it. For fresh seafood, go out of town to **Leith Docklands**, and if you're feeling wealthy and carnivorous, game on! For **live music** and **comedy** nights, peruse a copy of 'The List' magazine, which also tells you which of the many **clubs** is playing what. **Traditional live music** can be found in **pubs** around **Grassmarket**, while shiny arty **bars** pose around **Broughton and Chambers Streets**. There are stacks of **museums, art galleries, cinemas and concert venues**. For the upwardly mobile, get your Gucci **togs** on **George Street** and the oldest independent store in the World, Jenners, is a 'must'. For funky clothes head for **Cockburn Street,** all the well-known shops are on **Princes Street**, and **Grassmarket** and **Victoria Streets** have 'interesting' emporiums. 'Auld Reekie' was the name for **'Old Town'** (it had a 'heady aroma' in medieval times!). You'll find all the popular tourist **attractions** here – the **Castle** (see the **'Stone of Destiny'** – allegedly!), **Palace of Holyroodhouse, Holyrood Abbey** and lots of 'stuff' off the **Royal Mile** – go on, but avoid the souvenirs!

TOURIST INFORMATION ☎ 0131 473 3800
INFORMATION CENTRE, 3 PRINCES STREET,
EDINBURGH, EH2 2QP

HOSPITAL A & E ☎ 0131 536 1000
ROYAL INFIRMARY OF EDINBURGH,
1 LAURISTON PLACE, EDINBURGH, EH3 9YW

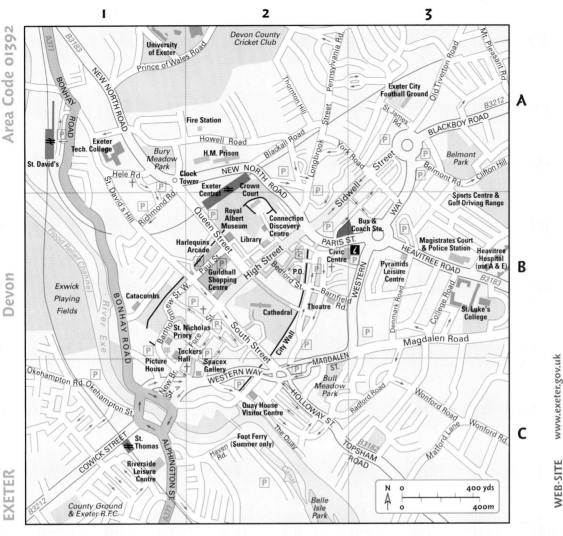

Area Code 01392 · Devon · EXETER

WEB-SITE www.exeter.gov.uk

LOCAL RADIO BBC RADIO DEVON 95.8 FM · CLASSIC GOLD 666 AM, GEMINI FM 97 & 103 FM

INDEX TO STREET NAMES

Once an outpost of the wild and woolly southwest, Exeter is now really easy to get to, the M5 takes you right to the door! This is as far west as the Romans got and yes, you can still see bits of their handiwork in large sections of the **Roman and Medieval city wall**, and in the (free) **Royal Albert Memorial Museum**. Moving smartly on to the nation's favourite pastime, you can spend a pleasant day ignoring history in over 600 **shops** in the city centre. Big High Street names? You guessed it, in the **High Street**! **Harlequins Shopping Mall** has lots of 'speciality' shops; the adjacent **Guildhall Shopping Centre** has big names and stalls. For 'alternative' small shops, boogie on down to **Fore Street and New Bridge Street**, while **Gandy Street** has yet more of yer individual stuff. Plenty of places to **refuel the tum**, from pub grub in quaint old hostelries, to Mexican and posh European cuisine. The nine or so **nightclubs**, nearly half of them in **The Quayside** (which also has arty **shops**, **cafés** and **pubs**), host varying sounds, check out local papers. There are **theatres and cinemas**, with **live concerts** at Westpoint. You can't miss **St. Peters Cathedral**, so you might as well go and get neck ache gazing at the longest unbroken Gothic vaulted ceiling in the whole world – or the Universe, probably! Next to Boots in the High Street, is the entrance to **medieval underground water inspection passages**! You can go on a spooky guided tour – not for the claustrophobic! Originally designed to save digging up the road every few months... um, excuse me, local underground service companies...!

TOURIST INFORMATION ☎ 01392 265700
CIVIC CENTRE, PARIS STREET, EXETER,
DEVON, EX1 1RP

HOSPITAL A & E ☎ 01392 411611
ROYAL DEVON & EXETER HOSPITAL (WONFORD),
BARRACK ROAD, EXETER, EX2 5DW

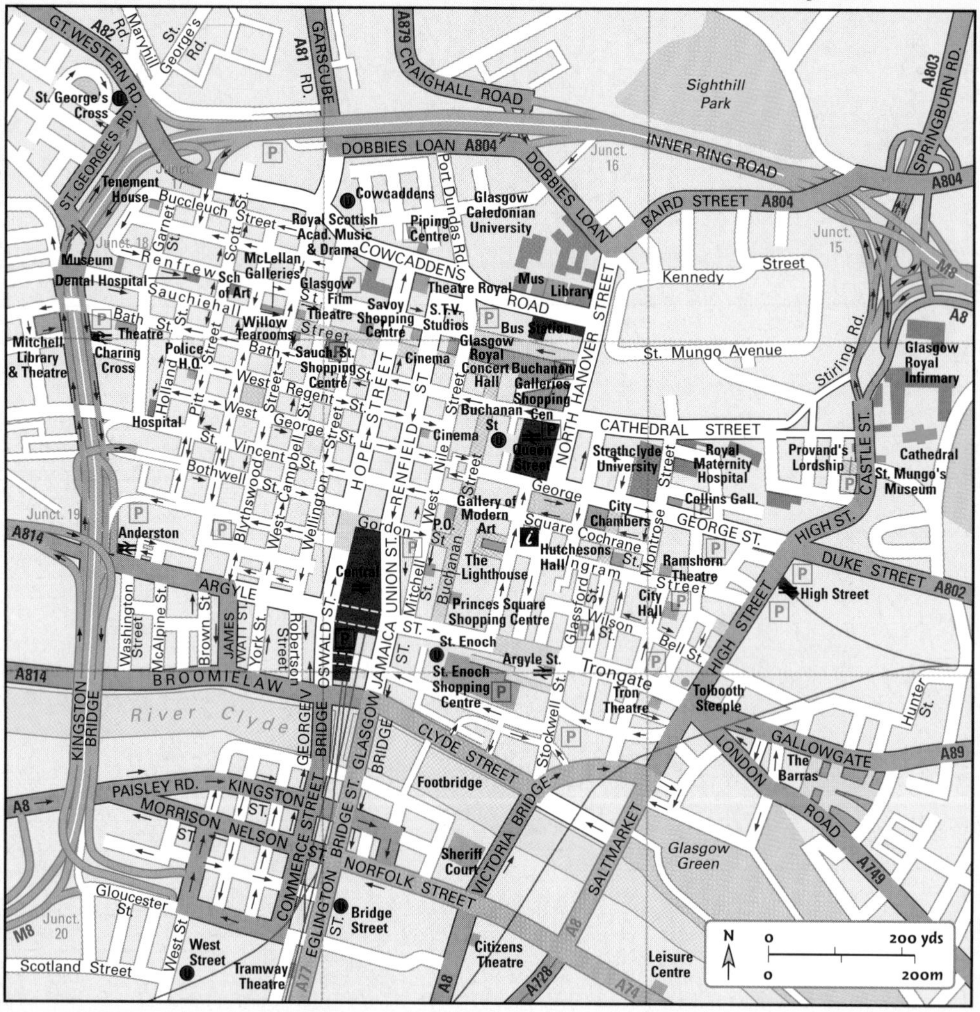

Area Code 0141

WEB-SITE www.glasgow.gov.uk

LOCAL RADIO BBC RADIO SCOTLAND 810 AM & 92.4-94.7 FM
CLYDE 1 102.5 FM, CLYDE 2 1152 AM, REAL RADIO 100.3 FM

INDEX TO STREET NAMES

Argyle Street	B1
Baird Street	A3
Bath Street	A1/B1
Bell Street	B3
Blythswood Street	B1
Bothwell Street	B1
Bridge Street	C2
Broomielaw	C1
Brown Street	B1
Buccleuch Street	A1
Buchanan Street	B2
Castle Street	B3
Cathedral Street	B2
Clyde Street	C2
Cochrane Street	B2
Commerce Street	C1
Cowcaddens Road	A2
Craighall Road	A2
Dobbie's Loan	A2
Duke Street	B3
Eglington Street	C1
Gallowgate	C3
Garnet Street	A1
Garscube Road	A1
George Square	B2
George Street	B3
George V Bridge	C1
Glasgow Bridge	C2
Glassford Street	B2
Gloucester Street	C1
Gordon Street	B2
Great Western Road	A1
High Street	B3
Holland Street	B1
Hope Street	B2
Hunter Street	C3
Ingram Street	B2
Inner Ring Road	A3
Jamaica Street	C2
James Watt Street	B1
Kennedy Street	A3
Kingston Bridge	C1
Kingston Street	C1
London Road	C3
Maryhill Road	A1
McAlpine Street	B1
Mitchell Street	B2
Montrose Street	B3
Morrison Street	C1
Nelson Street	C1
Norfolk Street	C2
North Hanover Street	B2
Oswald Street	C1
Paisley Road	C1
Pitt Street	B1
Port Dundas Road	A2
Renfield Street	B2
Renfrew Street	A1
Robertson Street	B1
Saltmarket	C2
Sauchiehall Street	A1
Scotland Street	C1
Scott Street	A1
Springburn Road	A3
St. George's Road	A1
St. Mungo Avenue	B3
St. Vincent Street	B1
Stirling Road	B3
Stockwell Street	C2
Trongate	B2
Union Street	B2
Victoria Bridge	C2
Washington Street	B1
Wellington Street	B1
West Campbell Street	B1
West George Street	B1
West Nile Street	B2
West Regent Street	B1
West Street	C1
Wilson Street	B2
York Street	B1

Glasgow is brilliant! – one of the coolest cities in Europe; don't be fooled by the view from the M8! The 'Weegies' are justifiably proud of their city of **culture, architecture and design.** The influence of **Charles Rennie Mackintosh** is everywhere – visit the **Glasgow School of Art** and gape! The many **art galleries** and **museums** are superb – most of them are free! **Entertainment?** Glasgow has everything from the highbrow to, well, good old Glaesga pubs! **City centre bars** are open seven days a week to around midnight and there are over 40 **clubs** catering for all tastes! (See 'The List' mag.) You'll find **live music** at around 20 venues every night, and top class **music** can be had at the **Royal Concert Hall** and loads of other places. **Hungry?** – Original, multi-cultural, quality, value food everywhere (forget deep fried choccie bars!) As for **shopping**, **Argyle Street** is the main shopping area, with Italian designer stuff to die for in, funnily enough, the **Italian Centre**. Fancy just 'High Street' shop browsing? Try the massive **Buchanan Galleries** and **Buchanan Street** for a start, with the ultra stylish **Princes Square** at the other end – High Street plus everything else! Then, after tea at **The Willow Tea Rooms** (more Rennie Mac stuff), wander down **Great Western Road** and **Byres Road** – interesting little shops (and **pubs**) that you just sort of find yourself in as if by magic (Harry!) All this plus festivals, history, parks.......Go for a week!

TOURIST INFORMATION ☎ 0141 204 4400
11 GEORGE SQUARE,
GLASGOW, G2 1DY

HOSPITAL A & E ☎ 0141 211 2000
WESTERN INFIRMARY, DUMBARTON ROAD,
GLASGOW, G11 6NT

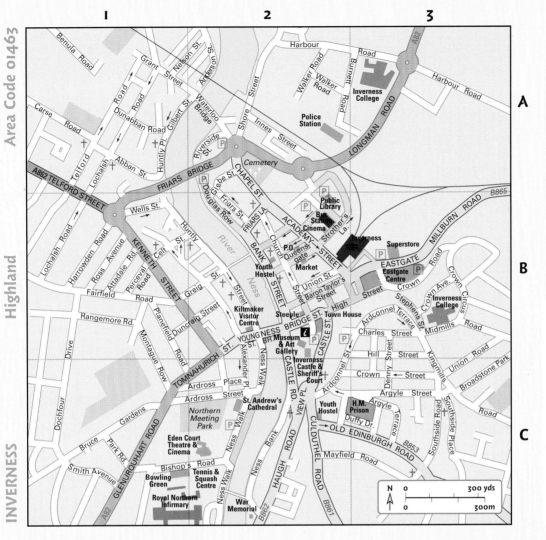

Area Code 01463

Highland

INVERNESS

INDEX TO STREET NAMES

Ah, the romantic Highlands, misty mountains, bagpipes and **NESSIE!** Loch Ness is only a few miles from Scotland's newest city, and if you've come all this way, you'll just have to take a coach and/or boat trip. In the city itself are several **shops** selling tartans, kilts and related goodies, while just outside of Inverness is the famous James Pringle Weavers Clan Tartan Centre, where you can see it being made. For larger stores visit Eastgate Shopping Centre and for 'quaint' shopping look in the indoor Victorian Market, though they are also dotted all over the place. The largest collection of rare and second-hand books in Scotland can be found in Leakey's in Greyfriars Hall. There is a **local museum and art gallery**, a **theatre**, a couple of **cinemas**, some **nightclubs** (see 'The List') and lots of **live music**, especially ceilidhs – have a fling! **Eating** out is not a problem; there are many cafes and restaurants catering for all tastes. Other 'must do's' around the city include watching **dolphins** in the Moray Firth, a trip to the haunting **Culloden Moor**, site of the 1746 Jacobite defeat, and if you're around when the **Highland games** are on, go and watch some cabers being tossed!

TOURIST INFORMATION ☎ 01463 234353
CASTLE WYND,
INVERNESS, HIGHLAND, IV2 3BJ

HOSPITAL A & E ☎ 01463 704000
RAIGMORE HOSPITAL, OLD PERTH ROAD,
INVERNESS, IV2 3UJ

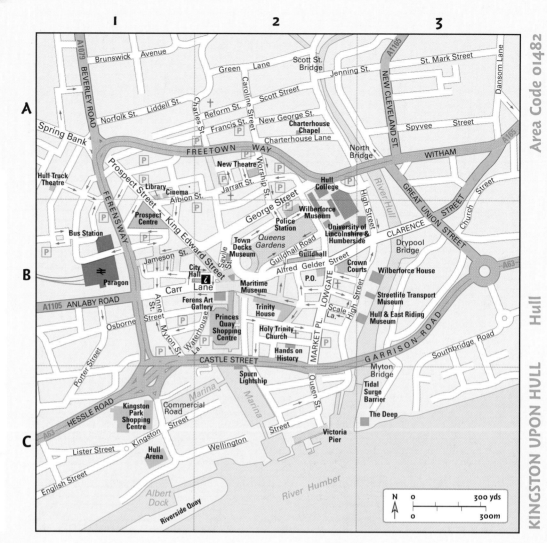

Area Code 01482

Hull

KINGSTON UPON HULL

WEB-SITE www.hullcc.gov.uk

LOCAL RADIO
BBC RADIO HUMBERSIDE 95.9 FM
MAGIC 1161 AM, VIKING FM 96.9 FM

INDEX TO STREET NAMES

By far the largest place of habitation in this part of the country, you may come to 'Ull just to catch the ferry to Rotterdam or Zeebrugge - but nay, tarry a while, merry make in one of the many pubs 'n clubs, or do 'a bit 'o shoppin'! Then there's the fascinating (if gory) story of whaling in the excellent Maritime Museum; see a blubber pot cauldron – that should make you join Greenpeace! Hull is making up for this part of its history though, 'The Deep' is Europe's deepest aquarium, it's part of the World Ocean Discovery Centre, carrying out research into all marine environments on the planet, so for all you budding marine biologists, this is a must! It's also got the only underwater lift in the world, through shark infested waters – stuff the science, this is fun! The Humber Bridge over the River Hull is pretty spectacular and so is the tidal barrage (over 30m, 100ft high!). For all round entertainment, go to the Marina area; it's surrounded by clubs and bars (lots more along Beverley Road). Close by is the shiny new Princes Quay, a four 'deck' shopping centre built on sturdy stilts over the formerly dilapidated Princes Dock. High Street and specialist shops without getting wet – hopefully! Otherwise, there's trendy stuff in Savile Street and browse the old Hepworth's Arcade – joke shop, retro clothes etc! The Hull Truck Theatre Company aims to show 'popular accessible theatre' (of 'Bouncers' fame), while annual festivals include jazz and the 'Hull Sea Fever' festival – sea shanties, rope craft, how–to–get–a–ship–in–a–bottle, Yo-ho-ho!

TOURIST INFORMATION ☎ 01482 223559
1 PARAGON STREET,
KINGSTON UPON HULL, HU1 3NA

HOSPITAL A & E ☎ 01482 328541
HULL ROYAL INFIRMARY, ANLABY ROAD,
KINGSTON UPON HULL, HU3 2JZ

Area Code 0113

West Yorkshire

LEEDS

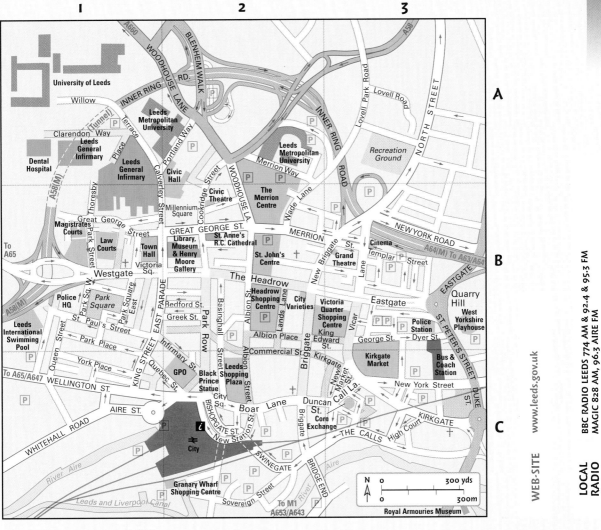

WEB-SITE   www.leeds.gov.uk

LOCAL RADIO   BBC RADIO LEEDS 774 AM & 92·4 & 95·3 FM   MAGIC 828 AM, 96·3 AIRE FM

INDEX TO STREET NAMES

Shopping – you'll think you've died and gone to heaven! First stop for Funky must be the **Corn Exchange**, clubbing gear to really weird stuff! The **Victoria Quarter** is a series of resplendent shopping arcades, with sharp designer stores (including Ms. Westwood's), as well as loads of other (slightly more affordable) frock and specialist shops. On **Briggate**, you'll find every High Street shop you can think of, as well as more exclusive names, such as Harvey Nick's. **Granary Wharf** looks a bit forbidding, but ignore the dark rushing waters of the River Aire and have a look in the 'crafty arty' shops. Then there's **The Headrow**, more shopping centres...so much shopping, so little time! As for **nightlife**, the **clubs** attract 'groovers' from all over the country, Leeds caters for every musical species, see www.northnightsout.co.uk/weekender/clubs. Needless to say, there are quite a few **pubs** as well! **Eating** out is easy, from 'bangers 'n mash' to lots of Italian, Asian and everything else up to really posh stuff. Fancy some **culture**? The **City Art Gallery** has an excellent collection of 20th century art and sculpture (including Henry Moore). There are a few good **theatres**, while the city has gone film mad! **Cinemas** are abundant – there's even an annual **Film Festival** in October. For **live popular music**, see what's on at **The Met** or **The Cockpit**, otherwise check the local paper. And finally! You must be absolutely 'tired' by now, so go to the Victorian Bramley Baths and have a Russian steam bath – oooh, luverly!

TOURIST INFORMATION ☎ 0113 242 5242
GATEWAY YORKSHIRE, THE ARCADE,
CITY STATION, LEEDS, W. YORKSHIRE, LS1 1PL

HOSPITAL A & E ☎ 0113 243 2799
LEEDS GENERAL INFIRMARY,
GREAT GEORGE STREET, LEEDS, LS1 3EX

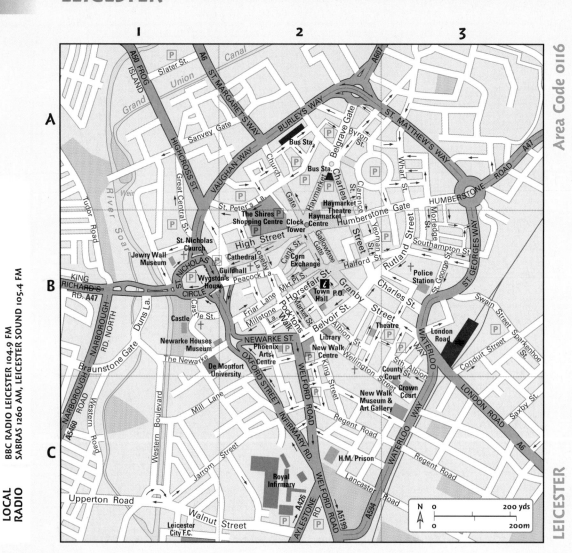

WEB-SITE www.leicester.gov.uk

LOCAL RADIO BBC RADIO LEICESTER 104.9 FM
SABRAS 1260 AM, LEICESTER SOUND 105.4 FM

INDEX TO STREET NAMES

Probably not the first place you'd think of for a top drawer **Indian meal**! but almost one third of the people here have Asian origins, the upshot of which is a colourful city, saved from the fate of 'fair to middlin'! The **Belgrave Road** has the largest sari **shop** not in India! plus ethnic art and jewellery. Some of the best **Asian restaurants** are down here too. In autumn, there is **Diwali**, the Hindu **Festival of Light**, puts Bonfire night to shame! Not to be outdone, in August, the **Afro-Caribbean's** hold the biggest **carnival** outside Notting Hill! For post Christmas depression, there's the annual **Leicester Comedy Festival** in February, and in summer, the **Abbey Park Festival** gives you a mini version of Glastonbury, without the mud and cowpats! Fancy a musical? Look no further than the **Haymarket Theatre**, or try The **Phoenix Arts Centre** for world dance and music, then The **De Montfort Hall** is the place for **live bands**. Oh, there's other food too by the way! Now for some **shopping**! **The Shires** shopping centre has around 75 shops, mainly the well-known names with some specialist shops. The smaller **Haymarket** shopping centre has more clothes, and for up-market designer wear, try **St. Martins** courtyard. The **High Street** is mainly for High Street clobber, and don't forget the **market** - the largest outdoor market in Europe no less! **Clubs and pubs** are alive and well, especially on Church Gate, Silver Street and High Street. There are also around ten **museums**, the strangest of which has to be the **Gas Museum** – go and marvel at a gas radio and gas hair-drier!

TOURIST INFORMATION ☎ 0116 299 8888
7-9 EVERY STREET, TOWN HALL SQUARE,
LEICESTER, LE1 6AG

HOSPITAL A & E ☎ 0116 254 1414
LEICESTER ROYAL INFIRMARY,
INFIRMARY SQUARE, LEICESTER, LE1 5WW

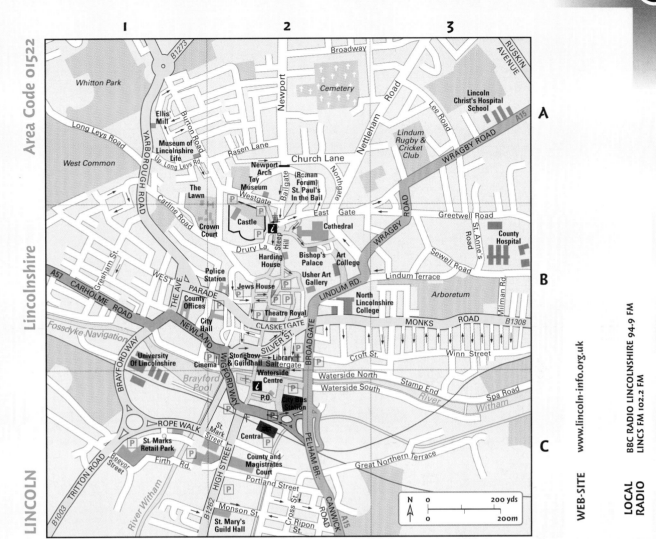

Area Code 01522

Lincolnshire

LINCOLN

WEB-SITE www.lincoln-info.org.uk

LOCAL RADIO BBC RADIO LINCOLNSHIRE 94·9 FM LINCS FM 102.2 FM

INDEX TO STREET NAMES

Christmas shopping - it's that sort of place! The 'Up hill' area around **Medieval Bailgate** and the **cathedral** (lovely carol service!) which fell down in 1185 due to a 6+ earthquake, (gosh!) has boutiques, gift and specialist shops. Walking down **Steep Hill** (and it is!), you'll probably get waylaid by the largest second hand bookshop in the UK, several cosy **tea shops** and **bistros**, designer jewellery, arty crafty shops etc. etc! Save some money for when you get to the 'Down hill' bit, the **High Street** features all the 'big ones', along with the **Waterside** shopping centre. Then there's the newest shopping centre, **St. Marks**, and **Silver Street** (famous names and unique stuff). As if that's not enough, come early December, there's an excellent **Christmas Market**, hundreds of stalls – bliss peeps! For **entertainment** there's the **Theatre Royal**, a couple of **cinemas** and a couple of **live music** venues. There are five or six **nightclubs** catering for most tastes, and **'new' pubs** mainly along the upper High Street. If you like **'traditional' pubs**, then climb back up Steep Hill! The range of **restaurants** includes British to Italian – the best up Steep Hill and around the cathedral. There are lots of **museums and galleries**, and for a bit of a breather, walk along to **Brayford Pool** (former Roman Harbour) and watch the pretty boats! (one of the barges is a disguised **pub** and **seafood restaurant** aha!) The **castle** holds one of the four original copies of the **Magna Carta** (grudgingly signed by bad King Johnny in 1215!) And finally, you can join in with the locals and have a 'bonza breakfast' and all sorts of Aussie fun in late January...don't ask!

TOURIST INFORMATION ☎ 01522 873213
9 CASTLE HILL, LINCOLN,
LINCOLNSHIRE, LN1 3AA

HOSPITAL A & E ☎ 01522 512512
LINCOLN COUNTY HOSPITAL,
GREETWELL ROAD, LINCOLN, LN2 5QY

1 2 3

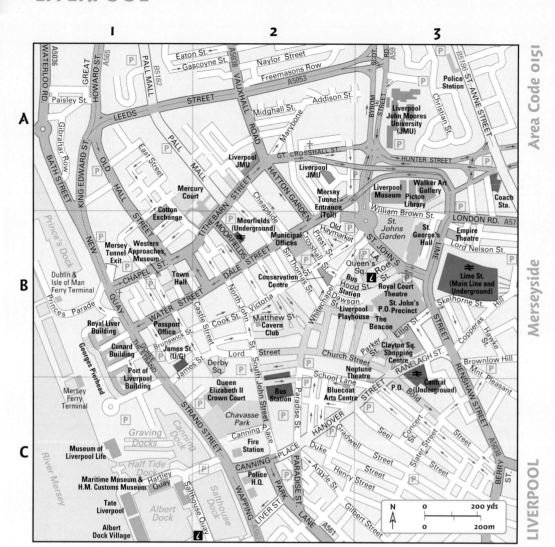

Area Code 0151

Merseyside

LIVERPOOL

WEB-SITE www.liverpool.gov.uk

LOCAL RADIO BBC RADIO MERSEYSIDE 95.8 FM
MAGIC 1548 AM, RADIO CITY 96.7 FM, JUICE 107.6 FM

INDEX TO STREET NAMES

Now you must have heard one of the ancestors raving on about 'The Beatles'! Well, Liverpool's the home of this famous '60s group. The old (rebuilt) **Cavern Club** (where they first played) is, allegedly, the best-known **live music club** in the world. There's a **Beatles Week** in August, lots of fans dancing and singing...! You can even go on a **Magical Mystery Tour**, which visits places mentioned in their songs. There are many **art galleries** and **museums** as in any major city, but some of these are really ace, the **Tate Gallery** for instance, cutting edge stuff – get an **'Eight Pass'**, which gives unlimited access to eight of the best for 12 months (www.visitliverpool.com). Other **entertainment** includes theatres (the **Bluecoat** shows more experimental works), **cinemas**, **classical music**, **popular music,** lots of **comedy** and **nightclubs** (Cream is the biggest and attracts people from afar!), most are in the centre. There are **'designer bars'** and **trad pubs**, with food from Russia, South America or France – the central area or the restored **Albert Docks** are good. **Shopping** – excellent! The roads off **Bold Street** house lots of cool, funky shops, as does the **Cavern Quarter** and **Quiggins** in School Lane – lots of independent retailers. **Albert Docks** has craft and gift shops and all the biggies are in Lord Street and Church Street, while you'll find **indoor shopping** in Clayton Square and St. John's. Take the **'Ferry 'cross the Mersey'** (Gerry and the ...never mind!) for a fine view of the city, and for fans of 'The Reds', you can have a tour of hallowed Anfield. For budding Frankie Dettori's, ride on a simulator at Aintree – it'll give your mates a laugh anyway!

TOURIST INFORMATION ☎ **09066 806886**
MERSEYSIDE WELCOME CENTRE, CLAYTON SQ.
SHOPPING CEN, LIVERPOOL, MERSEYSIDE, L1 1QR

HOSPITAL A & E ☎ **0151 525 5980**
UNIVERSITY HOSPITAL OF AINTREE, LOWER LANE,
FAZAKERLEY, LIVERPOOL, L9 7AL

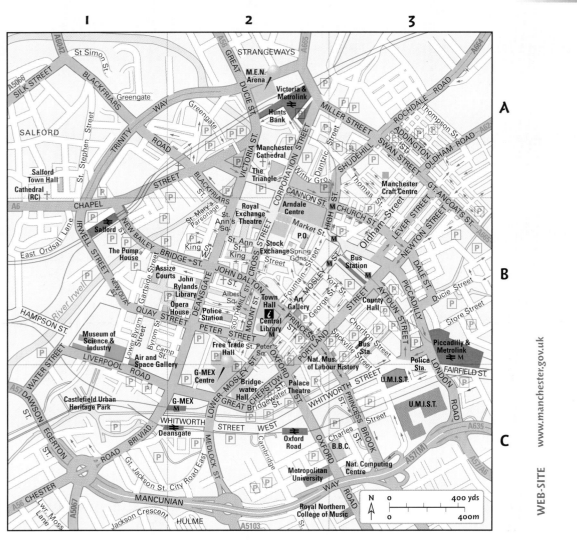

Area Code 0161

Greater Manchester

MANCHESTER

WEB-SITE www.manchester.gov.uk

LOCAL RADIO

BBC RADIO GMR 95.1 FM
MANCHESTER'S MAGIC 1152 AM, CAPITAL GOLD 1458 AM, GALAXY 102 FM,
KEY 103 FM

INDEX TO STREET NAMES

With the largest student population in England, **shopping, music, the arts, pubbing and clubbing** are more than adequately catered for! For **shops**, the **'Northern Quarter'** (up from Piccadilly Gardens) is funky city, while **The Triangle** and **King Street** require a platinum card or two for that 'must have dahling' designer stuff! Try **St. Ann's Square, Market Street, the Trafford Centre** (over 280 shops) and the **Arndale Centre** for the rest. Britain's largest **Chinatown** (behind the Piccadilly Plaza area) is a unique **shopping** and **dining** experience and has the only **Imperial Chinese Archway** in Europe! You can experience **rock/jazz/blues/pop/opera/classical/trad Irish music** etc. at venues such as **The Royal Northern College of Music, Manchester Academy** and **Roadhouse**. There's a huge **club scene** here with all tastes catered for in the (mainly) central area, gay clubs along the canal (in the Gay Village) and in the college clubs. Heard of 'matchstick men'? Well the works of L S Lowry at **Salford Quays** will show you what all the fuss is about. Other excellent **art** can be seen in the **Whitworth Art Gallery**, the **Cornerhouse** and many more. Everything you ever wanted to know about mummies can be experienced at the **Manchester Museum**, and if you like pushing buttons, go to the **Museum of Science and Industry** and be a child again! And yes, you can have a tour of **Old Trafford** if you're a 'Red Devils' supporter!

TOURIST INFORMATION ☎ 0161 234 3157/8
**MANCHESTER VISITOR CENTRE, TOWN HALL
EXTENSION, LLOYD ST, MANCHESTER, M60 2LA**

HOSPITAL A & E ☎ 0161 276 1234
**MANCHESTER ROYAL INFIRMARY,
OXFORD ROAD, MANCHESTER, M13 9WL**

1   2   3

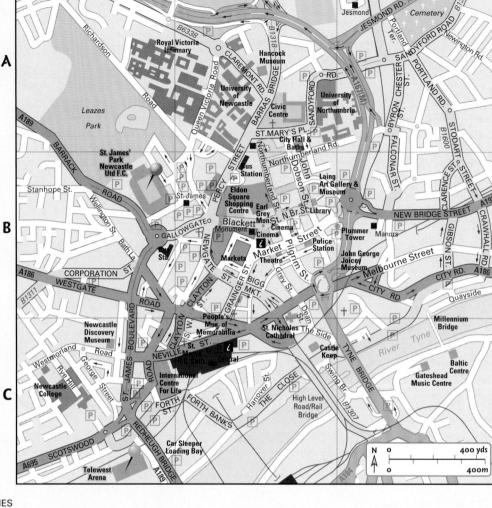

WEB-SITE www.newcastle.gov.uk

LOCAL RADIO BBC RADIO NEWCASTLE 95.4 FM MAGIC 1152 AM, METRO RADIO 97.1 FM, CENTURY FM 101.8 FM

INDEX TO STREET NAMES

You might ask a passing gent for directions to the nearest public conveniences, he might point to the lady next to him and say "Ax wor lass!" and she might say, "Aa divvint knaa!" then you can say "Oh, thanks" and walk off bewildered - great dialect, can be tricky! The language isn't all that's colourful, the city is full of energy, and you won't find a better place for a good night out! Some of the best **nightlife** in the country can be found in the new **Quayside** area, **Bigg Market** (good **pubs** – try a pint of 'Dog'!), **Haymarket** and **Osborne Road** – check out 'Paint it Red' and 'The Crack' mags. **Live music** can be found in most **pubs, student unions** and the **City Hall**, with really big acts appearing in **Newcastle Telewest Arena**. For top class **comedy**, go to **The Hyena Café**. Then there are all the **cinemas, theatres, art galleries and museums** – you won't have time in one weekend! Do fit in the **Laing Gallery**, The **BALTIC Centre for Contemporary Art**, the **Millennium Bridge** and **Life Interactive World** though – then **GO SHOPPING!** Spend the whole day hunting for bargains in **Greenmarket** and **Grainger Market**, or at the massive **MetroCentre** just over the river in Gateshead. **Northumberland Street** and **Eldon Shopping Centre** have more conventional stuff, while specialists and designer outlets are found in **Grainger Street** and **Eldon Gardens**.

Grainger Town has lots of trendy boutiques. As for **food**, you can still get 'stottie cakes', but there's everything else as well, from Indian takeaways to top class restaurants. So, it's 'broonsalroond' then!

Norfolk

NORWICH

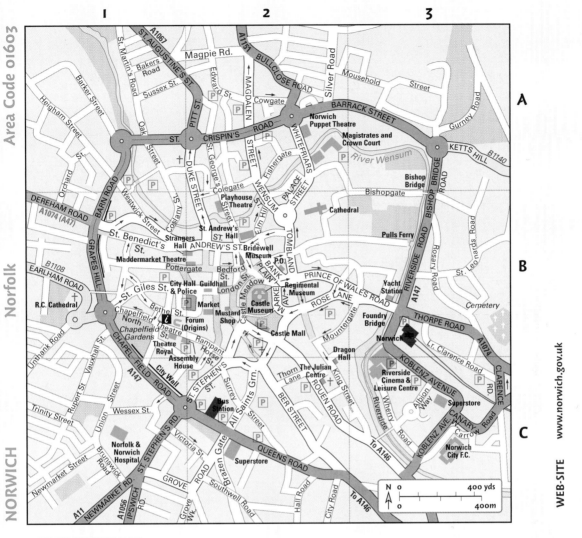

BBC RADIO NORFOLK 95.1 & 104.4 FM
CLASSIC GOLD AMBER 1152 AM, BROADLAND 102 102.4 FM

WEB-SITE www.norwich.gov.uk

LOCAL RADIO

INDEX TO STREET NAMES

The 'unofficial capital' of East Anglia, 'Naar'ch' has the honour of having more medieval churches than any other city in Europe! Don't let this put you off though; it also has lots of lurvly **shops** and a lively **nightlife**, with hundreds of **pubs**! **Shopping** is very diverse, wander around the **Pottergate** and **Lower Goat Lane** areas and you're in 'Hippie' Heaven! In fact all the little alleys radiating from the open-air **marketplace** (one of the country's largest) have interesting independent shops – clothes, books, crafts; and don't miss the **Royal Arcade** – more of the same and the **Colman's Mustard shop**! (visit the **museum** in **Bridewell Alley**), oh and **Elm Hill** (cobbled, medieval and more shops!) A stress-free shopping spree can be had round the elegant **London Street**, with nearby **Bedford Street** tempting your plastic with its designer wear. All your big stores are to the south of the centre, and **Castle Mall** has everything! **Gourmets** and **fast food** addicts will both be happy here, and there are some excellent veggie and 'wholefood' eateries. As for **culture**, several **theatres** (opera to fringe), several **live concert** venues, loads of **cinemas** (including 'Art House'), two main **Art Galleries** plus the renowned **Sainsbury Centre for Visual Arts** at the Uni, make this city no provincial backwater! The number of **clubbing venues** is growing all the time, with top name DJs dropping in to the new 'Mega clubs'. The **Waterfront** is a really excellent **alternative music** and **club night** venue. Then there's the cathedral, the castle (museums and dungeons!) and all those churches to visit!

TOURIST INFORMATION ☎ 01603 666071
THE FORUM, MILLENNIUM PLAIN,
NORWICH, NR2 1TF

HOSPITAL A & E ☎ 01603 286286
NORFOLK & NORWICH HOSPITAL,
BRUNSWICK ROAD, NORWICH, NR1 3SR

Area Code 0115

NOTTINGHAM

WEB-SITE www.nottinghamcity.gov.uk

LOCAL RADIO BBC RADIO NOTTINGHAM 103.8 FM CENTURY FM 106 FM, CLASSIC GOLD GEM 999 AM, TRENT FM 96.2 FM

(Map of Nottingham city centre with grid columns 1, 2, 3 and rows A, B, C. Labels include: Arboretum, Nottingham Trent University, General Cemetery, Royal Centre (inc. Royal Concert Hall and Theatre Royal), Bus Station, Victoria Shopping Centre, St Mary's Rest Garden, Victoria Park, R.C. Cathedral, The Albert Hall, Playhouse, Co-operative Arts Theatre, Cinema, Victoria Leisure Centre, Exchange Arcade Shopping Centre, Council House, Woolpack, Bowling Alley, Nottingham Arena, National Ice Centre, Tales of Robin Hood, The Lace Market Centre, The Caves of Nottingham, Broad Marsh Shopping Centre, The Galleries of Justice Museum, Costume Mus. & Lace Centre, Nottingham Castle Museum, Brewhouse Yard Mus., People's College, Bus Station, Crown Court, Magistrates Court, County Archives, Nottingham Station, Scale 400 yds / 400m)

INDEX TO STREET NAMES

One of the most popular places for hen nights, Nottingham has a **clubbing** scene to suit all tastes, from 70s retro to whatever came out last week! The vast selection of good **pubs** and places to stuff your face adds to its popularity, you can even have raw fish and seaweed on a conveyor belt! For a bit of culture, Nottingham has some unique contemporary **art exhibitions** and hosts the latest West End plays and musicals in its **theatres**, and the 'castle' (a 17th century mansion) houses exhibitions, a **museum** and an art gallery. One thing you really don't expect is the labyrinth of **caves** in the sandstone under the castle (guided tours only!) So was he gay, a myth and/or a Yorkshire man? No, how dare you; he was a fine upstanding young man from Nottinghamshire (with a rather dubious relationship with a 'maid'!) 'Learn' all about this most famous outlaw at the Tales of **Robin Hood** centre. **Shopping?** - this is definitely a 'shop 'til you drop' city! There are over 1300 shops, big stores to craft shops, some in the two huge shopping centres...And don't go home without buying some Nottingham lace doilies for your gran at the **Lace Centre!!**

TOURIST INFORMATION ☎ 0115 915 5330
1-4 SMITHY ROW,
NOTTINGHAM, NG1 2BY

HOSPITAL A & E ☎ 0115 924 9924
QUEENS MEDICAL CENTRE, UNIVERSITY HOSP,
DERBY ROAD, NOTTINGHAM, NG7 2UH

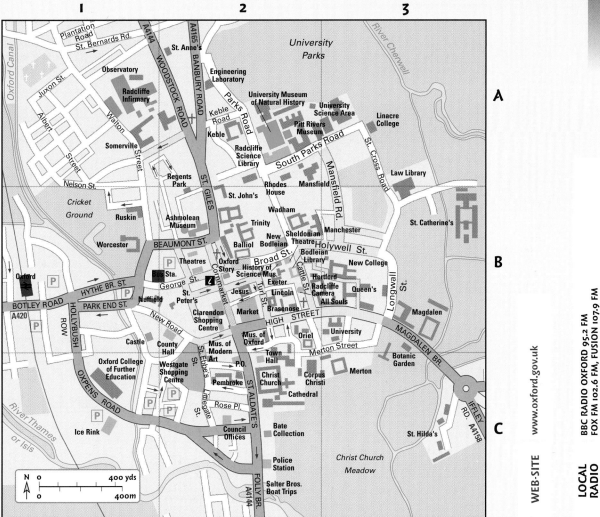

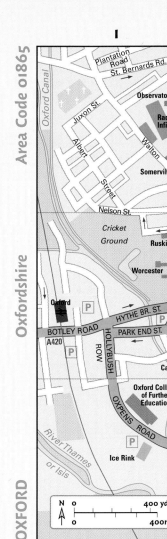

Area Code 01865

Oxfordshire

OXFORD

www.oxford.gov.uk

WEB-SITE

BBC RADIO OXFORD 95.2 FM
FOX FM 102.6 FM, FUSION 107.9 FM

LOCAL RADIO

INDEX TO STREET NAMES

You know that bit in 'Alice Through the Looking Glass' when she's in that shop run by a sheep and things keep moving around on the shelves? (What was Lewis Carroll on!)? Well anyway, that's **'Alice's Shop'** in **St. Aldate's**! Then **J.R.R. Tolkien** wrote **'The Hobbit'** and **'The Lord of the Rings'** here. More recently, some of **'Harry Potter and the Philosopher's Stone'** was filmed in **Christ Church College**, then of course there's **'Inspector Morse'** – guided tours available for all four! With so many literary connections, it's no surprise that you'll find loads of scrummy **bookshops** here; Broad Street has most of them, including the famous Blackwells. Staying with **shopping** (and why not!) if you just want the major retail chains, head for **Queen and Cornmarket Streets** or **Westgate and Clarendon Shopping Centres**. If you want funky independents, try **High Street, the Covered Market** (Oxford sausages!), **The Gallery** (next to Gloucester Green), **Walton, Jericho** and **St. Clements Streets** and over the River Cherwell (**punts** for hire!), the **Cowley Road** has all manner of ethnic and 'New Age' shops. There are so many stunning **buildings** in this 'City of Spires', you'll never see them all, but take a trip up the **Carfax Tower** for a superb view. The **Ashmolean Museum** is just huge and the **Pitt-Rivers Museum** has an amazing collection of ethnographic stuff (both free). **Food** is varied - both in price and country, and the **city centre** is crammed with **cafés**. Or why not grab some sarnies and picnic in the **Botanical Gardens**? There's plenty to do after dark, **theatres, cinemas, concerts, clubbing** (try the Uni) – consult WOW mag. oh, and wall to wall **pubs**!

TOURIST INFORMATION ☎ **01865 726871**
15-16 BROAD STREET,
OXFORD, OX1 3AS

HOSPITAL A & E ☎ **01865 741166**
JOHN RADCLIFFE HOSPITAL, HEADLEY WAY, HEADINGTON, OXFORD, OX3 9DU

PLYMOUTH

WEB-SITE www.plymouth.gov.uk

LOCAL RADIO BBC RADIO DEVON 103.4 FM
CLASSIC GOLD 1152 AM, PLYMOUTH SOUND 97 FM

Area Code 01752 · Devon · PLYMOUTH

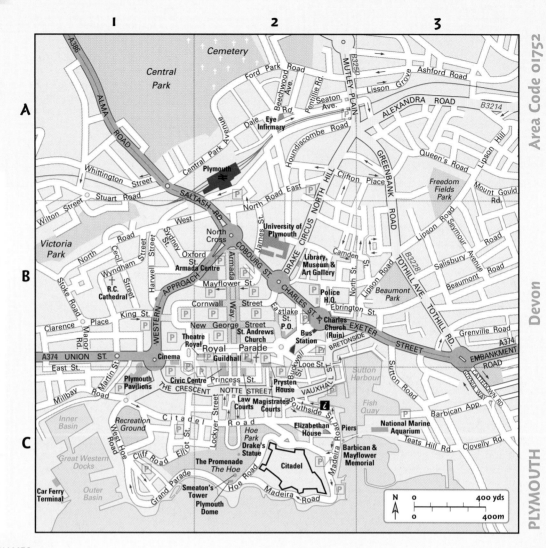

INDEX TO STREET NAMES

You can just see **Drake** on the **Hoe**, delaying the battle with the Armada with his bowls!.. in fact you can see him, well a rather tubby statue of him, on this very wide, and windy, esplanade! The Luftwaffe kindly contributed to the modern city centre shopping area Plymouth has today, with the four main **shopping streets** being **Royal Parade, New George, Cornwall and Mayflower**, these have all the major High Street stores, with **cafés, and bars, restaurants** and places to just sit. The **Barbican area** is much older, the narrow Tudor Streets have more independent and 'gifty' type shops (plus **art galleries** and **restaurants**); the **Barbican Centre** has lots of craft shops. If you're down this way, have a look in the **National Marine Aquarium**; amongst the fish, it has the largest collection of **Seahorse** species in Europe, the research here will hopefully contribute to their survival in the wild – and they're seriously cute! For a truly nautical experience (on a wet day), visit **Plymouth Dome**, you can do Elizabethan shippy things like 'splicing the main brace' and 'shivering yer timbers'! And 21st century things like seeing weather pictures arrive from satellites. When you're **hungry**, there's a load to choose from but try fresh seafood, in pubs or posh restaurants. Apparently, **Union Street** has an 'international reputation' for its **nightlife** – might be a bit feisty! Otherwise there's a varied selection of **nightclubs** and **pubs**. For **comedy** and **concerts**, see what's on at **Plymouth Pavilions**, or there are four theatres and a couple of cinemas (one has 15 screens). So, diddly dee diddly dee de de de de de de de de de (sing-a-long to Captain Pugwash – sorry!).

TOURIST INFORMATION ☎ 01752 264849 ISLAND HOUSE, 9 THE BARBICAN, PLYMOUTH, DEVON, PL1 2LS

HOSPITAL A & E ☎ 01752 777111 DERRIFORD HOSPITAL, DERRIFORD ROAD, CROWNHILL, PLYMOUTH, PL6 8DH

Area Code 023

PORTSMOUTH

WEB-SITE www.portsmouth.gov.uk

LOCAL RADIO
BBC RADIO SOLENT 96.1 FM
CAPITAL GOLD 1170 AM, OCEAN FM 97.5 FM, THE QUAY 107.4 FM,
WAVE 105.2 FM

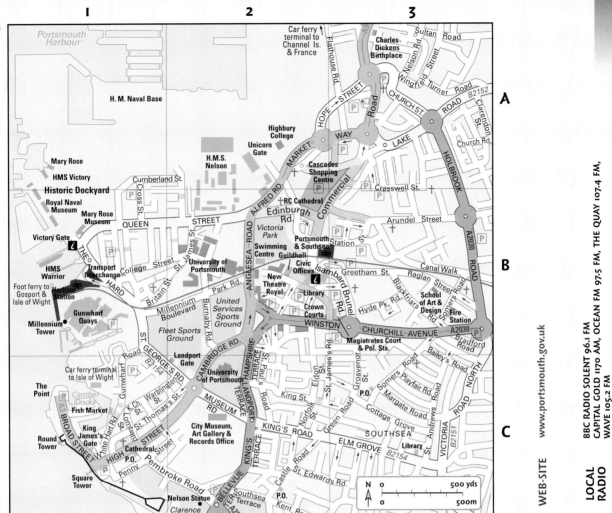

INDEX TO STREET NAMES

Home of the **British Navy**, you can't come to 'Pompey' without a visit to the **Historic Ships** – HMS Warrior (first iron battleship; Napoleon III said it was a "black snake amongst the rabbits" – perhaps it lost something in the translation!), HMS Victory (Nelson's ship – "Kiss me Hardy" and all that), and the remains of Henry VIII's Mary Rose (housed in a shed!) You might also see some huge modern **Naval Frigates** coming and going. **Old Portsmouth** is where the first spuds and baccy arrived – Raleigh has a lot to answer for! Having whizzed round there and taken some piccies to show Grandad, you'll be up for some **shopping**! **Gunwharf Quays** is a purpose built 'waterfront development' housing over 65 shops and several **bars** and **restaurants**, as well as a multi-screen **cinema, bowling alley, Jongleurs comedy club** and two **nightclubs** – just stay here then! The **Cascades** has all the High Street names under one roof, and **Commercial Road** next to it has more places to blow your cash! If you're looking for bargains and second-hand goodies then aim for **Fawcett Road**, a veritable mecca for ethnic and retro stuff. Museums specialising in the military and the sea abound, you can even visit a submarine (make sure you're not claustrophobic!) For **entertainment**, The **Guildhall** has **live bands**, **comedy** and **concerts**, while **clubs** and **nightclubs** can be found here and in neighbouring **Southsea**. There are lots of **pubs** here, some good ones in the **Guildhall** area. To **eat**, again you can't go wrong with seafood, and there are other hostelries with more cosmo dishes, including French – Nelson would turn in his grave!

TOURIST INFORMATION ☎ 023 9282 6722
THE HARD,
PORTSMOUTH, PO1 3QJ

HOSPITAL A & E ☎ 023 9228 6000
QUEEN ALEXANDRA HOSPITAL, SOUTHWICK
HILL ROAD, COSHAM, PORTSMOUTH, PO6 3LY

READING

Area Code 0118

WEB-SITE www.reading.gov.uk

LOCAL RADIO BBC RADIO BERKSHIRE 104.4 FM — CLASSIC GOLD 1431 AM, 2-TEN FM 97 FM

READING

INDEX TO STREET NAMES

Between 11am and 4pm, you can **shop** without having to use the 'Green Cross Code'; the whole of the town centre is closed to traffic. There's a big newish shopping complex called the **Oracle Centre**, which has over 80 stores (High Street stuff and others), with **Broad Street** (including a mall) being the other main shopping area – look out for the street entertainers! Then there's **Friar's Walk, King's Walk** (where you'll need a healthy bank balance! – some good **restaurants** here too) and more individual shops in **Harris Arcade**. If you're still alive after 4pm (having forgotten about the traffic!), grab a **bite to eat** in one of the many new **bars, cafés or restaurants** in the centre (fast food to classical Thai); otherwise, **Oxford Road** has lots of choice. For **pubs**, try Friar Street or Castle Street or there's lots of riverside pubby-clubs at the Oracle. If you're kicking your heels after dark, check out Blah Blah mag which will tell you what's on in the way of **live music** in the **pubs** and many **clubs** (varied and not too expensive). Alternatively, go for some classical vibes at the new **Concert Hall** or a good dose of **comedy** (and other stuff) at **The Hexagon** – or the **Uni**. Then there's the famous **Reading Festival** in late August (man!) and **WOMAD** – three days of world music at **Rivermead**, in early August. Don't forget the full-size Victorian replica (British version) of the **Bayeux Tapestry** in the **Museum** – all 70 metres of it! Well, if it's a wet day..!

TOURIST INFORMATION ☎ 0118 956 6226
TOWN HALL, BLAGRAVE STREET,
READING, RG1 1QH

HOSPITAL A & E ☎ 0118 987 5111
ROYAL BERKSHIRE HOSPITAL, LONDON ROAD,
READING, RG1 5AN

Area Code 0114

South Yorkshire

SHEFFIELD

WEB-SITE www.sheffield.gov.uk

LOCAL RADIO — BBC RADIO SHEFFIELD 88.6 FM / MAGIC AM, SOUTH YORKSHIRE 1548 AM, HALLAM FM 97.4 FM

(Map of Sheffield city centre with grid columns 1, 2, 3 and rows A, B, C)

N 0 — 300 yds / 0 — 300m

INDEX TO STREET NAMES

It's going to be really difficult to window **shop** here, so if you want funky and you're up to your overdraft limit, sell something and come anyway! There are at least six music shops stocking all sorts of specialist sounds and if you've just got nothing to wear, do pop along to **The Forum Centre** and get togged out (lots of colourful lava lamps etc here too!) Another good place for trendy stuff is the **Devonshire Quarter**, around Division Street. Those big turquoise coloured buildings you saw from the M1 are **Meadowhall**, it has absolutely everything you could want to buy – 1.25 million square feet of shopping apparently! As for **entertainment**, there's a huge choice; at night, check out the **bars** along **West Street** and **Division Street**, **Club** land is very lively and varied, and for mega **gigs**, try the **Arena** and **Don Valley Stadium** (see the Dirty Stop Out's Guide and the Sheffield Telegraph). For theatre try the **Crucible** (not just for snooker!); the **Lyceum** and **City Hall** also host classical events, then there's the **Roundhouse** and of course, the **Uni**. There are many **museums** and **art galleries** (try the **Cultural Industries Quarter**) for daytime amusement – 'Magna' is excellent, it's a science adventure centre – don't let the kids have all the fun! For **stuffing your face**, go Italian down the **Ecclesall Road**, posh in the **Devonshire Quarter**... or if you fancy something dubious on a stick or wrapped in some bread, this is kebab heaven! Lots more, no room!

TOURIST INFORMATION ☎ 0114 221 1900
1 TUDOR SQUARE,
SHEFFIELD, S1 2LA

HOSPITAL A & E ☎ 0114 243 4343
NORTHERN GENERAL HOSPITAL, HERRIES ROAD,
SHEFFIELD, S5 7AU

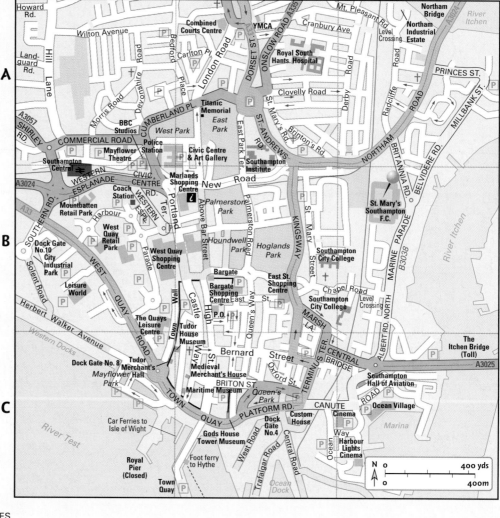

Area Code 023

SOUTHAMPTON

WEB-SITE www.southampton.gov.uk

LOCAL RADIO BBC RADIO SOLENT 96.1 FM
CAPITAL GOLD 1557 AM, POWER FM 103.2 FM, SOUTH CITY 107.8 FM,
WAVE 105.2 FM

INDEX TO STREET NAMES

If you like watching sailing boats (and don't mind that some people are just born rich!), then put on your deck shoes and mosey around **Ocean Village** – over 400 boats in the **Marina**, plus **shops**, **restaurants**, **bars** and **cinemas** all under cover. You can watch the really big stuff go off round the world if you're here during September… Coming back to the real world, **shops** can be found in the gigantic **WestQuay**, where you won't need boatloads of cash; undercover shopping in the heart of the city. The **Marlands shopping centre** is similar, while outdoors **Above Bar Street** is the main shopping street. If you want funky, then **The Bargate** has it all, from extreme sports gear to slinky club wear. Smaller independent shops can be found along **High Street, Carlton Place** and **Bedford Place**. Strut your navel stuff in Southampton's many **nightclubs** (two in the **Leisure World** entertainment centre), and a newer development, **pre-club bars**, are springing up everywhere – usually no jeans or trainers though! **Live entertainment** is often to be found in the **city pubs** – that should be jolly, Roger! With music and more in **The Gantry Arts Centre**. **The Guildhall** is a major live venue, while the **Mayflower theatre** hosts West End to ballet, and the **Nuffield** stages more contemporary stuff. For **fud**, all the **waterfront quays** and **shopping centres** have **café bars** and **restaurants**, but for something a bit different, set sail for **Oxford Street**. Incidentally, the Titanic left from here as well, and if you're a fan of the story, there's the **"Titanic Trail"**, a guided walking tour of the city – ice with your G & T?

TOURIST INFORMATION ☎ **023 8022 1106**
9 CIVIC CENTRE ROAD,
SOUTHAMPTON, SO14 7LP

HOSPITAL A & E ☎ **023 8077 7222**
SOUTHAMPTON GENERAL HOSP, TREMONA RD,
SHIRLEY, SOUTHAMPTON, SO16 6YD

Area Code 01782

STOKE-ON-TRENT

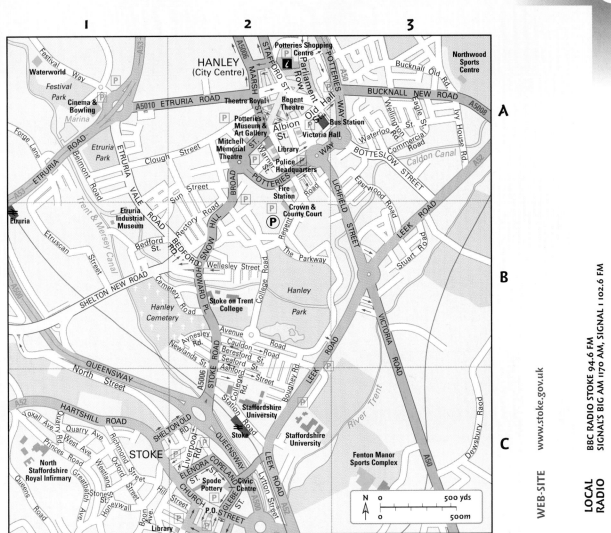

WEB-SITE   www.stoke.gov.uk

LOCAL RADIO   BBC RADIO STOKE 94.6 FM   SIGNAL'S BIG AM 1170 AM, SIGNAL 1 102.6 FM

INDEX TO STREET NAMES

This 'city' is in fact a 'Federation' of the six towns of Tunstall, Burslem, Hanley (generally counted as the 'city centre'), Stoke, Fenton and Longton. To make it even more confusing, the city is known as **"The Potteries"** ('cos of Messrs. Wedgwood, Spode etc). In spite of its recent problems, Stoke is still the largest producer of clay wear in the world! Lots of factories with lots of quaint **'Bottle Kilns'** with lots of **tours** (and **museums**) with lots of (bargain) **pottery** to buy for...whoever. So, having bought your prezzies, go to the **main shopping centre** in **Hanley**; it's called (you guessed it) the **Potteries Shopping Centre**! and buy yourself some goodies. There's everything from 'High Street' to second-hand jewellery to unique independents. Then there's **Freeport Talke Outlet Mall**, with discount designer stuff. Fancy a **snack**? Well, Stoke is the home of the **oatcake**!.. Alternatively there are a variety of **restaurants** serving easier to swallow fayre from Chinese to Italian. So, "Let Us Entertain You" (yes, Robbie comes from here!). The relatively new **'Cultural Quarter'** includes the **Victoria Hall** and **Regent** theatres (West End to drama), along with a variety of **restaurants, bars and clubs**. There are a couple of **cinemas** or work up a sweat in one of the **clubs** featuring dance music (look at www.movemag.com for details). Near the Trent and Mersey canal is an area called **Etruria**, here, there's **Festival Park**, and you'll find 'lots of things to see and do' including **laser gun fun**, a **Megabowl** and a **dry ski slope** – if you've got any energy left, well it's only 30 minutes to **Alton Towers**!

TOURIST INFORMATION ☎ **01782 236000**
POTTERIES SHOPPING CENTRE, QUADRANT RD,
STOKE-ON-TRENT, ST1 1RZ

HOSPITAL A & E ☎ **01782 715444**
NORTH STAFFORDSHIRE ROYAL INFIRMARY,
PRINCE'S ROAD, STOKE-ON-TRENT, ST4 7LN

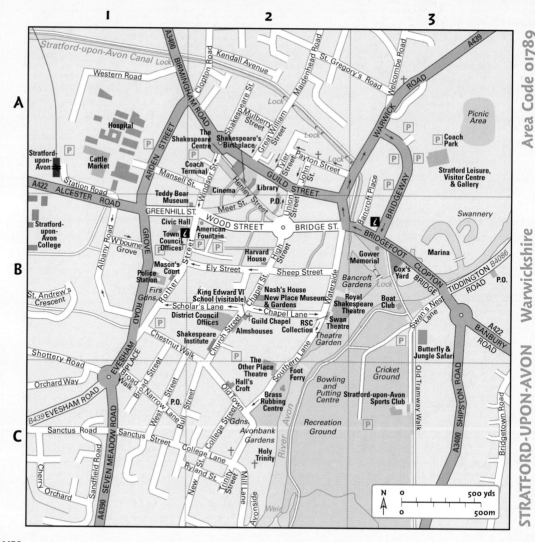

Area Code 01789 · Warwickshire · STRATFORD-UPON-AVON

WEB-SITE www.stratford.gov.uk

LOCAL RADIO BBC RADIO COVENTRY & WARWICKSHIRE 94.8 & 103.7 FM
FM 102 THE BEAR 102 FM

INDEX TO STREET NAMES

To go or not to go! Let's face it; if you come here you do need to have an interest in 'the bard'. There's **Shakespeare's Birthplace Museum**, his grave, his **'Centre'**, and nearby, his **Mum's house** and even the house where the **first husband of Shakespeare's granddaughter lived**! not to mention three **theatres** (on the banks of the River Avon) that stage the plays wot he wrote. To be fair, the theatres do show other more contemporary works, especially **The Other Place**. **The Royal Shakespeare** is the biggest and most traditional and the **Swan** has a central stage, which puts you in the play! You can have a **behind the scenes tour** which is really good, especially if you're thinking of a career in that area. For other culture, **The Gallery** is a new contemporary art gallery that's well worth a visit. There are lots of places for that 'pre-play' **picnic** on the river, and there's even a **microbrewery** where you can sample 'Jester Ale'! If you want excellent **food**, from English to Indian, in lovely old buildings with really friendly service, you couldn't find anywhere better – try **Sheep Street** and **Bridge Street** for a start; what's more, they serve food at times which fit in with theatre performances! For a real treat, and to feel unashamedly English, it's got to be afternoon tea in the **Hathaway Tea Rooms** on the **High Street**! **Faster food** and **live music** can also be found in the **pubs and bars** – sometimes. **Shopping**...well, lots of souvenir shops and 'quaint' shops with the odd 'normal' one thrown in – try **Bridge Street**. There are one or two shops bordering on the funky, but most cater for tourists, and as for **nightclubs**... nooo!

TOURIST INFORMATION ☎ 01789 293127
BRIDGEFOOT, STRATFORD-UPON-AVON,
WARWICKSHIRE, CV37 6GW

HOSPITAL A & E ☎ 01926 495321
WARWICK HOSPITAL, WAKIN ROAD,
WARWICK, CV34 5BW

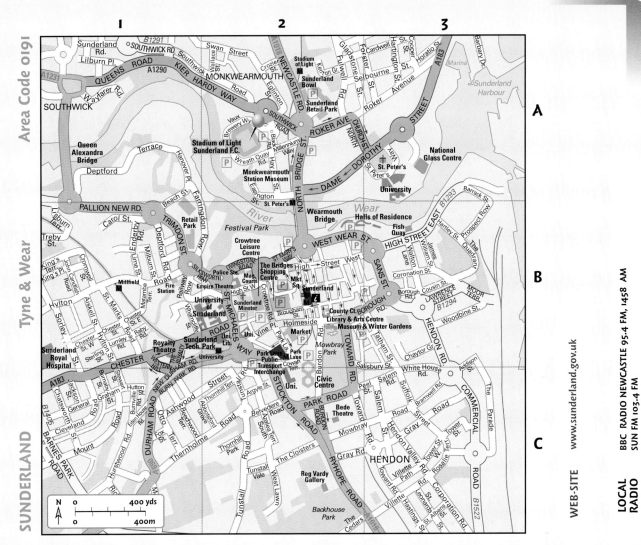

Area Code 0191

Tyne & Wear

SUNDERLAND

WEB-SITE www.sunderland.gov.uk

LOCAL RADIO: BBC RADIO NEWCASTLE 95.4 FM, 1458 AM / SUN FM 103.4 FM

INDEX TO STREET NAMES

If you want something colourful, unique and funky to adorn your room, come here. Glass has been made in this area for 1300 years, and the **National Glass Centre** on the north bank of the river Wear has designer crafts people working on site, with a luverly shop (yes, some of it you'd have to sell the family jewels to buy, but they sell marbles too!) - they also have an award winning **restaurant** called Throwingstones! There's a church around here too, **St Peter's**, one of the oldest churches in the country (674 AD) and it has the oldest stained glass in the country too, gosh! Inside, are the remains of the monastery where the **'Venerable Bede'** (lovely name!), the **'Father of English History'**, lived and worked, double gosh! Back to the **shopping** theme, **The Bridges shopping centre** has all the big names you'd expect (and cake and ice-cream!), while 'traditional' streets with specialist and independent shops are scattered around; the **city centre** has the High Street names. If you feel like a bit of a stroll, and it's a nice day, climb Penshaw Hill and look at the **Penshaw Monument**, built in the style of a Greek Temple... er, then climb down again! Alternatively, flock to one of the beaches at **Seaburn** or **Roker**, clean and sandy! For a wet day, the **Vardy Gallery** at the **Uni** has cutting edge art – and it's free! **Food** is tasty, everything from Fish 'n chips to Caribbean, while for the evening, there are plenty of **pubs 'n clubs**, **High Street West and East**, and **Holmeside** will get you started. More cultured stuff can be had at the **Empire**, **Royalty** and other **theatres**, or for something completely different, watch the bunny at **Sunderland Greyhound Racing Stadium**!

TOURIST INFORMATION ☎ 0191 553 2000
50 FAWCETT STREET, SUNDERLAND, SR1 1RF

HOSPITAL A & E ☎ 0191 565 6256
SUNDERLAND DISTRICT GENERAL HOSPITAL, KAYLL ROAD, SUNDERLAND, SR4 7TP

SWANSEA

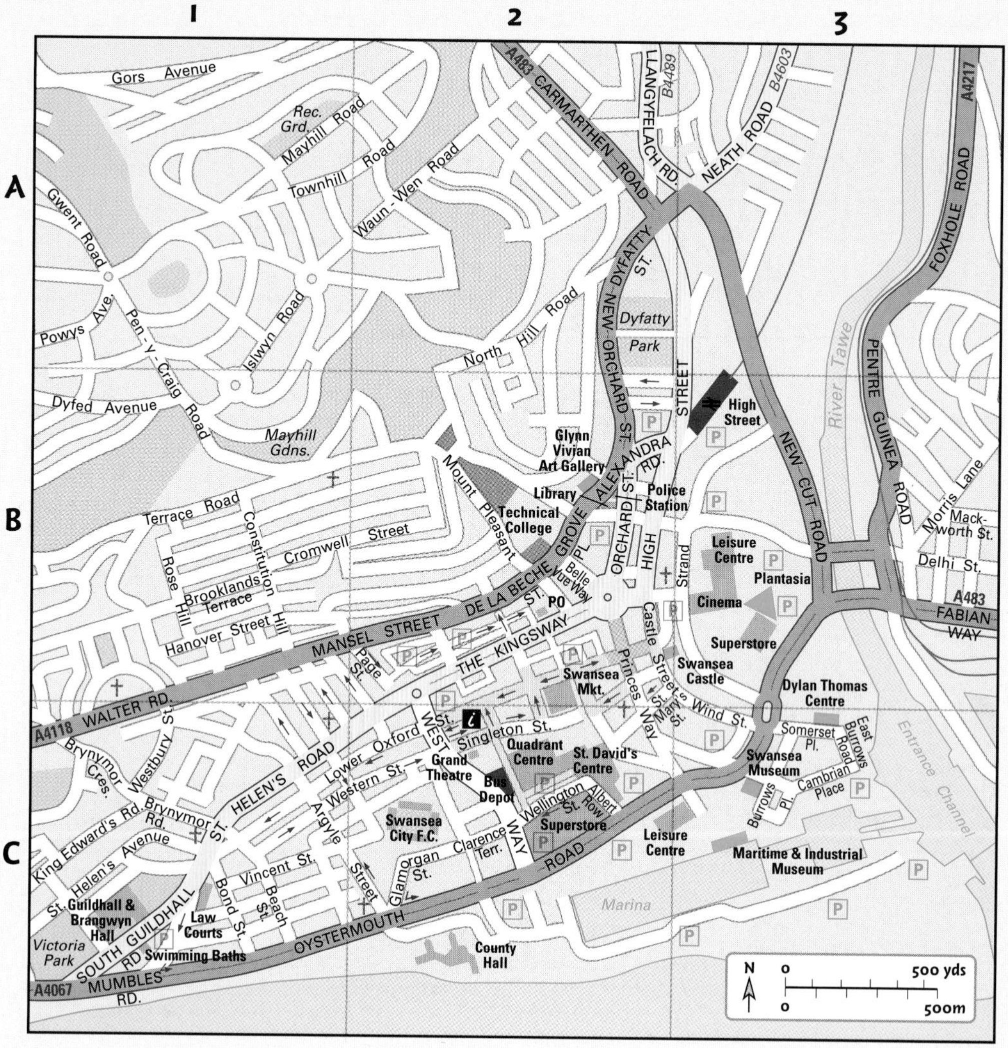

Area Code 01792

SWANSEA

Map of Swansea city centre with grid references (columns 1–3, rows A–C).

WEB-SITE www.swansea.gov.uk

LOCAL RADIO BBC RADIO WALES 93.9 FM
SWANSEA SOUND 1170 AM

INDEX TO STREET NAMES

Let's start with **nightlife**. Swansea is, allegedly, a 'cool place to party', 90% of the nightclubs are along **The Kingsway**, with more along the **'Mumbles Mile'** – be warned, it heaves in summer! Then along and around **Wind Street** there are loads of **wine bars** and pubs. For **entertainment**, check out who's on where in the **'Gig Guide'** in the **Evening Post** on Fridays; good places are the **Taliesin Arts Centre** at the Uni and the **Irish pubs** – of course! Some of the **music festivals** include the week long **'Tune Town'** – local rock bands in **Castle Square** (free!), **Swansea Maritime & Sea Shanty Festival** (July) – All things nautical and lots of jolly songs! Then there's **'The Ponty'** in August – world music and dance. If you like **classical**, then there's the **Swansea Festival of Music and Arts** in October, (**Brangwyn Hall** has all the classical stuff the rest of the year). **Food**? No problem. If you want a barbie on the beach, go to **Swansea Market**, fresh local produce including fresh fish and cockles (get some laverbread too, made with seaweed!). Otherwise, the city can provide trad Welsh, Mediterranean, Lebanese, veggie...Of course, there's **shopping** too! **The Quadrant Shopping Centre** houses some of the largest retail stores in Wales as well as smaller independents and boutiques. The city centre is pedestrianised; **Oxford Street, High Street** and **Kingsway** have most of the rest. For a **cultural** hour or so, visit the **Glynn Vivian Art Gallery** - good Welsh art, and of course, the **Dylan Thomas Centre**, an exhibition of Swansea's famous son 'Under Milkwood' and all that. And if it's a really luverly day, taker yer Barbie and drive a few miles out to **Gower** - beeeooootiful!

TOURIST INFORMATION ☎ 01792 468321
WESTWAY,
SWANSEA, SA1 3QG

HOSPITAL A & E ☎ 01792 702222
MORRISTON HOSPITAL, MORRISTON,
SWANSEA, SA6 6NL

Area Code 01793

SWINDON

1 **2** **3**

A

B

C

WEB-SITE www.swindon.gov.uk

LOCAL RADIO BBC WILTSHIRE SOUND 103.6 FM CLASSIC GOLD 1161 AM, GWR FM 97.2 FM

N 0 400 yds / 400m

INDEX TO STREET NAMES

You can split Swindon into three distinct areas from the 'having fun' point of view. There's **'New Town'**, which has pedestrianised, mostly undercover, shopping – **The Parade**, **The Big Top Market** and the **Brunel Shopping Centre** (with all the High Street names and around 100 'speciality' shops) for a start. You'll also find smaller independent shops, a good selection of **restaurants**, the **Wyvern Theatre** and town centre **clubs** and **pubs**. Then there's **'Old Town'**, which has more 'traditional' shopping with some good funky **shops**, buzzing **nightclubs**, good **pubs**, an **Arts Centre** which shows **theatre, comedy** etc, an **Art Gallery** housing a great collection of 20th century stuff, and excellent **restaurants** (Drove Road and Bath Road are the rough dividing lines, with Old Town to the east and south). If you head **north of the railway**, you'll find the **Great Western Outlet Village**, at the time of writing, the biggest covered outlet in Europe! What's more, it's not in a new purpose built concrete monstrosity, but in the amazingly well restored home of the **Brunel locomotive works** – top marks Swindon! Not only top brands, but up to 50% off High Street prices! You can spend all day here, and they've thoughtfully provided several **cafés**, a good selection of **restaurants** and a large **food court** done up like an old Victorian railway station - complete with the **'City of Truro'** steam engine; there's also a **steam museum** next door! – Sorry, a touch of the bobble hats there! – Oh why not, who had a train set when they were little then!

TOURIST INFORMATION ☎ 01793 530328
37 REGENT STREET,
SWINDON, SN1 1JL

HOSPITAL A & E ☎ 01793 536231
PRINCESS MARGARET HOSPITAL, OKUS ROAD,
SWINDON, SN1 4JU

WINCHESTER

Area Code 01962

Hampshire

WINCHESTER

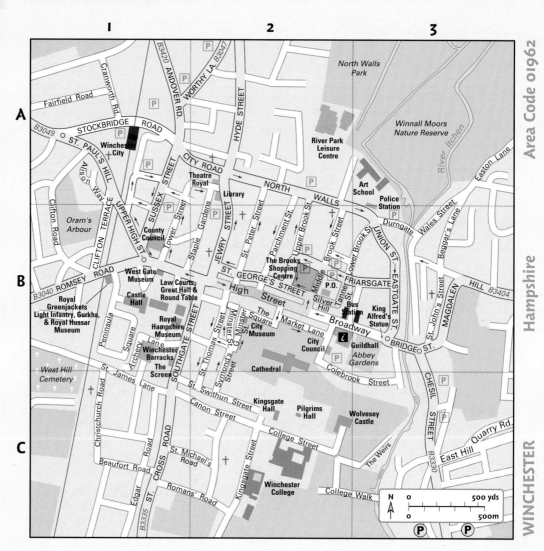

WEB-SITE
www.winchester.gov.uk

LOCAL RADIO
BBC RADIO SOLENT 96.1 FM
OCEAN FM 96.7 FM, WIN 107.2 FM

INDEX TO STREET NAMES

A city of sublime temptation for the dedicated **shopper**! Lots of ethnic, gift, 'retro funky', craft, book and designer jewellery emporiums, especially in the side streets. All the Big names loiter around the pedestrianised **precinct**, the **High Street** and the **Brooks shopping centre**. The **restaurants** here are top class, so all you foodies should have a treat; old **pubs** and **teashops** are part of the scenery, so afternoon tea with boiled eggs and cream cakes is almost compulsory! If you're here in mid-summer (usually early July-ish), you could catch the **'Hat Fair'** in the city centre; it's a bit like banana surprise – no bananas! Instead you'll find Britain's longest running **street theatre festival**, with sword swallowing, world music, and all sorts of 'off the wall' goings on! For **live music**, the **Guildhall** and **Tower Arts Centre** (which also does 'alternative' **comedy** etc) are decent venues and the **Theatre Royal** shows some good plays. For a luxury **cinematic** experience, **'The Screen'** in **Southgate Street** not only shows all the latest films but it has a licensed bar, coffee, ice cream and big squidgy seats from Paris! Only one or two **nightclubs**, but hey, you can't have everything! Being such an ancient place, you've got to have a quick whizz round the **history** – it was **Venta Belgarum** under the Romans (5th largest town in Britain!), then **King Alfred** burnt the cakes and made it his capital (**statue** at the bottom of **Broadway**), after **Cromwell** took over, everything went downhill. See the **cathedral** – superb, nice 'Green Man', the **'Arthurian' round table** in the **Great Hall** – fake! and **Winchester College** – oldest public school in England originally for 'poor scholars' – bit pricey now one thinks!

TOURIST INFORMATION ☎ 01962 840500
GUILDHALL, THE BROADWAY, WINCHESTER
HAMPSHIRE, SO23 9LJ

HOSPITAL A & E ☎ 01962 863535
ROYAL HAMPSHIRE COUNTY HOSPITAL,
ROMSEY ROAD, WINCHESTER, SO22 5DG

Area Code 01904

YORK

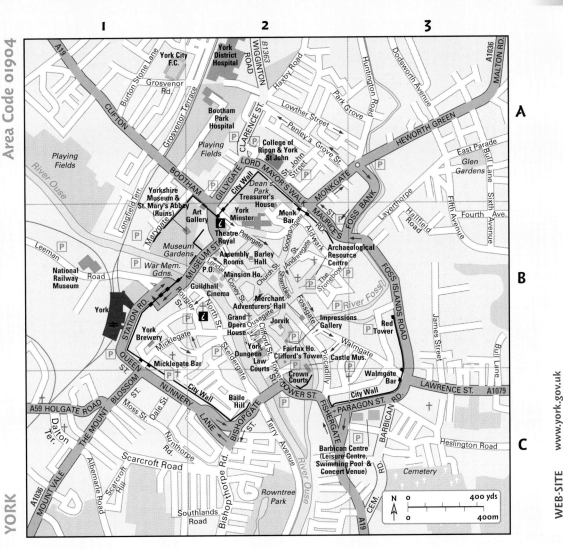

WEB-SITE www.york.gov.uk

LOCAL RADIO BBC RADIO YORK 103.7 FM MINSTER FM 104.7 FM, GALAXY 105 105.1 FM

INDEX TO STREET NAMES

Go to **Betty's Tea Rooms**, the **Art Deco** surroundings are a bit special, not to mention the posh nosh! There are lots of **cafés, tearooms** and **coffee bars** in York, and the twilight hours offer **international cuisine** from English to Indian. As for **watering holes**, there's reputedly one for every day of the year; trad English (whatever that is), wine bars, pre-club bars and real ale pubs (**Micklegate** has a good run of them). **Shopping**, oh yes, if your money is waiting to burn, York has a match! Some of it's a bit 'twee' but you could spend a week in **Swinegate, Stonegate, Fossgate, The Shambles** and **Goodramgate** – designer boutiques, specialist shops, and gift shops – Chrissy shopping heaven! Historically, York is a bit of an onion, Roman under Viking, under Saxon under medieval, and since you're here, visit the **Jorvik Viking Centre** and make your own coin with a big hammer! **York Minster** is another 'must do'; it has the world's largest medieval stained glass window (faces east, go in the morning), the famous Rose window and a 400-year-old wooden clock! The Romans had a hand in the **city wall** (well there's a surprise!), what you can see is mostly medieval though, but you can run round the two-and-a-half miles for free! **Entertainment**? Around four **cinemas**, and the same number of **theatres**, including the **Arts Centre** for more experimental stuff.

There are some **nightclubs** but most people head for Leeds. For **live music**, try the **Barbican Centre**, and city centre **pubs** (see www.thisisyork.co.uk). Finally, if you're here in February, you can run around in a pointy helmet at '**Jolablot**', the annual Viking festival...!

TOURIST INFORMATION ☎ **01904 554488**
TIC TRAVEL OFFICE, 20 GEORGE HUDSON ST.,
YORK, YO1 6WR

HOSPITAL A & E ☎ **01904 631313**
YORK DISTRICT HOSPITAL, WIGGINTON ROAD,
YORK, YO31 8HE

F

G

Index to London street names

Index to Britain

Index to Britain

Index to Britain

Index to Britain

International ferry & airport information

FERRY INFORMATION

International vehicle ferry journeys from Britain with details of journey length, season of operation and operator

Cairnryan to Larne
1 hr - 2hrs 15 mins
All year
P&O Irish Sea

Douglas to Belfast
2 hrs 45 mins
Summer only
Isle of Man Steam Packet Co

Douglas to Dublin
2 hrs 45 mins - 4 hrs 45 mins
Summer only
Isle of Man Steam Packet Co

Dover to Calais
45 mins
All year
Hoverspeed

Dover to Calais
1 hr 15 mins
All year
P&O Stena Line

Dover to Calais
1 hr
All year
SeaFrance

Dover to Oostende
2 hrs
All year
Hoverspeed

Dover to Zeebrugge
4 hrs 30 mins
All year
P & O Stena Line

Fishguard to Rosslare
1 hr 50 mins - 3 hrs 30 mins
All year
Stena Line

Fleetwood to Larne
8 hours
All year
P&O Irish Sea

Harwich to Esbjerg
19 hrs
All year
DFDS Seaways

Harwich to Hamburg
20 hrs
All year
DFDS Seaways

Harwich to Hoek van Holland
3 hrs 40 mins
All year
Stena Line

Heysham to Belfast
4 hrs
Summer only
Seacat

Heysham to Douglas
3 hrs 30 mins
All year
Isle of Man Steam Packet Co

Holyhead to Dublin
1 hr 50 mins - 3 hrs 15 mins
All year
Irish Ferries

Holyhead to Dublin
3 hrs 45 mins
All year
Stena Line

Holyhead to Dún Laoghaire
1 hr 40 mins
All year
Stena Line

Hull to Rotterdam
14 hrs
All year
P&O North Sea Ferries

Hull to Zeebrugge
14 hrs
All year
P&O North Sea Ferries

Lerwick to Bergen
12 hrs 30 mins
Summer only
Smyril Line

Lerwick to Seydisfjordur
31 hrs
Summer only
Smyril Line

Lerwick to Torshavn
13 hrs
Summer only
Smyril Line

Liverpool to Belfast
8 hrs
All year
NorseMerchant Ferries

Liverpool to Douglas
2 hrs 30 mins - 4 hrs
All year
Isle of Man Steam Packet Co

Liverpool to Dublin
3 hrs 45 mins
All year
Isle of Man Steam Packet Co

Liverpool to Dublin
7 hrs
All year
NorseMerchant Ferries

Liverpool to Dublin
6 hrs 30 mins - 8 hrs
All year
P&O Irish Sea

Mostyn Quay to Dublin
6 - 8 hrs
All year
P&O Irish Sea

Newcastle to Amsterdam
15 hrs
All year
DFDS Seaways

Newcastle to Bergen
22 hrs - 26 hrs
All year
Fjord Line

Newcastle to Göteborg
25 hrs
All year
DFDS Seaways

Newcastle to Haugesund
21 hrs 30 mins
All year
Fjord Line

Newcastle to Kristiansand
17 hrs
All year
DFDS Seaways

Newcastle to Stavanger
19 hrs
All year
Fjord Line

Newhaven to Dieppe
2 hrs
Summer only
Hoverspeed

Pembroke to Rosslare
3 hrs 45 mins
All year
Irish Ferries

Plymouth to Roscoff
6 hrs - 7 hrs 30 mins
All year
Brittany Ferries

Plymouth to Santander
24 hrs
Summer only
Brittany Ferries

Poole to Cherbourg
2 hrs 15 mins
Summer only
Condor Ferries

Poole to Cherbourg
4 hrs 15 mins - 5 hrs 45 mins
All year
Brittany Ferries

Poole to Guernsey
2 hrs 30 mins
Summer only
Condor Ferries

Poole to Jersey
3 hrs - 3 hrs 45 mins
Summer only
Condor Ferries

**Poole to St Malo
(via Guernsey or Jersey)**
4 hrs 35 mins
Summer only
Condor Ferries

Portsmouth to Bilbao
35 hrs
All year
P&O Portsmouth

Portsmouth to Caen
6 hrs - 6 hrs 15 mins
All year
Brittany Ferries

Portsmouth to Cherbourg
2 hrs 45 mins - 7 hrs
All year
P&O Portsmouth

Portsmouth to Guernsey
6 hrs 30 mins
All year
Condor Ferries

Portsmouth to Jersey
10 hrs
All year
Condor Ferries

Portsmouth to Le Havre
5 hrs 30 mins
All year
P&O Portsmouth

Portsmouth to St. Malo
8 hrs 45 mins - 10 hrs 30 mins
All year
Brittany Ferries

Rosyth to Zeebrugge
16 hrs 30 mins
All year
Superfast Ferry Scotland

Stranraer to Belfast
1 hr 45 mins - 3 hrs 15 mins
All year
Stena Line

Swansea to Cork
10 hrs
All year
Swansea Cork Ferries

Troon to Belfast
2 hrs 30 mins
All year
Seacat

Troon to Larne
4 hrs
All year
P&O Irish Sea

Weymouth to Guernsey
2 hrs - 2 hrs 15 mins
All year
Condor Ferries

Weymouth to Jersey
3 hrs 15 mins - 3 hrs 35 mins
All year
Condor Ferries

FERRY OPERATORS

Contact details for the ferry operators who run the ferries listed above

Brittany Ferries
0870 90 12 400
www.brittany-ferries.co.uk

Condor Ferries
01305 761551
www.condorferries.co.uk

DFDS Seaways
08705 333 000
www.dfdsseaways.co.uk

Fjord Line
0191 296 1313
www.fjordline.co.uk

Hoverspeed
0870 240 8070
www.hoverspeed.co.uk

Irish Ferries
08705 171717
www.irishferries.ie

Isle of Man Steam Packet Co
08705 523 523
www.steam-packet.com

NorseMerchant Ferries
0870 600 4321
www.norsemerchant.com

P&O Irish Sea
0870 24 24 777
www.poirishsea.com

P&O North Sea Ferries
0870 129 6002
www.ponsf.com

P&O Portsmouth
023 9230 1000
www.poportsmouth.com

P&O Stena Line
0870 0600 0600
www.posl.com

Seacat
08705 523 523
www.steam-packet.com

SeaFrance
08705 711 711
www.seafrance.com

Smyril Line
01224 572615
www.smyril-line.fo

Stena Line
08705 707070
www.stenaline.co.uk

Superfast Ferry Scotland
0800 0681 676
www.superfastscotland.com

Swansea Cork Ferries
01792 456116
www.swansea-cork.ie

AIRPORT INFORMATION

Airports in Britain which offer international & scheduled flights

Aberdeen
Farburn Terrace
Dyce
ABERDEEN
AB21 7DU
01224 722331
www.baa.co.uk/main/airports/aberdeen

Birmingham International
Birmingham
WEST MIDLANDS
B26 3QJ
0121 767 5511
www.bhx.co.uk

Blackpool
Squires Gate Lane
BLACKPOOL
FY4 2QY
01253 343434
www.blackpoolairport.com

Bournemouth International
Hurn
CHRISTCHURCH
BH23 6DB
01202 364000
www.bourneintairport.co.uk

Bristol International
BRISTOL
BS48 3DY
0870 1212747
www.bristolairport.co.uk

Cardiff International
Rhoose
BARRY
CF26 3BD
01446 711111
www.cial.co.uk

East Midlands International
Castle Donington
DERBY
DE74 2SA
01332 852852
www.eastmidlandsairport.com

Edinburgh
EDINBURGH
EH12 9DN
0131 333 1000
www.baa.co.uk/main/airports/edinburgh

Glasgow
Abbotsinch
PAISLEY
PA3 2PF
0141 887 1111
www.baa.co.uk/main/airports/glasgow

Glasgow Prestwick International
PRESTWICK
KA9 2PL
01292 511000
www.gpia.co.uk

Humberside International
Grimsby Road
Kirmington
Ulceby
SOUTH HUMBERSIDE
DN39 6YH
01652 688456
www.humberside-airport.co.uk

Kirkwall
Kirkwall
ORKNEY
KW15 1TH
01856 872421
www.hial.co.uk/kirkwall-airport.html

Leeds Bradford International
Leeds
WEST YORKSHIRE
LS19 7TU
0113 250 9696
www.lbia.co.uk

Liverpool John Lennon
LIVERPOOL
L24 1YD
0151 288 4000
www.liverpooljohnlennonairport.com

London City
Royal Dock
LONDON
E16 2PB
020 7646 0088
www.londoncityairport.com

London Gatwick
Gatwick
WEST SUSSEX
RH6 0JH
0870 000 2468
www.baa.co.uk/main/airports/gatwick

London Heathrow
Hounslow
MIDDLESEX
TW6 1JH
0870 0000 123
www.baa.co.uk/main/airports/heathrow

London Luton
Percival Way
LUTON
LU2 9LY
01582 405100
www.london-luton.co.uk

Lydd
Lydd
KENT
TN29 9QL
01797 322411
www.lydd-airport.co.uk

Manchester
MANCHESTER
M90 1QX
0161 489 3000
www.manairport.co.uk

Newcastle International
Woolsington
NEWCASTLE UPON TYNE
NE13 8BU
0191 286 0966
www.newcastleairport.com

Norwich International
Amsterdam Way
NORWICH
NR6 6JA
01603 411923
www.norwichinternational.com

Plymouth City
Crownhill
PLYMOUTH
PL6 8BW
01752 204090
www.eghd.com

Southampton International
SOUTHAMPTON
SO18 2NL
023 8062 0021
www.baa.co.uk/main/airports/southampton

Stansted
Stansted
ESSEX
CM24 1RW
0870 0000 303
www.baa.co.uk/main/airports/stansted

Teesside International
DARLINGTON
DL2 1LU
01325 332811
www.teessideairport.com

Motorway number	Junction	Service provider	Service Name	On-site services
A1(M)	1	Welcome Break	South Mimms	
A1(M)	10	Extra	Baldock	
A1(M)	17	Extra	Peterborough	
A1(M)	34	Moto	Blyth	
A1(M)	61	RoadChef	Durham	
A1(M)	64	Moto	Washington	
M1	2–4	Welcome Break	London Gateway	
M1	11–12	Moto	Toddington	
M1	14–15	Welcome Break	Newport Pagnell	
M1	15A	RoadChef	Rothersthorpe	
M1	16–17	RoadChef	Watford Gap	
M1	21–21A	Welcome Break	Leicester Forest East	
M1	22	Moto	Leicester	
M1	23A	Moto	Donington Park	
M1	25–26	Moto	Trowell	
M1	28–29	RoadChef	Tibshelf	
M1	30–31	Welcome Break	Woodall	
M1	38–39	Moto	Woolley Edge	
M2	4–5	Moto	Medway	
M3	4A–5	Welcome Break	Fleet	
M3	8–9	RoadChef	Winchester	
M4	3	Moto	Heston	
M4	11–12	Moto	Reading	
M4	13	Moto	Chieveley	
M4	14–15	Welcome Break	Membury	
M4	17–18	Moto	Leigh Delamere	
M4	23A	First Motorway	Magor	
M4	30	Moto	Cardiff Gate	
M4	33	Moto	Cardiff	
M4	36	Welcome Break	Sarn Park	
M4	47	Moto	Swansea	
M4	49	RoadChef	Pont Abraham	
M5	3–4	Moto	Frankley	
M5	8	RoadChef	Strensham (South)	
M5	8	RoadChef	Strensham (North)	
M5	13–14	Welcome Break	Michael Wood	
M5	19	Welcome Break	Gordano	
M5	21–22	RoadChef	Sedgemoor (South)	
M5	21–22	Welcome Break	Sedgemoor (North)	
M5	24	Moto	Bridgwater	
M5	25–26	RoadChef	Taunton Deane	
M5	28	Margram	Cullompton	
M5	29–30	Moto	Exeter	
M6	3–4	Welcome Break	Corley	
M6	10–11	Moto	Hilton Park	

On-site services

(pump)	Fuel	(wheelchair)	Disabled facilities	(fork & knife)	Food	£	Service shops
i	Information	(bed)	Accommodation	££	Other shops	(people)	Conference facilities

Motorway number	Junction	Service provider	Service Name	Fuel	Disabled facilities	Food	Service shops	Information	Accommodation	Other shops	Conference facilities
M6	14–15	RoadChef	**Stafford (South)**	✓	✓	✓	✓		✓	✓	
M6	14–15	Moto	**Stafford (North)**	✓	✓	✓	✓	✓		✓	✓
M6	15–16	Welcome Break	**Keele**	✓	✓	✓	✓				
M6	16–17	RoadChef	**Sandbach**	✓	✓	✓	✓				
M6	18–19	Moto	**Knutsford**	✓	✓	✓	✓	✓		✓	
M6	27–28	Welcome Break	**Charnock Richard**	✓	✓	✓	✓		✓		
M6	32–33	Moto	**Lancaster**	✓	✓	✓	✓	✓	✓	✓	
M6	35A–36	Moto	**Burton-in-Kendal (North)**	✓	✓	✓	✓	✓	✓	✓	
M6	36–37	RoadChef	**Killington Lake (South)**	✓	✓	✓	✓		✓		
M6	38–39	Westmorland	**Tebay**	✓	✓	✓	✓		✓		✓
M6	41–42	Moto	**Southwaite**	✓	✓	✓	✓	✓	✓	✓	
M8	4–5	RoadChef	**Harthill**	✓	✓	✓	✓				✓
M9	9	Moto	**Stirling**	✓	✓	✓	✓	✓	✓	✓	
M11	8	Welcome Break	**Birchanger Green**	✓	✓	✓	✓		✓		✓
M18	5	Moto	**Doncaster North**	✓	✓	✓	✓	✓	✓	✓	
M20	8	RoadChef	**Maidstone**	✓	✓	✓	✓	✓	✓		
M23	11	Moto	**Pease Pottage**	✓	✓	✓	✓	✓	✓	✓	
M25	5–6	RoadChef	**Clacket Lane**	✓	✓	✓	✓	✓	✓		
M25	23	Welcome Break	**South Mimms**	✓	✓	✓	✓		✓	✓	✓
M25	30	Moto	**Thurrock**	✓	✓	✓	✓	✓	✓	✓	
M27	3–4	RoadChef	**Rownhams**	✓	✓	✓	✓		✓		
M40	8	Welcome Break	**Oxford**	✓	✓	✓	✓		✓		✓
M40	10	Moto	**Cherwell Valley**	✓	✓	✓	✓	✓	✓	✓	✓
M40	12–13	Welcome Break	**Warwick**	✓	✓	✓	✓		✓		✓
M42	2	Welcome Break	**Hopwood Park**	✓	✓	✓	✓			✓	
M42	10	Moto	**Tamworth**	✓	✓	✓	✓	✓	✓	✓	✓
M48	1	Moto	**Severn View**	✓	✓	✓	✓	✓	✓	✓	
M50	4	Welcome Break	**Ross Spur**	✓	✓	✓	✓				
M56	14	RoadChef	**Chester**	✓	✓	✓	✓	✓	✓		
M61	6–7	First Motorway	**Bolton West**	✓	✓	✓	✓		✓		✓
M62	7–9	Welcome Break	**Burtonwood**	✓	✓	✓	✓		✓		
M62	18–19	Moto	**Birch**	✓	✓	✓	✓	✓	✓	✓	✓
M62	25–26	Welcome Break	**Hartshead Moor**	✓	✓	✓	✓		✓		✓
M62	33	Moto	**Ferrybridge**	✓	✓	✓	✓	✓		✓	
M65	4	Supermart	**Blackburn Interchange**	✓	✓	✓	✓		✓		
M74	4–5	RoadChef	**Bothwell (South)**	✓	✓	✓	✓				
M74	5–6	RoadChef	**Hamilton (North)**	✓	✓	✓	✓	✓	✓		✓
M74	11–12	Cairn Lodge	**Happendon**	✓	✓	✓	✓				✓
M74	12–13	Welcome Break	**Abington**	✓	✓	✓	✓		✓		✓
A74(M)	16	RoadChef	**Annandale Water**	✓	✓	✓	✓		✓		
A74(M)	22	Welcome Break	**Gretna Green**	✓	✓	✓	✓		✓		✓
M90	6	Moto	**Kinross**	✓	✓	✓	✓	✓	✓	✓	

208

Great Britain distance chart

Distances between two selected towns in this table are shown in miles and kilometres. In general, distances are based on the shortest routes by classified roads.

DISTANCE IN KILOMETRES

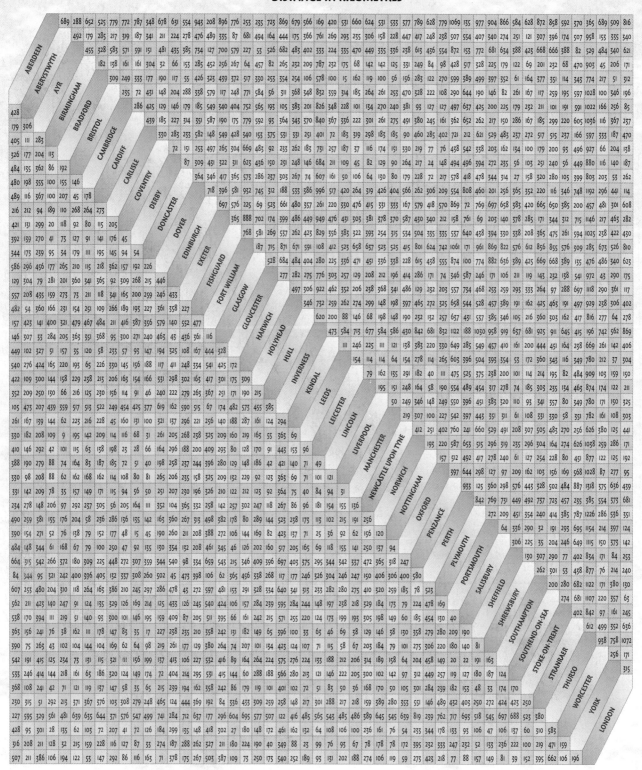

DISTANCE IN MILES